Kaplan Method for Problem Solving

1) Study the question stem and the answers.

2) Determine what the question asks.

3) Choose an approach, or combine approaches:

   a) Use a strategy.

      i) Picking Numbers

      ii) Backsolving

   b) Do the straightforward math.

   c) Guess strategically.

      i) Use logic to eliminate answers.

      ii) Estimate the value of the correct answer.

      iii) Be wary of answer choices that are structurally different from others.

      iv) On Roman numeral questions, try to verify or disprove one or more statements and any related answer choices.

      v) On "which of the following" questions, be partial to the latter choices

4) Read the question again, making sure your answer makes sense.

Kaplan Method for Data Sufficiency

1) From the question stem, determine what type of information would be needed to answer the question.

   - Determine whether the question requires a "yes/no" answer or a "value" answer.

   - If the stem contains an algebraic expression, see if the expression can be put in a simpler form.

   - Determine what type of information would be needed to answer the question.

2) Evaluate each statement separately.

   - For yes/no questions, seek to find a single answer to the question.

   - For value questions, seek to find a single value.

   - Determine the sufficiency of one statement.

   - Determine the sufficiency of the other statement.

   - Keep track of your options as you go.

   - If (2) is insufficient, the answer must be (A), (C), or (E).

   - If (2) is sufficient, the answer must be (B) or (D).

   - If (1) is insufficient, the answer must be (B), (C), or (E).

   - If (1) is sufficient, the answer must be (A) or (D).

   - Do not let information from one statement influence your decision about the other statement.

3) Evaluate the statements in combination, if necessary.

4) When combining the statements, treat them as one long statement.

Dealing With Word Problems

The key to solving word problems is translation. Rather than having an equation set up for you, *you* have to decide what arithmetic or algebraic operations to perform on which numbers.

Your job is to translate the problem from English into math. A phrase like "three times as many as John has" can be translated as 3j; the phrase "four fewer than Susan" can be translated as "s − 4."

Here's a general approach to any word problem:

1. Read through the whole question once, without lingering over details, to get a sense of the overall problem.

2. Identify and label the variables or unknowns in a way that makes it easy to remember what they stand for.

3. Translate the problem into one or more equations, sentence by sentence. Be careful of the order in which you translate the terms. For example, consider the phrase: "5 less than 4x equals 9." The *correct* way to translate it is: "$4x − 5 = 9$." But many students make the mistake of writing the terms in the order in which they appear in words: "$5 − 4x = 9$."

4. Solve the equation(s).

5. Check your work, if time permits.

STRATEGIES AND TEST-DAY TIPS

Picking Numbers:
Pick Numbers that are permissible and manageable.

Backsolving:
Start with choice (B) or (D).

Equations and Variables:
n distinct linear equations are needed to solve for n variables.

DATA SUFFICIENCY
1 (A) #1 is Suff.; #2 is Not Suff.
2 (B) #2 is Suff.; #1 is Not Suff.
T (C) #1 is Not Suff.; #2 is Not Suff.; #1 AND #2 are Suff.
E (D) #1 is Suff.; #2 is Suff.
N (E) #1 is Not Suff.; #2 is Not Suff.; #1 AND #2 are Not Suff.

OTHER FORMULAS AND THINGS TO KNOW:

$$\text{Speed} = \frac{\text{Distance}}{\text{Time}} \qquad \text{Average} = \frac{\text{Sum of the terms}}{\text{Number of terms}} \qquad \text{Average Speed} = \frac{\text{Total Distance}}{\text{Total Time}} \qquad \text{Rate} = \frac{\text{Quantity of } A}{\text{Quantity of } B}$$

$$\% \text{ Increase} = \frac{\text{New Amount} - \text{Original Amount}}{\text{Original Amount}} \times 100\% \qquad \% \text{ Decrease} = \frac{\text{Original Amount} - \text{New Amount}}{\text{Original Amount}} \times 100\%$$

EXPONENT RULES:

$$x \cdot x = x^2 \qquad (x^a)^b = x^{ab}$$

$$x^{-a} = \frac{1}{x^a} \qquad \frac{x^a}{x^b} = x^{a-b}$$

$$x^0 = 1 \qquad (\text{negative})^{\text{odd}} = \text{negative}$$

$$x^a x^b = x^{a+b} \qquad (\text{negative})^{\text{even}} = \text{positive}$$

RADICAL RULES:

$$\sqrt{a}\sqrt{b} = \sqrt{ab}$$

$$\frac{\sqrt{a}}{\sqrt{b}} = \sqrt{\frac{a}{b}}$$

$$a\sqrt{c} + b\sqrt{c} = (a+b)\sqrt{c}$$

$$\sqrt{a} + \sqrt{b} \neq \sqrt{a+b}$$

$$(\sqrt{a})^2 = a$$

NUMBERS:

0 is an even integer.

1 is *not* prime.

2 is the lowest prime number.

Mode: the most common number(s) in a set

Median: the middle term in a set of ascending or descending numbers; when the set has an even number of numbers, the average of the two middle terms.

Only (odd) × (odd) and (odd) + (even) yield odd numbers.

MISCELLANEOUS:

$$ab + ac = a(b + c) \qquad |-x| = |x|$$

$$x\% \text{ of } y = y\% \text{ of } x \qquad \frac{a+b}{c} = \frac{a}{c} + \frac{b}{c}$$

Test Prep and Admissions
kaptest.com

GMAT Verbal Skills
READING COMPREHENSION | CRITICAL REASONING | SENTENCE CORRECTION

Kaplan Method for Reading Comprehension

1) Read the passage, write a Passage Map, and note Topic, Scope, and Purpose.
2) Read the question stem, determining which type of question it is.
3) Answer the question, following the Kaplan strategies for that question type.

   a) On Global questions, use your Passage Map, Topic, Scope, and Purpose/Main Idea to prephrase an answer.
   b) On Detail questions, use your Passage Map to locate the relevant text in the passage. If necessary, read that portion of the passage again. Then prephrase a response.
   c) On Inference questions, search for the answer choice that follows from the passage.
   d) On Logic questions, determine the author's intentions in a particular part of the passage, and prephrase an answer.

KAPLAN METHOD FOR CRITICAL REASONING

1) Read the question stem and determine the type of question.
2) Read the stimulus.
3) Follow the strategy appropriate for the question type.

   a) For an Assumption question, find the conclusion, evidence, and central assumption(s), then prephrase an answer before going to the answer choices.
   b) For a Strengthen or Weaken question, find the conclusion, evidence, and central assumption(s), then prephrase an answer that confirms (strengthens) or denies (weakens) a central assumption before going to the answer choices.
   c) For a Flaw question, find the conclusion, evidence, and central assumption(s), then prephrase a choice that indicates the logical fallacy of the assumption.
   d) For an Explain question, search the answer choices for a statement that, if true, could explain how the statements in the stimulus could all be true.
   e) For an Inference question, accept that the stimulus is true and locate the answer choice that must follow from the stimulus.

Kaplan Method for Sentence Correction

1) Read the original sentence carefully, looking for errors.
   • Look for classic errors.
   • If you find an error in the sentence, eliminate choice (A), which repeats the underlined part.
   • Eliminate any other answer choice that contains the same error you found.
   • Realize that the sentence is sometimes correct as written, making choice (A) correct.
2) Scan the answer choices.
   • Scan vertically for differences in the wording that will help you zero in on the types of errors being tested.
   • Once you know what wording is at issue, determine which alternative is preferable.
3) Eliminate choices until only one remains.
   • As soon as you find one error, eliminate that answer choice.
   • Eliminate other answer choices that repeat the error.
   • Scan the remaining choices for other differences by which you can zero in on other errors.
   • If you have to guess, go for the shortest answer that's clear and unambiguous.
   • Confirm your answer by reading your choice back in the sentence.

GMAT AWA Essay Skills
ISSUE ESSAY | ARGUMENT ESSAY

Kaplan Method for an Issue Essay

1) Take the issue apart.
   • Determine the conclusion and the (offered or implied) counter-conclusion.
   • Consider the circumstances under which the conclusion would be true/untrue.
2) Select the points you will make. Decide whether to agree or disagree, naming 2–4 reasons.
3) Organize:
   • Paragraph 1: Restate the issue, agree/disagree, and state two to four reasons.
   • Paragraphs 2–4: Elaborate on reasons, using evidence, testimony, and anecdotes.
   • Second to last paragraph: Present and refute an alternative argument.
   • Last paragraph: Summarize your points.
4) Type your essay.
5) Proofread.

Kaplan Method for an Argument Essay

1) Take the argument apart.
   • Determine the conclusion, evidence, and assumptions.
   • Consider the circumstances under which the assumptions are valid/invalid.
   • Consider what would strengthen/weaken the argument.
2) Select the points you will make. What weaknesses/strengths of the argument are critical? For which of those you can marshal evidence?
3) Organize:
   • Paragraph 1: Demonstrate that you understand the argument, list weaknesses, and describe what could strengthen the argument.
   • Paragraph 2: Detail assumptions on which the argument hinges, describe what would be required to validate the assumptions, and list gaps between existing evidence and what's necessary.
   • Paragraph 3: Discuss poorly defined terms, and their effect on the argument.
   • Final paragraph: Discuss what could strengthen the argument, and summarize your points.
4) Type your essay.
5) Proofread.

COMMON GMAT IDIOMS

able to (ability to)

among vs. between (Use among to refer to 3+ items; between to refer to 2 items.)

as vs. like (Use like to compare nouns; as to compare actions)

associate with

at least as . . . as

between . . . and . . .

compare to vs. compare with (Compare with is more common than compare to on the GMAT.)

connection between

consequence of

continue to

credit with

different from

distinguish between . . . and . . .

distinguish . . . from . . .

each other vs. one another (In GMAT English, each other is used to refer to 2 things; one another is used for 3+.)

either . . . or . . .

extent to which (common on the GMAT)

fewer vs. less (Fewer describes countable things; less describes an uncountable quantity.)

if vs. whether (Whether is far more common than if on the GMAT. If is reserved for conditional "if–then" statements.)

like vs. such as (Such as is far more common than like on the GMAT.)

more than

neither . . . nor . . .

not only . . . but also . . .

not so much . . . as . . .

perceive as

prohibit from

regard as

so . . . as to be . . .

so . . . that

superior to

use as

BORDERS.

Kaplan Publishing
Published by Simon & Schuster
1230 Avenue of the Americas
New York, NY 10020

Contributing Editor: Justin Serrano
Executive Editor: Jennifer Farthing
Project Editor: Ruth Baygell
Production Manager: Michael Shevlin
Page Layout: Evan Smith Rakoff
Cover Design: Cheung Tai

Manufactured in the United States of America
Published simultaneously in Canada

January 2005

10 9 8 7 6 5 4 3 2 1

ISBN: 0-7432-7411-3

For bulk sales, contact your local Borders store and ask to speak to the Corporate Sales Representative.

Test Prep and Admissions

GMAT®

Diagnostic Test and Practice Questions

A BORDERS EXCLUSIVE

By the Staff of Kaplan Test Prep and Admissions

Simon & Schuster

NEW YORK · LONDON · SYDNEY · TORONTO

GMAT® is a registered trademark of the Graduate Management Admission Council.

TABLE OF CONTENTS

HOW TO USE THIS BOOK

You are planning to take the GMAT and you don't have much time. Where to begin? The first step is to assess your strengths and weaknesses, so you can focus your study time. This book helps you do just that.

Here's how to use the *GMAT Diagnostic:*

STEP ONE: TAKE THE DIAGNOSTIC GMAT TEST

Take the full-length practice test—timed—as a test run for the real thing. The explanations for every question are included at the end so you can understand your mistakes.

STEP TWO: IDENTIFY YOUR STRENGTHS AND WEAKNESSES

Check your answers to the diagnostic, and note how many you got right and how many you got wrong. Look for patterns. Did Sentence Correction questions trip you up? Did you ace the Problem Solving questions? Try not to limit your review only to the questions you got wrong. Read all the explanations—even for the questions you got right—to reinforce key concepts and sharpen your skills. If necessary, go back to the questions to better understand the material and concepts on which you will be tested.

STEP THREE: CREATE A CUSTOMIZED STUDY PLAN

Based on your performance on the diagnostic test and the amount of time you have available to study before the GMAT, you can use the content in Section Three to create a customized study plan. Think about what you learned in Step Two and about the material you need to focus your study time on. Then, realistically determine how much time you have to devote to GMAT study. Use the information and tools in this section to build your plan. Then stick to it—your study plan only works for you if you follow it!

STEP FOUR: REVIEW TO REINFORCE AND BUILD SKILLS

Section Three provides you with targeted quizzes to help you conquer the content you need to know to score high on the GMAT. Based on your study plan, take the quizzes here to help prepare you for test day.

ABOUT THE GMAT

The GMAT is a standardized test that helps business schools assess the qualifications of students entering into their programs. Though many factors play a role in admissions decisions, the GMAT score is usually an important one. And, generally speaking, being average just won't cut it. While the median GMAT score is somewhere around 500, you need a score of at least 600 to be considered competitive by the top B-schools.

The first thing to know about the GMAT is that it is a computer-adaptive test; that is, a test taken on computer at a private workstation, scheduled at your convenience in a test-center near you. In a computer-adaptive test, you see only one question at a time. Instead of having a predetermined mixture of basic, medium, and hard questions, the computer selects questions for you based on how well you are doing. You cannot skip a question, and you cannot move around within a section to check a previous answer.

The GMAT measures basic verbal, mathematical, and analytical writing skills, and contains three sections: Analytical Writing Assessment (AWA) Quantitative (Math), and Verbal. First, you'll begin with the two AWA sections—30 minutes to type each essay into a computer. Then come the two 75-minute multiple-choice sections: Quantitative (Math) and Verbal. The Quantitative section contains 37 math questions in two formats: Problem Solving and Data Sufficiency. The Verbal section includes 41 questions in three types: Reading Comprehension, Sentence Correction, and Critical Reasoning.

Overall scaled scores range between 200 and 800. Because the test is graded on a preset curve, the scaled score will correspond to a certain percentile. So an overall score of 590, let's say, corresponds to the 80th percentile, meaning that 80 percent of test takers scored at or below that same level. The percentile helps business school admissions officers to see where you fall in a large pool of applicants.

For complete registration information about the GMAT, download the GMAT Information Bulletin from **mba.com/mba/TaketheGMAT**.

Section One

DIAGNOSTIC ASSESSMENT

CHAPTER ONE
Diagnostic Test

HOW TO TAKE THIS DIAGNOSTIC TEST

Before taking the Diagnostic Test, find a quiet place where you can work uninterrupted for approximately 3 and a half hours. Make sure you have a comfortable desk, several pencils, and some scratch paper.

Time yourself according to the time limits shown at the beginning of each section. It's okay to take a short break between sections, but for the most accurate results, you should go through all three sections in one sitting.

Use the answer sheet on the following page to record your answers to the multiple-choice sections. Do not skip a question. In the actual test-taking environment, you won't be able to skip from question to question, so make sure to mimic those same conditions here. If you are having trouble figuring out an answer, take your best guess and move on.

Also, on the real CAT test, you won't be able to go back and check your work, so choose your answers wisely. Type your essays into a computer.

You'll find the answer key and scoring information in chapter 3. Good luck!

GMAT Diagnostic Test
Answer Sheet

Remove (or photocopy) the answer sheet and use it to complete the practice test.
See the answer key following the test when finished.

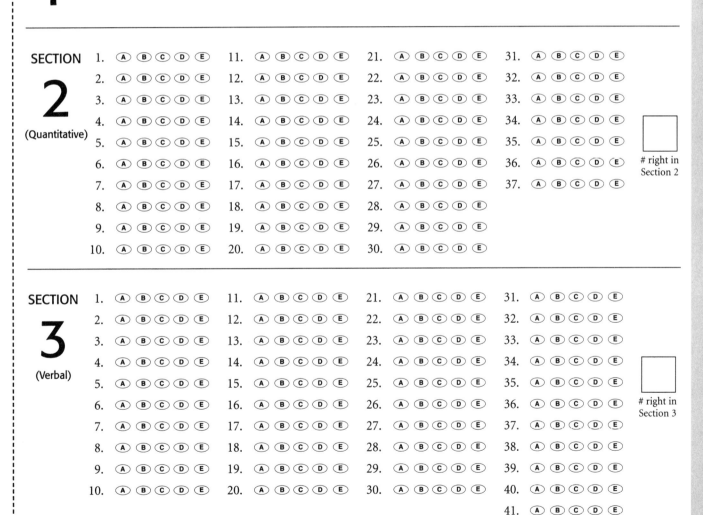

SECTION

1

Section One is the Analytical Writing Assessment.
Lined pages on which you will write your essay can be found in that section.

SECTION

2

(Quantitative)

1. Ⓐ Ⓑ Ⓒ Ⓓ Ⓔ	11. Ⓐ Ⓑ Ⓒ Ⓓ Ⓔ	21. Ⓐ Ⓑ Ⓒ Ⓓ Ⓔ	31. Ⓐ Ⓑ Ⓒ Ⓓ Ⓔ
2. Ⓐ Ⓑ Ⓒ Ⓓ Ⓔ	12. Ⓐ Ⓑ Ⓒ Ⓓ Ⓔ	22. Ⓐ Ⓑ Ⓒ Ⓓ Ⓔ	32. Ⓐ Ⓑ Ⓒ Ⓓ Ⓔ
3. Ⓐ Ⓑ Ⓒ Ⓓ Ⓔ	13. Ⓐ Ⓑ Ⓒ Ⓓ Ⓔ	23. Ⓐ Ⓑ Ⓒ Ⓓ Ⓔ	33. Ⓐ Ⓑ Ⓒ Ⓓ Ⓔ
4. Ⓐ Ⓑ Ⓒ Ⓓ Ⓔ	14. Ⓐ Ⓑ Ⓒ Ⓓ Ⓔ	24. Ⓐ Ⓑ Ⓒ Ⓓ Ⓔ	34. Ⓐ Ⓑ Ⓒ Ⓓ Ⓔ
5. Ⓐ Ⓑ Ⓒ Ⓓ Ⓔ	15. Ⓐ Ⓑ Ⓒ Ⓓ Ⓔ	25. Ⓐ Ⓑ Ⓒ Ⓓ Ⓔ	35. Ⓐ Ⓑ Ⓒ Ⓓ Ⓔ
6. Ⓐ Ⓑ Ⓒ Ⓓ Ⓔ	16. Ⓐ Ⓑ Ⓒ Ⓓ Ⓔ	26. Ⓐ Ⓑ Ⓒ Ⓓ Ⓔ	36. Ⓐ Ⓑ Ⓒ Ⓓ Ⓔ
7. Ⓐ Ⓑ Ⓒ Ⓓ Ⓔ	17. Ⓐ Ⓑ Ⓒ Ⓓ Ⓔ	27. Ⓐ Ⓑ Ⓒ Ⓓ Ⓔ	37. Ⓐ Ⓑ Ⓒ Ⓓ Ⓔ
8. Ⓐ Ⓑ Ⓒ Ⓓ Ⓔ	18. Ⓐ Ⓑ Ⓒ Ⓓ Ⓔ	28. Ⓐ Ⓑ Ⓒ Ⓓ Ⓔ	
9. Ⓐ Ⓑ Ⓒ Ⓓ Ⓔ	19. Ⓐ Ⓑ Ⓒ Ⓓ Ⓔ	29. Ⓐ Ⓑ Ⓒ Ⓓ Ⓔ	
10. Ⓐ Ⓑ Ⓒ Ⓓ Ⓔ	20. Ⓐ Ⓑ Ⓒ Ⓓ Ⓔ	30. Ⓐ Ⓑ Ⓒ Ⓓ Ⓔ	

right in
Section 2

SECTION

3

(Verbal)

1. Ⓐ Ⓑ Ⓒ Ⓓ Ⓔ	11. Ⓐ Ⓑ Ⓒ Ⓓ Ⓔ	21. Ⓐ Ⓑ Ⓒ Ⓓ Ⓔ	31. Ⓐ Ⓑ Ⓒ Ⓓ Ⓔ
2. Ⓐ Ⓑ Ⓒ Ⓓ Ⓔ	12. Ⓐ Ⓑ Ⓒ Ⓓ Ⓔ	22. Ⓐ Ⓑ Ⓒ Ⓓ Ⓔ	32. Ⓐ Ⓑ Ⓒ Ⓓ Ⓔ
3. Ⓐ Ⓑ Ⓒ Ⓓ Ⓔ	13. Ⓐ Ⓑ Ⓒ Ⓓ Ⓔ	23. Ⓐ Ⓑ Ⓒ Ⓓ Ⓔ	33. Ⓐ Ⓑ Ⓒ Ⓓ Ⓔ
4. Ⓐ Ⓑ Ⓒ Ⓓ Ⓔ	14. Ⓐ Ⓑ Ⓒ Ⓓ Ⓔ	24. Ⓐ Ⓑ Ⓒ Ⓓ Ⓔ	34. Ⓐ Ⓑ Ⓒ Ⓓ Ⓔ
5. Ⓐ Ⓑ Ⓒ Ⓓ Ⓔ	15. Ⓐ Ⓑ Ⓒ Ⓓ Ⓔ	25. Ⓐ Ⓑ Ⓒ Ⓓ Ⓔ	35. Ⓐ Ⓑ Ⓒ Ⓓ Ⓔ
6. Ⓐ Ⓑ Ⓒ Ⓓ Ⓔ	16. Ⓐ Ⓑ Ⓒ Ⓓ Ⓔ	26. Ⓐ Ⓑ Ⓒ Ⓓ Ⓔ	36. Ⓐ Ⓑ Ⓒ Ⓓ Ⓔ
7. Ⓐ Ⓑ Ⓒ Ⓓ Ⓔ	17. Ⓐ Ⓑ Ⓒ Ⓓ Ⓔ	27. Ⓐ Ⓑ Ⓒ Ⓓ Ⓔ	37. Ⓐ Ⓑ Ⓒ Ⓓ Ⓔ
8. Ⓐ Ⓑ Ⓒ Ⓓ Ⓔ	18. Ⓐ Ⓑ Ⓒ Ⓓ Ⓔ	28. Ⓐ Ⓑ Ⓒ Ⓓ Ⓔ	38. Ⓐ Ⓑ Ⓒ Ⓓ Ⓔ
9. Ⓐ Ⓑ Ⓒ Ⓓ Ⓔ	19. Ⓐ Ⓑ Ⓒ Ⓓ Ⓔ	29. Ⓐ Ⓑ Ⓒ Ⓓ Ⓔ	39. Ⓐ Ⓑ Ⓒ Ⓓ Ⓔ
10. Ⓐ Ⓑ Ⓒ Ⓓ Ⓔ	20. Ⓐ Ⓑ Ⓒ Ⓓ Ⓔ	30. Ⓐ Ⓑ Ⓒ Ⓓ Ⓔ	40. Ⓐ Ⓑ Ⓒ Ⓓ Ⓔ
			41. Ⓐ Ⓑ Ⓒ Ⓓ Ⓔ

right in
Section 3

Section 1
ANALYSIS OF ISSUE ESSAY

(30 minutes)

"The emergence of a new competitor is always harmful to a company. The new competitor forces the company to become reactionary and short-sighted, rather than sticking to its long-term strategy."

Discuss the extent to which you agree or disagree with the opinion stated above. Support your views with reasons and/or examples from your own experience, observations or reading.

Sprint has a plan for $39.99 in which you'll have unlimited texting, free internet service and free calling after 5:30 for a month only; T-mobile has a plan for $35.23 in which you'll have unlimited texting, free calling after 4:00, free downloadible games, free background customization, and free music downloads for 3 months only. When Sprint hears of the new deal, they'll try to better their plan and add more accessories for a lower price. The two phone companies will be resilient in their plans and will try to suceed one another.

ANALYSIS OF ARGUMENT ESSAY

(30 minutes)

The following appeared as part of a campaign by a publishing company to sell more advertising space in its monthly news magazine, the *Halcyon.*

"Advertising in the *Halcyon* has helped many companies increase their sales. For example, Pallas Textile Mills began advertising in the *Halcyon* one year ago and has seen its business increase by 15 percent since that time. You, too, can use our magazine to make your business more profitable."

Discuss how well-reasoned you find this argument. In your discussion be sure to analyze the line of reasoning and the use of evidence in the argument. For example, you may need to consider what questionable assumptions underlie the thinking and what alternative explanations or counter-examples might weaken the conclusion. You can also discuss what sort of evidence would strengthen or refute the argument, what changes would make it more logically sound, and what, if anything, would help you better evaluate its conclusion.

_____

_____

_____

_____

_____

_____

_____

_____

_____

Section 2
QUANTITATIVE SECTION

Time—75 minutes
37 Questions

Directions: The following questions are either Problem Solving or Data Sufficiency.

Problem Solving questions are those with five listed answer choices. In each of these, select the best answer choice, and mark the corresponding oval on your exam grid. Note that figures are drawn as accurately as possible except when it is stated that a figure is not drawn to scale. All figures lie in a plane unless otherwise indicated.

Data Sufficiency questions are those which have a question stem followed by two statements containing certain data. Your task is to determine whether the data provided by the statements are sufficient to answer the question. The answer choices for all of these questions are always the same. They are the following:

(A) Statement (1) BY ITSELF is sufficient to answer the question, but statement (2) by itself is not.

(B) Statement (2) BY ITSELF is sufficient to answer the question, but statement (1) by itself is not.

(C) Statements (1) and (2) TAKEN TOGETHER are sufficient to answer the question, even though NEITHER statement BY ITSELF is sufficient.

(D) EITHER statement BY ITSELF is sufficient to answer the question.

(E) Statements (1) and (2) TAKEN TOGETHER are NOT sufficient to answer the question, requiring more data pertaining to the problem.

Based upon the statements' data, your knowledge of mathematics, and your familiarity with everyday facts (such as the number of minutes in an hour), select the best answer choice, and mark it on your answer grid. A figure accompanying a Data Sufficiency question will conform to the information in the question stem, but will not necessarily conform to the information in the two statements. Figures are not necessarily drawn to scale. Note that you may assume that the positions of points, angles, regions, etc., exist in the order shown and that angle measures are greater than zero. All figures lie in a plane unless otherwise indicated.

1. $x^2 + kx + 8 = 0$. What is the value of k ?

    (1) One factor of the equation is $(x + 4)$.
    (2) One factor of the equation is $(x + 2)$.

2. If x is an integer, then $x(x + 2)(x + 3)$ is

    (A) odd whenever x is odd
    (B) even only when x is even
    (C) even only when x is odd
    (D) divisible by 3 when x is odd
    (E) divisible by 2

3. A team begins its season by winning 10 games and losing 14 games. What is the least number of games that the team must play in the remainder of the season so that the team can win at least $\frac{5}{7}$ of all of its games in the season?

    (A) 25
    (B) 30
    (C) 35
    (D) 49
    (E) 74

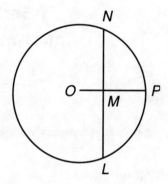

4. What is the length of the diameter of the circle above with center O ?

    (1) The ratio of the length OM to the length of MP is 1 to 3.
    (2) Radius OP bisects chord NL.

5. Each table at a reception seats the same number of guests. Enough guests were invited to fill exactly 32 tables. If 27 more guests arrived than were invited, how many more tables would be needed to seat them?

    (1) 288 guests were invited to the reception.
    (2) Exactly 9 people can be seated at each table.

6. If it is true that $-6 \leq n \leq 10$, which of the following must be true?

    (A) $n < 8$
    (B) $n = -6$
    (C) $n > -8$
    (D) $-10 < n < 7$
    (E) none of the above

7. Each runner during a race is labeled with a unique one-letter code or a unique two-letter code, where the two letters are different. Different orders of the same two different letters are considered to be different two-letter codes. The codes use the 26-letter English alphabet. What is the maximum number of runners that can receive unique codes for the race?

    (A) 325
    (B) 351
    (C) 377
    (D) 650
    (E) 676

8. If $a \neq 0$, is $a > 0$?

    (1) $a + b = 9$
    (2) $ab = 14$

9. Circle O is inscribed within square $ABCD$. Square $EFGH$ is inscribed within circle O. What is the ratio of the area of $ABCD$ to the area of $EFGH$?

    (A) $1 : \sqrt{2}$
    (B) $1 : 2$
    (C) $2 : 1$
    (D) $4 : 1$
    (E) $4 : \sqrt{2}$

10. The amount of time that three consultants worked on a special project was in the ratio of 2 to 3 to 7. If the three consultants worked a total of 144 hours on the project, how many hours did the consultant who worked the greatest number of hours spend on the project?

    (A) 24
    (B) 36
    (C) 60
    (D) 73
    (E) 84

11. When 50 is divided by x, the remainder is $x - 6$. Which of the following could be the value of x ?

    (A) 3
    (B) 4
    (C) 6
    (D) 7
    (E) 9

12. In January, a candy store sold 10 boxes of truffles at $45.00 a box. In February, the store sold 15 boxes of truffles at $42.50 a box. By what amount did the monthly revenue from sales of boxes of truffles increase from January to February?

    (A) $25.00
    (B) $37.50
    (C) $187.50
    (D) $450.00
    (E) $637.50

13. If a, b, and c are positive numbers, is $a > b > c$?

    (1) $a^2 > ab$
    (2) $ac > c^2$

14. A rectangular shipping crate has dimensions of 5 feet, 4 feet, and 3 feet. What is the greatest possible straight-line distance, in feet, between any two points on the crate?

    (A) 6
    (B) 7
    (C) $\sqrt{57}$
    (D) $5\sqrt{2}$
    (E) $5\sqrt{3}$

15. Jane and Richard together have a total of t dollars. Jane has v dollars more than 3 times the number of dollars that Richard has. Which of the following is the number of dollars that Jane has?

    (A) $\dfrac{3t + v}{4}$

    (B) $\dfrac{3t + 2v}{4}$

    (C) $\dfrac{2t + v}{4}$

    (D) $\dfrac{2t - v}{4}$

    (E) $\dfrac{t - v}{4}$

16. Is $4^k > 1,000$?

    (1) $4^{k + 1} > 4,000$
    (2) $4^{k - 1} = 256$

17. What is the largest possible value of x if $(x + 16)(x + 3)(x + 5) = 0$?

    (A) -4
    (B) -3
    (C) -2
    (D) 3
    (E) 5

18. $\dfrac{(3)(-2.4) - (9)(0.8)}{60} =$

    (A) -2.4
    (B) -0.24
    (C) 0
    (D) 0.24
    (E) 2.4

19. During a certain month, a courier service completed 78% of its first 100 deliveries on time and 60% of its remaining deliveries on time. If the courier service completed 72% of its deliveries on time for the entire month, what was the total number of deliveries that the company made?

    (A) 180
    (B) 156
    (C) 150
    (D) 138
    (E) 120

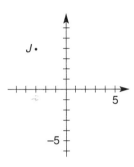

20. What are the coordinates of point *J* in the figure above?

    (A) (–3, –4)
    (B) (–3, 4)
    (C) (3, 4)
    (D) (4, –3)
    (E) (4, 3)

21. If the sum of *r*, *s*, and *t* is 180, what is the value of *r*?

    (1) $r = 2s$
    (2) $s + t = 150$

22. What is the average of *p*, *q*, and *r* ?

    (1) $p + 3q - 2r = 5$
    (2) $4p + 2q + 7r = -5$

23. A teacher must seat six students in two rows of three seats each. If one troublesome student must sit in the front row, and the others may sit in either row, how many possible seating arrangements does the teacher have to choose from?

    (A) 360
    (B) 270
    (C) 120
    (D) 72
    (E) 36

24. $m \neq 0$ and $5m + \dfrac{4 - 2m^2}{m} = \dfrac{n}{m}$, then $n =$

    (A) $-3m^2 + 4$
    (B) $3m^2 + 4$
    (C) $9 - 2m^2$
    (D) $5m^2 - 2m + 4$
    (E) $5m^2 - 3m + 4$

25. Is *x* positive?

    (1) $|x + 6| > 6$
    (2) $|x - 6| > 6$

26. A bag contains only *b* blue marbles and *r* red marbles. 4 blue marbles and 5 red marbles are then added to the bag. If one marble is selected at random from the bag, what is the probability that the selected marble will be red?

    (A) $\dfrac{r}{r + r}$
    (B) $\dfrac{r}{r + 4}$
    (C) $\dfrac{r + 5}{r + 9}$
    (D) $\dfrac{r + 5}{r + r + 5}$
    (E) $\dfrac{r + 5}{r + r + 9}$

27. If *a* and *b* are positive integers, what is the value of *ab* ?

    (1) *a* is 200 percent more than *b*
    (2) *b* is a prime number less than 3

28. $a + b = 8$. Is $ab > 8$?

   (1) $a^2 - b^2 = 32$

   (2) $a^2 + b^2 = 40$

29. If n is an integer and $100 < n < 120$, what is the value of n ?

   (1) There is a remainder of 3 when n is divided by 4.

   (2) There is no remainder when n is divided by 5.

30. If a is positive, is $a + 1$ a prime number?

   (1) a is a prime number greater than 3

   (2) $a + 2$ is not a prime number

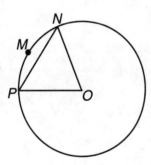

31. If the circle with center O above has a circumference of 24π and $OP = NP$, what is the perimeter of sector $OPMN$?

   (A) 24

   (B) $12 + 4\pi$

   (C) 36

   (D) $24 + 4\pi$

   (E) $24 + 6\pi$

32. If $4a = 16$ and $\dfrac{3}{b} = 5$, then what is the value of $\dfrac{3a}{5a + 4b}$?

   (A) $\dfrac{3}{20}$

   (B) $\dfrac{12}{23}$

   (C) $\dfrac{15}{28}$

   (D) $\dfrac{3}{5}$

   (E) $\dfrac{23}{12}$

33. If $a < b < c$, which of the following must be true?

   I. $a < b^2$

   II. $b - a < c$

   III. $a^2 < b^2 < c^2$

   (A) None

   (B) I only

   (C) II only

   (D) III only

   (E) II and III

34. Is the positive integer x greater than 4 ?

   (1) x has exactly three distinct positive integer factors

   (2) x is odd

35. If an object travels at a constant rate of 720,000 meters per hour, how many meters will it travel in one second?

   (A)   2
   (B)   20
   (C)   200
   (D)   2,000
   (E) 200,000

36. Which of the following variables cannot be equal to 0 if $(v + w)(x - y - z)(x + y + z)z = 3$?

   (A) v
   (B) w
   (C) x
   (D) y
   (E) z

37. The average speed of a car decreased by 3 miles per hour every successive 8-minute interval. If the car traveled 4.8 miles in the sixth 8-minute interval, what was the average speed of the car, in miles per hour, in the first 8-minute interval?

   (A) 35
   (B) 40
   (C) 48
   (D) 51
   (E) 53

Section 3
VERBAL SECTION

Time—75 minutes
41 Questions

Directions: This section consists of Sentence Correction questions, Critical Reasoning questions, and Reading Comprehension questions.

Sentence Correction questions consist of sentences that are either partly or entirely underlined. Below each sentence are five versions of the underlined portion of the sentence. The first of these, choice (A), duplicates the original version. The four other versions revise the underlined portion of the sentence. Read the sentence and the four revisions carefully, and select the best version. If the original version seems better than the revised versions, select the first choice, (A). If not, choose one of the revised versions. Choose answers according to the norms of standard written English for grammar, word choice, and sentence construction. Your selected answer should express the intended meaning of the original sentence as clearly and precisely as possible, while avoiding ambiguity, awkwardness, or unnecessarily wordy constructions.

Critical Reasoning questions consist of a set of statements, followed by a question. Analyze the statements, then select the answer choice that is the most appropriate response to the question. No specialized knowledge of any particular field is required for answering these questions.

Reading Comprehension questions refer to a specified passage. Your choice is to be based on what is stated or implied in the passage, and not on your own knowledge. You may refer to the passage while answering the questions.

1. Numerous studies of chemotherapy patients over the last 10 years have shown that patients who had regularly attended support groups or received counseling experienced significantly fewer side effects and shorter recovery times than did patients who had not. Clearly, although the mainstream scientific community has been slow to acknowledge it, psychological support has an effect on the body's ability to heal.

   Which of the following, if true, would most strengthen the argument above?

   (A) The survival rates for chemotherapy patients in the study were virtually identical regardless of whether or not they received support.

   (B) The patients who did not attend support groups chose not to do so, even though they were healthy enough to attend.

   (C) Many medical doctors believe that the mind plays a role in the causation and prevention of illness.

   (D) The majority of chemotherapy patients must undergo more than one round of treatment.

   (E) Some hospitals do not conduct support groups on their premises for chemotherapy patients and their families.

2. Which of the following best completes the passage below?

   In the parole hearings held in the last month, three-quarters of the prisoners up for parole claimed to feel remorse for the crimes they had committed. However, this number may overestimate the number of prisoners up for parole who were truly remorseful, because _____.

   (A) some prisoners who were not remorseful may have claimed to be remorseful during the parole hearing

   (B) some prisoners who claimed to be remorseful may have been more remorseful than others

   (C) some prisoners who were remorseful may not have claimed to be remorseful during the parole hearing

   (D) some prisoners who did not claim to be remorseful may, in fact, have been remorseful

   (E) some prisoners not up for parole are probably remorseful

3. Economist: When stock market indices were increasing, the federal deficit decreased, but after stock market indices began to fall, the federal deficit increased. The perception of bad economic conditions, therefore, decreased the federal government's willingness to reduce deficit spending.

The economist's argument relies on her assumption that

(A) perceived economic conditions have worsened over the years
(B) the federal deficit will always increase when the stock market indices decrease
(C) the government's perception of bad economic conditions depends, in large measure, on the direction in which stock market indices are moving
(D) the government's ability to reduce deficit spending depends upon its perception of economic conditions
(E) economic conditions are bad when the government increases deficit spending

4. Concerned by the steep rise in expenditures in the last quarter, the department manager ordered her senior staff <u>should prepare a list of</u> cost-cutting measures for immediate implementation.

(A) should prepare a list of
(B) would prepare a list of
(C) to be preparing a list of
(D) to prepare a list of
(E) to be listing

5. All human languages feature utterances that can be characterized as curses: verbal exclamations in response to surprise, anger, or frustration. Traditionally, neuroscientists believed that verbal cursing behavior was modulated by the same speech centers in the brain that initiate and control other forms of speech. More recent research, however, has begun to produce conclusions inconsistent with that assumption.

Which of the following pieces of evidence, if true, contradicts the belief that verbal cursing behavior originates in the same speech centers as other types of speech?

(A) The frequency of verbal cursing behavior and the readiness with which individuals curse correlate with the frequency of verbal cursing behavior exhibited by their parents or other primary caregivers.
(B) While some people demonstrate verbal cursing behavior readily in response to relatively low levels of stimuli, other people hardly ever curse at all.
(C) When people move from one social group to another, the frequency of their verbal cursing behavior varies in response to the level prevalent in different groups.
(D) People who have suffered damage or loss to the physical mechanisms required to produce speech, the larynx or parts of the mouth, still exhibit gestures and expressions associated with verbal cursing behavior when frustrated.
(E) Aphasiacs, people who have suffered damage to speech centers in the brain and are unable to speak normally, still exhibit verbal cursing behavior when under stress.

6. <u>Other than the importance of eating more vegetables and less sugar, many people fail to realize that exercising is also an important part of a healthy diet</u>.

   (A) Other than the importance of eating more vegetables and less sugar, many people fail to realize that exercising is also an important part of a healthy diet

   (B) In addition to the importance of eating more vegetables and less sugar, many people fail to realize that exercising is also an important part of a healthy diet

   (C) Many people know the importance of eating more vegetables and less sugar, but fail to realize that exercising is also an important part of a healthy diet

   (D) Many people who realize the importance of eating more vegetables and less sugar also fail to realize that exercising is also an important part of a healthy diet

   (E) Many people, failing to realize that exercising is also an important part of a healthy diet, know the importance of eating more vegetables and less sugar

7. <u>Communicating effectively, anticipation of customer needs, and learning from mistakes are</u> all crucial to great customer service, whether one works out of her home or heads a Fortune 500 company.

   (A) Communicating effectively, anticipation of customer needs, and learning from mistakes are

   (B) Communicating effectively, anticipation of customer needs, and learning from mistakes is

   (C) Communicating effectively, anticipating customer needs, and learning from mistakes are

   (D) Effective communication, anticipation of customer needs, and the ability to learn from mistakes is

   (E) Effective communication, anticipation of customer needs, and learning from mistakes are

Questions 8 through 10 are based on the following passage:

Controversy has surrounded the utility and efficacy of intelligence tests since their very inception. Intelligence tests produce a quantitative score known as the intelligence quotient (IQ). IQ
(5) scores serve primarily as an evaluation of an individual's cognitive ability and potential. Opponents of testing argue that the intelligence quotient may not provide an accurate picture of an individual's skills. Test questions do not
(10) measure social abilities; instead, they assess only minimally the types of thought and behavior required for real life situations. Because the scoring guides are standardized, extremely imaginative or original answers may fail to accrue
(15) deserved points. Although scores can serve as valuable indices of potential and ability, they may also reflect personal attitudes and test-taking sophistication. Lastly, because of the value placed on IQ scores, intelligence tests administered by
(20) unqualified or uninterested individuals have the potential to damage or grossly alter a client's life. For example, testers who fail to consider such factors as an individual's socioeconomic status, ethnicity, current health, and family
(25) circumstances may not understand the motivations behind certain responses. In the worst case scenario, poor test administrators may mistake a hearing, speech, or vision impediment for signs of retardation or low IQ.
(30) Nonetheless, if intelligence tests are administered and interpreted correctly, they are invaluable sources of information about an individual. They provide objective, quantitative scores that allow us to compare individuals in
(35) equivalent ways. In addition, the tests generate a measure of individual ability that remains constant over time. Furthermore, intelligence scores may reveal hidden strengths or weaknesses in individuals. This, in turn, allows society to
(40) understand an individual and provide him or her with better treatment options, educational opportunities, and special programs for individuals. IQ scores also may be used to track the effectiveness of such programs
(45) longitudinally. The merits of the Head Start program, for example, were first recognized by examining the increase in IQ scores of participants. However, perhaps the most salient argument for intelligence tests is that they
(50) eliminate subjective criteria and potential biases from the evaluation process. It is only through intelligence tests that psychologists and educators are able to gain essential information about a person's current cognitive functioning.

8. Which of the following best describes the organization of the passage?

   (A) A scientific hypothesis is presented and dismissed as inadequate.
   (B) Two competing schools of thought are discussed and then unified using theoretical analysis.
   (C) A cognitively-based phenomenon is described through systematic observation.
   (D) The merits of an argument are considered, then rejected in favor of the opposing position.
   (E) A paradox is presented and resolved using scientific evidence.

9. Opponents of intelligence testing would most likely agree with which of the following statements?

   (A) Intelligence tests should incorporate some assessment of social skills and pragmatic thought.
   (B) Test scores should never be used in evaluating individuals.
   (C) Creative answers are superior to those in the scoring guide.
   (D) Intelligence scores may reflect a wide variety of genetic and environmental effects.
   (E) Most administrators of IQ tests are not qualified to interpret the results.

10. Why does the author refer to individual factors in lines 23–25?

   I.   To emphasize the breadth of factors affecting IQ scores

   II. To illustrate the conceivable pitfalls of poor test interpretation

   III. To explicate potential psychological damage of labeling children based on IQ scores

   (A) I only
   (B) II only
   (C) III only
   (D) I and II
   (E) II and III

11. Recent government studies show that a woman <u>earns about seventy-six cents for every dollar that</u> a man with comparable skills in a comparable job earns.

   (A) earns about seventy-six cents for every dollar that
   (B) earns about seventy-six cents on every dollar which
   (C) earning seventy-six cents for about every dollar that
   (D) who earns about seventy-six cents for every dollar that
   (E) earns about seventy-six cents for every dollar of that which

12. A university offered its students a reduced-cost bus pass for use on buses operated by the public bus company. The university paid the full fare to the bus company and sold the pass at a discount to students. After several months of use, however, the university's administration determined that the program was unduly expensive to administer and discontinued it. As a result, the public bus company lost a sizable amount of revenue.

   Which of the following can be correctly inferred from the statements above?

   (A) Without the pass, many students stopped riding public buses.
   (B) Public buses are the only public transportation option for students.
   (C) The university could not afford to develop an alternate scheme for student transportation.
   (D) Students make up a significant proportion of the population in the city in which the university is located.
   (E) After the pass was discontinued, most students began walking to classes.

13. The number of people sentenced to death by state courts in State X has dropped significantly this year, compared to the number for the last five years. State legislators attribute this decrease entirely to the deterrent effect of the controversial public broadcast last January of the execution of serial killer John Doe.

    Which of the following, if true, would most seriously weaken the state legislators' explanation for the decrease in the number of death sentences?

    (A) For the last six years, State X has reported the highest number of death sentences of all the states that authorize the death penalty.

    (B) The number of households that watched the broadcast of the John Doe execution was much lower than expected.

    (C) Federalization of many capital offenses has removed the majority of the most heinous homicide cases from the state courts.

    (D) A civil rights group has been successful in obtaining a judicial order enjoining the state from broadcasting any executions until the Supreme Court reviews the legality of such broadcasts.

    (E) The homicide rate in State X has dropped by ten percent this year.

14. The defective thermometers will sometimes fail to register <u>a fever when it is present and indicate that there is one</u> when it is not.

    (A) a fever when it is present and indicate that there is one

    (B) a fever when it is present and indicate that it is present

    (C) when a fever is present and indicate that there is one

    (D) when a fever is present and indicates its presence

    (E) the presence of a fever when it is there and indicates its presence

15. To give creditors a better recourse for collecting debts, Parliament in 18th century England passed severe bankruptcy <u>laws; a debtor, for example, could have his ear cut off or even be</u> put to death.

    (A) laws; a debtor, for example, could have his ear cut off or even be

    (B) laws including a debtor having his ear cut off or being

    (C) laws in which a debtor could have his ear cut off or even be

    (D) laws; a debtor, for example, could have his ear cut off or even being

    (E) laws so that a debtor could have his ear cut off or even be

16. One result of the family's long ordeal at sea was <u>the appreciation of the fact that as a person dehydrates, their</u> minds tend to wander.

    (A) the appreciation of the fact that as a person dehydrates, their

    (B) the appreciation of the fact that as people dehydrate, their

    (C) to appreciate that when a person dehydrates, his or her

    (D) to appreciate that when people dehydrate, their

    (E) appreciating that as people dehydrate, their

17. Employee: Installing a nap room in our offices would boost employee morale. Other companies in our industry have recently installed nap rooms and they report a tremendous boost in employee morale. If we want to improve our productivity, then one way to do so is to install a nap room.

    Which of the following, if true, would most strengthen the author's argument?

    (A) The companies that have recently installed nap rooms have generated increased profits.
    (B) The companies that have installed nap rooms have also taken other effective measures to boost employee morale.
    (C) Nap rooms, once installed, are seldom used because workers feel awkward sleeping in the workplace.
    (D) Studies have shown that workers with positive attitudes can increase productivity by almost 20%.
    (E) Many analysts see installing a nap room as a sign that a company is progressive in its human resources policies.

18. Hayes Diner's plan to expand its dining area is ill-conceived. Since the diner is not expanding its kitchen as well, the restaurant will not be able to handle the additional orders and will lose business due to its poor service.

    Which of the following statements, if true, most weakens the prediction above?

    (A) The new dining area will only serve counter drinks and pre-cooked pastries.
    (B) Currently, the kitchen at Hayes Diner is understaffed, requiring workers to work occasional double shifts.
    (C) The new dining area will accommodate seven additional four-person tables.
    (D) Two other diners have opened in the same neighborhood as Hayes Diner.
    (E) The Hayes Diner has hired two new wait staff members to serve in the new dining area.

19. One should not attempt to operate a motor vehicle if <u>you have not been trained to do it</u>.

    (A) you have not been trained to do it
    (B) one has not been trained to do it
    (C) you have not been trained to do so
    (D) one have not been trained to do it
    (E) one has not been trained to do so

20. Of all the possible weather conditions that threaten American farms, tornadoes <u>are maybe the more difficult for prediction</u>.

    (A) are maybe the more difficult for prediction
    (B) are maybe the more difficult to predict
    (C) are probably the most difficult to predict
    (D) are maybe the most difficult for prediction
    (E) are, it may be, the more difficult to predict

Questions 21 through 23 are based on the following passage:

The under-valuation of work that has traditionally been done by women, such as jobs in the retail clothing industry, could be addressed in a number of different ways. One (5) method is for women to organize into unions, and then collectively bargain with—or exert pressure on—management to commit to increases in wage levels. (Evidence that this method is effective exists: women in unions (10) earn one-third more than do non-union women.) Another is to lobby for a change in the differing pay scales that persist between predominantly female industries and those, such as auto manufacturing, that are made up (15) largely by males.

The collective actions described above are sometimes difficult to engender. The majority of women in the workforce are employed in industries—catering and domestic and home- (20) based workers, to name a few—in which it is often difficult to organize. Indeed, women's access to employment itself is impeded by factors such as childcare and unequal access to education and training; once employed, women (25) face discrimination and poor access to economic resources, including land, capital, credit, and technology.

But today's inequities and challenges notwithstanding, women workers should try to (30) reshape or otherwise influence their work situations themselves rather than simply hoping that laws and other external means will remedy the problem for them.

21. According to the author, the best tool for correcting the wage discrepancy between men and women is to

(A) increase the wages of women and men in a single industry
(B) negotiate as a group with those who have the ability to alleviate the problem
(C) change the dynamic of collective bargaining
(D) rely on civil rights law to remedy economic grievances
(E) reduce unionization of industries that are predominantly female

22. According to the author, which of the following may be achieved through the processes of unionization and collective bargaining?

(A) Overcoming market pressures that keep wages in some industries lower than in others
(B) Encouraging worker flexibility in adjusting a new pay scale to economic conditions
(C) Helping workers to apply group pressure on their employers
(D) Aiding in determining the degree to which women are being underpaid
(E) Changing the pay relationship between unionized and non-unionzed workers within a single industry

23. Based on the information given in the passage, the author would be most likely to agree that

    (A) pay inequity for women exists because of the lack of unionization in traditionally female occupations

    (B) government regulation of industry to achieve pay equity for women is unnecessary because management has the power to effectively determine wages

    (C) unionization would solve all industry problems relating to the valuation of women's work

    (D) government regulation may play a role in achieving pay equity for women in industries in which collective bargaining has not been successful in doing so

    (E) poor access to economic resources hamper the collective actions of not only women workers but men also

24. Since pollution-causing human activities can cause an increase in average global temperatures, the mild winters in the area could be a result of the high concentration of vehicle exhaust emitted in the region. However, some scientists argue that the mild winters are a result of the increased rate of conversion of commercial areas to industrial areas.

    Which of the following, if true, strengthens the scientists' argument?

    (A) Although commercial property areas tend to emit significantly less pollution than industrial areas, they still emit more than the vehicles in the area on a given day.

    (B) Most of the people who work in commercial areas drive to work each day.

    (C) New strict laws in the area require buildings in the industrial areas to reduce their emissions by 60% in the next 5 years.

    (D) Vehicle exhaust is comprised largely of carbon monoxide, the same pollutant emitted by the industrial areas.

    (E) In response to consumer demand, exhaust levels per vehicle have steadily decreased in recent years.

25. Reducing the serotonin deficit caused by a breakdown in the passage of serotonin molecules from the presynaptic cell to receptors on the postsynaptic cell has been identified as a successful treatment for clinical depression for many individuals. A new series of drugs, Selective Serotonin Reuptake Inhibitors, prevent the presynaptic cell from reuptaking serotonin, thereby allowing normal amounts of serotonin to reach the receptors on the postsynaptic cell.

Which of the following can be correctly inferred from the above statements?

(A) If too much serotonin is released to the receptors, a person will feel extremely euphoric.

(B) Taking a Selective Serotonin Reuptake Inhibitor is currently the only successful treatment for clinical depression.

(C) Individuals who have normal levels of serotonin uptake do not run the risk of suffering from depression.

(D) By not taking a Selective Serotonin Reuptake Inhibitor, individuals with depression run the risk of depleting their serotonin levels.

(E) Taking a Selective Serotonin Reuptake Inhibitors reduces the incidence of depression in some people.

Questions 26 through 30 are based on the following passage:

Just south of Louisiana's barrier islands, a large portion of the Gulf of Mexico is completely devoid of marine life. Dubbed "the dead zone" by fishermen and scientists alike, the
(5) region has grown since its discovery in 1974, when it was small patches of lifeless water near the Louisiana shoreline. Starting near the Mississippi Delta, today it sometimes stretches as far as Texas; in the summer of 2000 it covered
(10) as many square miles as does the state of New Jersey.

The dead zone follows complicated cycles with compound causes. In late spring, intense sunshine separates the water into layers, forcing
(15) nitrogen-rich, warm, fresh water to skim over cooler, saltier, heavier Gulf water. The nitrogen-rich water provides algae a fertile field in which to multiply. The surface is covered by massive concentrations of algae that rain dead cells and
(20) fecal pellets to the seafloor, where bacteria decomposing the cells and pellets deplete oxygen in the water. At the same time, the discrete layer of lighter fresh water on top of the heavier Gulf water keeps air from reaching and
(25) refreshing the hypoxic zone. Later, strong winds over the Gulf resuscitate bottom waters by mixing them with the oxygen-rich river water above.

This pattern could spell environmental
(30) disaster for the Gulf of Mexico. Floods in the Midwest in 1993 poured huge amounts of nutrient-rich runoff from waterlogged cities and agricultural lands into the Gulf, and the dead zone doubled in size. The pollution that finds its
(35) way to the Gulf is traceable in large part to farmers upstream on the Mississippi. Sediment samples of the land before European settlement in the agricultural regions of the Great Plains showed lower nutrient levels. By 1950,
(40) sophisticated farming methods poured by-products of fertilizers and chemicals into the

river. Another fifteen percent of this pollution comes from municipal wastewater plants.

Resolving the problem of polluted
(45) waterways will require intensive research on all farms bordering the Mississippi. Solutions are likely to include a reduction of agricultural sources of nitrogen as well as control of livestock waste. A more comprehensive response calls for
(50) the creation of wetlands or wooded buffer zones along the river, which would remove nitrogen from water traveling downstream. Another proposed solution includes the removal of nitrogen and phosphorus from wastewater.

26. As used by the author, the phrase "the pollution that finds it way to the Gulf" (lines 34–35) can be best understood as referring to:

(A) combined industrial, agricultural, and urban wastes

(B) phosphorus from municipal wastewaters

(C) nitrogen from fertilizers used by modern farmers

(D) dead cells and fecal pellets rained down by algae masses

(E) Gulf water high in salt concentration

27. An assumption made by the author in discussing the causes and solutions to the dead zone problem is that:

(A) farmers will modify their techniques to benefit the environment of the Mississippi Delta

(B) fisherman are at odds with the farmers when it comes to the best solution

(C) the dead zone is the only environmental problem faced by the Gulf of Mexico

(D) the dead zone hasn't always existed in some shape or size in the Gulf

(E) algae are indicative of a healthy aquatic ecosystem

28. Given the information in the passage, efforts to eliminate the environmental hazards that exist in the Gulf of Mexico involve all of the following EXCEPT:

    (A) limitations of untreated wastewater permitted into the river
    (B) investigation of nitrogen run-off from farms bordering the Mississippi River
    (C) control of the sources of nitrogen entering the river
    (D) creation of wetlands or wooded buffer zones to act as nitrogen filters
    (E) a study of sediment levels in the area surrounding the dead zone

29. The primary purpose of the passage as a whole is to:

    (A) neutralize and resolve a debate
    (B) identify and discuss a problem
    (C) criticize and discredit an opinion
    (D) explain and criticize a policy
    (E) detail and support a position

30. Which of the following best describes the organization of the passage?

    (A) Several solutions to a long-term problem are compared and contrasted.
    (B) The historical roots and consequences of a problem are explored.
    (C) The mechanism of a problem is dissected and societal implications are considered.
    (D) The source and mechanism of a problem are identified and solutions are proposed.
    (E) Sources of a problem are assessed and action is demanded.

31. An environmental organization is currently conducting a series of demonstrations to protest logging of old growth forest by Corporation Y. In order to place further pressure on Corporation Y, the leaders of the environmental organization are considering conducting simultaneous demonstrations at nearby plastics production facilities also owned by Corporation Y.

    Which of the following questions is LEAST directly relevant to the environmentalists' decision of whether demonstrating at the plastics plant will help discourage Corporation Y from carrying on with its logging operations?

    (A) Would decreases in production at the plastics plant due to demonstrations significantly impact Corporation Y's income?
    (B) Does Corporation Y have other plastics plants that can pick up the slack for loss of production capacity at the plant where the protests are taking place?
    (C) Have other environmentalists been able to stop other corporations from logging operations in similar situations?
    (D) Have other political action organizations been able to achieve their goals by employing similar tactics?
    (E) Do other corporations that carry on logging operations also own plastics plants?

32. It is dangerous to own certain animals as pets unless you have received proper training in how to handle them. Some children have purchased dangerous pets sold at a local pet store. The store is endangering the safety of the children.

The argument above assumes which of the following?

(A) The government should provide instruction in the proper handling of dangerous pets.

(B) Sales of snakes to people without proper training in handling them should be outlawed.

(C) Children are inherently less capable of handling dangerous pets than adults.

(D) The owners of the local pet store are indifferent to the needs of the community.

(E) The store does not provide proper training to the children purchasing the dangerous pets.

33. Color blindness, a disorder whose most common manifestation is an inability to distinguish red from green, is much more common <u>between white males than between</u> women or members of other races.

(A) between white males than between

(B) between white males and

(C) in white males and

(D) in white males than in

(E) in white males than it is in

Questions 34 through 35 are based on the following passage:

Multi-party initiatives are becoming increasingly popular among the members of the parliament of Country W. Although legislation proposed under the auspices of more
(5) than one party may not adhere as strictly to the agenda of each party involved as legislation proposed by only one party, the political backing of the voting blocs represented by the cooperating parties make such proposals more
(10) likely to pass. The benefit of multi-party initiatives is that legislation important to the general welfare of Country W that might otherwise have foundered in inter-party disagreements can effectively be enacted.

34. Which of the following statements by a minister of Party C in the government of Country W is most consistent with the beliefs of an individual political party in the situation described above?

(A) "Our party would rather compromise on some issues and also see other parties compromise on their issues than run the risk of not having legislation that we propose pass."

(B) "Our party would rather give up a few minor points of ideology than risk having the issues important to our constituents not be addressed as a result of the government's inability to pass any new laws."

(C) "Our party would rather participate in an environment that fosters inter-party cooperation than persist in constant conflict with other parties."

(D) "Our party would rather have other parties join in support of our legislation than join in supporting the proposals of other parties."

(E) "Our party would rather have our proposals passed because they represent what is best for the welfare of our country than to become engaged in the agendas of other parties."

35. Which of the following can be inferred from the passage above?

    (A) Multi-partisan initiatives deal with proposals too large and complex for a single party to have passed into law.

    (B) Multi-partisan initiatives produce a confluence of ideas that results in legislation that is generally better overall for the welfare of Country W.

    (C) Multi-partisan initiatives have in the past been less common in the government of Country W than now.

    (D) Jointly-supported proposals represent only the interests of the parties that back their passage into law.

    (E) Jointly-supported proposals are not any more likely to be passed into law than proposals presented by individual parties.

36. Global climate-change models used by the Institute for Environmental Studies predict that the higher the average global temperature rises, extreme weather conditions will occur more.

    (A) extreme weather conditions will occur more

    (B) the greater the occurrence of extreme weather conditions

    (C) extreme weather conditions will occur

    (D) the occurrence of extreme weather conditions will be more

    (E) more extreme weather conditions will occur

37. Using sophisticated technology, a hurricane can be detected in its incipient stage and early warnings can be issued to the media.

    (A) Using sophisticated technology, a hurricane can be detected in its incipient stage and early warnings can be issued

    (B) A hurricane can be detected in its incipient stage, using sophisticated technology, and early warnings can be issued

    (C) In its incipient stage, a hurricane can be detected using sophisticated technology, and giving early warnings

    (D) Using sophisticated technology, meteorologists can detect a hurricane in its incipient stage and issue early warnings

    (E) Meteorologists, using sophisticated technology, are detecting a hurricane in its incipient stage and could issue early warnings

38. Although earlier poets introduced Dido as <u>the founder of Carthage, Virgil is credited as having invented</u> her encounter with Aeneas.

    (A) the founder of Carthage, Virgil is credited as having invented
    (B) being the founder of Carthage, Virgil is credited as having invented
    (C) the founder of Carthage, Virgil is credited with having invented
    (D) being the founder of Carthage, Virgil is credited as the one who invented
    (E) the founder of Carthage, Virgil is credited to have invented

39. Joshua Tree National Monument was designated a National Park in <u>1994; as a result</u> a total of 55 National Parks under the jurisdiction of the National Park Service.

    (A) 1994; as a result
    (B) 1994, to result in
    (C) 1994, resulting in
    (D) 1994; and the result was
    (E) 1994, as a result

40. Scientists determined that the acreage of healthy forests in North and Central America had <u>declined by a 59% decrease</u> over the previous several centuries.

    (A) declined by a 59% decrease
    (B) declined by 59%
    (C) decreased by a 59% decline
    (D) a 59% decrease
    (E) decline by 59%

41. Prior to purchasing a corporate bond, investors are advised to request important information <u>regarding the note, including its maturity date, interest rate, and whether its credit rating is very secure or highly speculative, which depends on the seller's financial status.</u>

    (A) regarding the note, including its maturity date, interest rate, and whether its credit rating is very secure or highly speculative, which depends on the seller's financial status
    (B) regarding the note, including its maturity date, interest rate, and credit rating, which may range from very secure to highly speculative depending on the seller's financial status
    (C) regarding the note, which includes the maturity date, interest rate, and its credit rating, which may range between very secure and highly speculative, depending on the seller's financial status
    (D) in regards to the note, including the maturity date and interest rate, and also its credit rating, which ranges from the very secure to the highly speculative, depending on the financial status of the seller
    (E) in regard to them, including maturity date, interest rates, and if the credit rating is very secure or highly speculative, which is dependent on the sellers' financial status

CHAPTER TWO

Diagnostic
Answers and Explanations

ANSWER KEY: ANALYTICAL WRITING ASSESSMENT

For both essays in the AWA, you will be evaluated on how well you:

- organize, develop, and express your ideas about the issue presented
- provide relevant supporting reasons and examples
- control the elements of standard written English

For the Issue essay, you must analyze the issue and explain your views. There is no correct answer. For the Argument essay, you must critique the argument presented. You are *not* being asked to present your own views on the subject.

The AWA score is an average of the scores given for the two essays. Scores range from 0 to 6 (best). Each essay is given two, independent ratings, one of which may be performed by an electronic system that evaluates more than 50 structural and linguistic features, including organization of ideas, syntactic variety, and topical analysis. If the two ratings differ by more than one point, an additional evaluation will be made.

The following table will give you a general idea of the guidelines a GMAT grader will have in mind when reading your essays:

6: Outstanding Essay

- Insightfully presents and convincingly supports an opinion on the issue or a critique of the argument
- Ideas are very clear, well organized, and logically connected
- Shows superior control of language: grammar, stylistic variety, and accepted conventions of writing; minor flaws may occur

5: Strong Essay

- Presents and strongly supports an opinion on the issue or a critique of the argument
- Ideas are generally clear and well organized; connections are logical
- Shows solid control of language: grammar, stylistic variety, and accepted conventions of writing; minor flaws may occur

4: Adequate Essay

- Presents and adequately supports an opinion on the issue or a critique of the argument
- Ideas are fairly clear and adequately organized; logical connections are satisfactory
- Shows satisfactory control of language: grammar, stylistic variety, and accepted conventions of writing; some flaws may occur

3: Limited Essay

- Succeeds only partially in presenting and supporting an opinion on the issue or a critique of the argument
- Ideas may be unclear and poorly organized
- Shows less than satisfactory control of language: contains significant mistakes in grammar, usage, and sentence structure

2: Seriously Flawed Essay

- Shows little success in presenting and supporting an opinion on the issue or a critique of the argument
- Ideas lack organization
- Meaning is impeded by many serious mistakes in grammar, usage, and sentence structure

1: Fundamentally Deficient Essay

- Fails to present a coherent opinion on the issue or a critique of the argument
- Ideas are seriously disorganized
- Lacks meaning due to widespread severe mistakes in grammar, usage, and sentence structure

0: Unscorable Essay

- Essay completely ignores topic

Following are two sample essays in response to the AWA assignments. Both essays would earn a perfect score.

Sample Issue Essay (Score 6)

"The emergence of a new competitor is always harmful to a company. The new competitor forces the company to become reactionary and short-sighted, rather than sticking to its long-term strategy."

Discuss the extent to which you agree or disagree with the opinion stated above. Support your views with reasons and/or examples from your own experience, observations or reading.

If the author of the given statement were able to support his or her position with specific examples or direct observation, one might find it easy to agree with. However, as written, I cannot agree with the opinion offered. In fact, the statement is itself as "reactionary and short-sighted" as the author claims a company facing competition might be. With the following examples of companies continuing unaffected or even improving their business in the face of new competition, it becomes clear that emerging competition is not always deleterious.

To state that competition is always harmful is to ignore several examples of companies that not only exist, but thrive in competitive markets. For example, Internet provider America Online (AOL) has faced, and many would argue, overcome the competitors that have emerged and evolved since the early days of the Internet. Even facing hundreds of new competitors has not harmed AOL.

Despite what the author stated above, a new competitor does not truly *force* the original company to do anything. To illustrate the concept that a new competitor does not compel an established business to react, consider Starbucks coffee franchises. Most cities and towns have at least one Starbucks shop. When a new, or even several new, coffee shops open in the same city, it will hardly force Starbucks to do anything. A new competitor that offers coffee at a lower price or serves a specialty dessert would not force Starbucks to lower their own prices or change their menu. In addition, new competition could fail for any reason, from an undesirable location to a poorly planned menu. In these cases, a struggling or failing new business would not affect the original company.

Clearly, new competition is a factor in adapting or reacting business, however specialization is not necessarily detrimental. One industry that has specialized in the face of competition is the travel industry. Travel agencies have faced heavy competition with the advent and evolution of online booking of hotels, flights, car rentals, cruises, and other travel arrangements. In this case, competition led to specialization. For example, some travel agencies chose to specialize in tour packages for senior citizens, a segment of the population that is perhaps less likely to use the Internet to search for and book travel plans. Other travel agencies focus strictly on last minute discount travel, something consumers under time constraints might not have time to do themselves. Again, the idea that new competition is damaging or that reactionary changes are negative is proved untrue.

Finally, assuming a company does have a long-term strategy, its options when facing nascent competition are myriad. The original company can continue to follow its long-term design, if that's what its market warrants, or it can choose to be original in its approach. It is important to note that any company that has a long-term strategy that is so inflexible that it can't adapt to new rivals may fail anyway. For this reason, a company's long-term plan should include provisions for shifts in the economy, the market, the consumer's needs and interests, or technology. For example, large booksellers were probably unaware 30 years ago about how much online shopping would affect the bookselling market. The long-term strategy many stores may have had was to keep a clean and well-stocked store and to sell quality books at the lowest prices. However, with online orders becoming so considerable many large booksellers have built their own websites and included an online shopping element to their businesses. Although this is reactionary, it still ultimately falls within their long-term plans. Additionally, in this example, the reaction is not at all short-sighted, but is indeed a strategic business move.

In reviewing the examples of the ways that competition does not harm and can actually improve business, the author's statement exemplifies a reactionary and short-sighted opinion. Clearly, competition is beneficial to the businesses, and ultimately to the consumers, who find products and services improving and diversifying as a result of emerging rivals.

Sample Argument Essay (Score 6)

The following appeared as part of a campaign by a publishing company to sell more advertising space in its monthly news magazine, the *Halcyon*.

> "Advertising in the *Halcyon* has helped many companies increase their sales. For example, Pallas Textile Mills began advertising in the *Halcyon* one year ago and has seen its business increase by 15 percent since that time. You, too, can use our magazine to make your business more profitable."

Discuss how well-reasoned you find this argument. In your discussion be sure to analyze the line of reasoning and the use of evidence in the argument. For example, you may need to consider what questionable assumptions underlie the thinking and what alternative explanations or counter-examples might weaken the conclusion. You can also discuss what sort of evidence would strengthen or refute the argument, what changes would make it more logically sound, and what, if anything, would help you better evaluate its conclusion.

The stated conclusion that advertising in Halcyon magazine will increase sales for companies who choose to do so may, in fact, be true. However, as written the argument is poorly reasoned, lacks quantitative information that would strengthen the conclusion, and contains questionable assumptions.

The first part of the statement includes the first two terms that need to be quantified. To say that "advertising in the Halcyon has helped many companies increase their sales," is ineffective in proving such a conclusion. First, the author of this statement needs to quantify "many." Without knowing actually how many companies have been helped, potential advertisers cannot make an informed decision. For example, the publisher of the Halcyon might consider five companies many, however that is not the kind of track record that would impress potential advertisers. In addition, the amount of which sales have increased for those companies would also need to be measured for the argument to better support the conclusion.

Although one example is given that specifies a company that has had increased sales since advertising with the Halcyon, it too suffers from questionable assumptions. The first is that the 15% increase that Pallas Textile Mills has seen since advertising in the magazine is actually a result of those ads. To fully support its claim, the Halcyon would have to show direct causation from the ad campaign to that increase in sales. Also, the author of the statement fails to mention the nature of the Mills' advertising.

Perhaps that company used a full-page color ad in all 12 issues, from which one might expect a greater increase in sales.

The second assumption that the statement makes is that a 15% increase is actually an improvement. For example, if Pallas Mills typically sees a 56% increase in sales annually, this paltry increase would really show a slowing in business after advertising in the Halcyon. By providing evidence from both the Halcyon and the advertiser, the argument would be more sound and effective.

In addition to the questionable assumptions made, a lack of evidence regarding the directive "use our magazine" also weakens the argument. The Halcyon provides no information about the magazine itself. The publisher should include information such as the cost and size of available advertising space, the distribution of the magazine, and the demographics of the readers. These facts would strengthen the statement tremendously. For example, the Halcyon is a news magazine, but perhaps its target audience is college students in and around the Boston area and the distribution is only about 3,000 issues per month. In this case, it is illogical for retirement communities in Arizona to advertise in the Halcyon with the intention of increasing sales. Clearly, without accurate quantifiable information, companies should not assume that advertising with this particular magazine will be effective.

Finally, the publisher of the Halcyon asserts that advertising can "make your business more profitable." That may seem like a soothing fact. However, it is not logically sound. The Halcyon makes no claim as to how much profits will increase, nor does it make any provision if profits actually decline. This statement would be bolstered by an arrangement for money back on ads that do not generate increased sales, or even a discount on future advertising space in the event that their assertion of larger profits is untrue.

The conclusion that any company that advertises in the Halcyon is certainly an appealing one. However, upon closer examination, the evidence to support this claim is too weak. With more direct evidence, educated assumptions, and stronger explanations, the publisher of the Halcyon could make a strong argument and in turn, see its own business increase considerably.

ANSWER KEY: QUANTITATIVE SECTION

1. D	14. D	27. C
2. E	15. A	28. D
3. A	16. D	29. C
4. E	17. B	30. A
5. D	18. B	31. D
6. C	19. C	32. C
7. E	20. B	33. A
8. C	21. B	34. C
9. C	22. C	35. C
10. E	23. A	36. E
11. D	24. B	37. D
12. C	25. E	
13. E	26. E	

1. D

Statement (1) tells us that one factor of the left side of the equation is $(x + 4)$. If we call the other factor $(x + a)$, where a is a constant, then $(x + 4)(x + a) = x^2 + kx + 8$. If we multiply out $(x + 4)(x + a)$ using FOIL, we obtain $(x + 4)(x + a) = x^2 + (a + 4)x + 4a$. So $x^2 + (a + 4)x + 4a = x^2 + kx + 8$. The constant terms $4a$ and 8 must be equal. So $4a = 8$. Then $a = 2$. So the other factor must be $(x + 2)$. So $x^2 + kx + 8 = (x + 2)(x + 4)$. When we multiply out $(x + 2)(x + 4)$, by using FOIL, the resulting equation is $x^2 + 6x + 8 = 0$. So $k = 6$. Statement (1) is sufficient.

Statement (2) tells us that one factor is $(x + 2)$. Once we know that, the other factor must be $(x + 4)$. Once again $x^2 + kx + 8 = (x + 2)(x + 4)$, and when we use FOIL on $(x + 2)(x + 4)$, the resulting equation is again $x^2 + 6x + 8 = 0$. So $k = 6$. Therefore, Statement (2) is also sufficient.

2. E

Since most of the choices deal with even versus odd, it is best to think in those terms. If x is an integer, whether even or odd, the expression above

must be even. This is because we have the factors $(x + 2)$ and $(x + 3)$. If x is even, the first 2 factors, x and $x + 2$, will be even. Let $x = 2$; $x + 2 = 4$, which is even, and $x + 3 = 5$, which is odd. If x is odd, the third factor, $x + 3$, will be even. Let $x = 3$; $x + 2 = 5$, which is odd, and $x + 3 = 6$, which is even. If the product of a group of integers contains at least one even integer, the product will be even, because an even integer times any integer yields an even integer. All even numbers are divisible by 2. Therefore, answer choice (E) is correct.

3. A

The team won 10 out of its first 24 games. The least number of games necessary occurs when the team wins the rest of its games. Suppose that x more games are played and that the team wins these next x games. Then the team will have won a total of $10 + x$ games out of a total of $24 + x$ games. The fraction of the games that the team will have won is $\frac{10 + x}{24 + x}$. We want this fraction to be at least $\frac{5}{7}$. So $\frac{10 + x}{24 + x} \geq \frac{5}{7}$. Solve this inequality for x. To begin, multiply both sides of the inequality $\frac{10 + x}{24 + x} \geq \frac{5}{7}$ by the positive quantity $7(24 + x)$, which will keep the direction of the inequality the same and enable us to get rid of the fractions. Then $7(10 + x) \geq 5(24 + x)$, $70 + 7x \geq 120 + 5x$, $2x \geq 50$, and $x \geq 25$. The least number of games that the team must play in the remainder of the season is 25.

4. E

To get the diameter of a circle, we need the radius, area, or circumference. From statement (1), all that we know is that the radius is 4 times the length of *OM*. There are an infinite number of lengths of *OM* and *MP* that are in the ratio of 1 to 3, so statement (1) is insufficient.

For statement (2), knowing that *OP* bisects *NL* does not give any information that will get us to the length of the diameter, so it too is insufficient.

Statements (1) and (2) together do not provide any of the measurements above that will allow us to calculate the radius.

5. D

To determine how many tables are necessary to accommodate the extra guests, we must divide 27 by the number of people that can be seated at a table. We know that 32 tables are already filled, so if we knew the total number of invited guests, we could divide that by 32 to determine how many people fit at a table.

Statement (1) tells us the total number of invited guests, so it is sufficient.

Statement (2) tells us how many people can be seated at a table, so it is also sufficient.

6. C

We should start with answer choice (D) and move up the choices to see if any choice MUST be true. Choice (D) may be true, but if $7 \leq n \leq 10$, then this statement is not true. Choice (C) must be true because all possible values of *n* specified by the inequality in the question stem are greater than –8. This is the correct choice. We can stop here. Choice (B) is incorrect because there are more values within the range in the question stem than just –6. Choice (A) may be true, but does not have to be. If $8 \leq n \leq 10$, choice (A) is not true.

7. E

We need to add the number of runners with single letters, and the number of runners with two letters where the two letters are different. We can have 26 runners represented by the single letters A through Z. For the two letter codes, the first letter can be any of the 26 letters. The second letter can be any of the other 25 letters since the two letters must be different. So the number of possible codes is $26(25) = 650$.

Therefore, the maximum number of runners that can receive unique codes for the race is $26 + 650 = 676$.

8. C

Statement (1) is insufficient because it tells us nothing about either *a* or *b*, individually. *a* and *b* could be anything, as long as their sum is 9.

Statement (2) is insufficient because if $ab = 14$, all we know is that either both variables are positive *or* both variables are negative.

Together the two statements are sufficient because we know from Statement (2) that the variables *a* and *b* are either both positive or both negative. When we combine this information with statement (1), we see that both *a* and *b* must be positive, because adding two negative numbers results in a negative number, so adding two negative numbers cannot yield a positive result. So $a > 0$.

9. C

To conceptualize this problem, it may be helpful to draw a diagram.

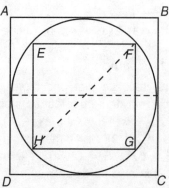

The first step is recognizing the role of the diameter of the circle in both squares. In *ABCD*, the diameter is equal to any side of the square. In *EFGH*, the diameter is equal to a diagonal running from one corner of the square to the opposite corner.

Algebraically, we can solve for a side of each square in terms of the diameter and then examine the ratio of the two areas. The area of *ABCD* in terms of the diameter is simply d^2, since the diameter is equal to the length of a side of *ABCD*. The area of *EFGH* is a little bit more difficult to determine. Since the diameter of the circle is equal to the diagonal of *EFGH*, and we know that the diagonal of a square is equal to $x\sqrt{2}$, where *x* is equal to the length of a side, we can let $d = x\sqrt{2}$. Therefore, *x* (the length of a side of *EFGH*) is equal to $\dfrac{d}{\sqrt{2}}$, and the area of *EFGH* is equal to $\left(\dfrac{d}{\sqrt{2}}\right)^2 = \dfrac{d^2}{2}$. Now we can calculate the ratio of the area of *ABCD* to the area of *EFGH*.

The ratio is $\dfrac{d^2}{\left(\dfrac{d^2}{2}\right)} = d^2\left(\dfrac{2}{d^2}\right) = 2$.

We could also pick numbers. When doing so, we should keep this in mind—we know that the diagonal of a square forms a 45/45/90 triangle with two sides, and the hypotenuse of such a triangle is given by $x\sqrt{2}$, where *x* is the length of a side of the square, which is a leg of the right triangle. Knowing that, let's choose as our diameter $2\sqrt{2}$. That means that the area of *ABCD* is given by $d^2 = (2\sqrt{2})^2 = 8$. We can find a side length for *EFGH* by setting $2\sqrt{2} = x\sqrt{2}$ and solving for *x*, which gives us $x = 2$. That means that the area of *EFGH* is $2^2 = 4$. The ratio, then, of the area of *ABCD* to the area of *EFGH* is 8:4, which we can reduce to 2:1. If we were forced to resort to guessing on this problem, we could eliminate choices (A) and (B) with a fairly basic understanding of this: since *ABCD* is bigger than *EFGH*, the first number in the ratio needs to be

bigger than the second, which is only the case in the last three answer choices.

10. E

This may be set up using the equation $2x + 3x + 7x = 144$, where *x* is equal to the coefficient by which each part of the proportion must be multiplied to equal the number of hours worked by each person. This equation simplifies to $12x = 144$. Therefore, $x = 12$. The consultant who worked the most hours worked $7x = 7(12) = 84$ hours.

11. D

This is a "Which of the following…" question, so it is a good strategy to start with choice (E) and move up the choices. If $x = 9$, then 50 divided by 9 has a remainder of 5. A remainder of $x - 6$ is $9 - 6 = 3$, not 5. Now let's try choice (D). If *x* is 7, then 50 divided by 7 has a remainder of 1. In this case, a remainder of $x - 6$ is $7 - 6 = 1$. This is correct.

12. C

In January, the store sold 10 boxes of truffles at $45.00 a box. So the revenue in January was $45.00 × 10 which is $450.00.

In February, the store sold 15 boxes of truffles at $42.50 a box. So the revenue in January was $42.50 × 15 which is $637.50.

The increase in revenue from January to February is $637.50 − $450.00 = $187.50.

13. E

Since we know that *a*, *b*, and *c* are all positive, we can divide both sides of statement (1) by *a*, without any implications caused by negative values or zero. Statement (1) then becomes $a > b$. This tells us nothing about *c*, so it is insufficient.

For the same reason, we can divide both sides of the inequality $ac > c^2$ of statement (2) by *c*, to get the inequality $a > c$. This tells us nothing about *b*, so it is insufficient.

When we combine the statements, we know that *a* is greater than both *b* and *c*, but we do not know which is the larger of *b* and *c*.

14. D

It is helpful to sketch a diagram to make the situation more concrete. The diagram includes dotted lines for the distances we need to determine.

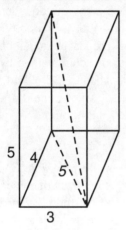

The best place to start is to find the hypotenuse of the right triangle with the lengths of the two legs given in the problem. Since we have legs of lengths 3 and 4, we know this hypotenuse has a length of 5 since 3:4:5 is a common Pythagorean triplet. This side is now one of the legs of a new triangle. The other leg is the dimension not yet used, which was 5. Now we have a right triangle with both legs of length 5. This is a 45/45/90 triangle. Therefore, the ratio of the sides is $x : x : x\sqrt{2}$. So the hypotenuse, which represents the greatest straight-line distance between any two points in the crate, is $5\sqrt{2}$.

15. A

We can write two equations here. The first equation can be translated into the equation $J + R = t$, where J and R represent the numbers of dollars that Jane and Richard have, respectively. The second equation would be $J = 3R + v$. A good way to solve for the number of dollars that Jane has is to first solve the second equation, $J = 3R + v$, for R in

terms of J. We have $J = 3R + v$, $J - v = 3R$, and then $R = \frac{J - v}{3}$. We can now substitute $\frac{J - v}{3}$ for R into the first equation, $J + R = t$, to get $J + \frac{J - v}{3} = t$. We can now solve for J in terms of v and t as follows:

$$J + \frac{J - v}{3} = t$$

$$\frac{J - v}{3} = t - J$$

$$J - v = 3(t - J)$$

$$J - v = 3t - 3J$$

$$-v - 3t = -4J$$

$$J = \frac{-v - 3t}{-4} = \frac{v + 3t}{4}$$

16. D

Look at statement (1). Dividing both sides of the inequality $4^{k + 1} > 4,000$ by the positive quantity 4 keeps the direction of the inequality the same and we have that $4^k > 1,000$. We can answer the question with a YES. Statement (1) is sufficient. Eliminate (B), (C), and (E).

Look at statement (2). Here we have the equation $4^{k - 1} = 256$. Multiplying both sides of this equation by 4, we have $4(4^{k - 1}) = 4(256)$, and then $4^k = 1,024$. We see that since $4^k = 1,024$, $4^k > 1,000$. We can answer the question with a YES. Statement (2) is sufficient.

17. B

When the product of a group of terms is 0, at least one of the terms must equal 0. Here, $(x + 16)(x + 3)(x + 5) = 0$. So at least one of the factors $x + 16$, $x + 3$, and $x + 5$ must be 0. Therefore, x may equal −16, −5, or −3. The largest possible value of x is −3.

18. B

$$\frac{(3)(-2.4) - (9)(0.8)}{60} = \frac{-7.2 - 7.2}{60} = \frac{-14.4}{60} = -0.24$$

19. C

We can write an equation to express the situation as follows: $.78(100) + 0.60(T - 100) = 0.72T$, where T represents the total number of deliveries. We then solve this equation as follows:

$78 + 0.6T - 60 = 0.72T$

$$18 = 0.12T$$

$$T = \frac{18}{0.12}\left(\frac{100}{100}\right) = \frac{1800}{12} = 150$$

We could also solve this question using Backsolving. Let's begin with choice (C). Suppose that the total number of deliveries is 150. Then 78 of the first 100 were on time. 60 percent of the remaining 50 deliveries were time, or 30 of the next 50 were on time. Therefore, there were a total of 78 + 30 = 128 deliveries on time. The overall percent of deliveries that were made on time is $\frac{108}{150} = \frac{54}{75}$ $= \frac{18}{25} = 72\%$.

This works, so choice (C) is the correct answer.

20. B

We simply need to find both the x and y coordinates and locate the correct answer choice. Point J is –3 units in the x-direction and +4 units in the y-direction. Therefore, the correct answer is (–3, 4).

21. B

Since we know the sum of the three variables, we could solve for r if you knew the sum of s and t, or if we had two more distinct equations containing r, s, or t.

Without any information about t, Statement (1) is insufficient. Statement (2) gives us the sum of s and t, which we could then subtract from 180 to find r. Statement (2) is sufficient.

22. C

To get the average of p, q, and r, we need either the values of all 3 variables, or the sum of the 3 variables.

Statement (1) is one equation with the 3 variables p, q, and r. This does not help at all, so statement (1) is insufficient.

Statement (2) is one equation with the 3 variables p, q, and r. This does not help at all, so statement (2) is insufficient.

Taking the two statements together, we can add the corresponding sides of the equations in statements (1) and (2) to get $5p + 5q + 5r = 0$. If we divide both sides of this equation by 5, we have $p + q + r = 0$. We now have the sum of the three variables and we could get the average by dividing both sides by 3. Therefore, the two statements taken together are sufficient.

23. A

This is a word problem involving permutations (key word: "arrangements"). We need to identify how many students there are, and what restrictions are placed on their seating arrangement.

Starting with the back row, the teacher can choose from five students (all but the troublesome one) to seat first. In the successive seats in the back row, she can choose from 5, 4, and 3, respectively. Moving to the front row, 2 students and the troublemaker remain. Thus, she can choose from 3, 2, and 1 students for the three seats in the front row. To calculate the number of possible permutations, we multiply all of these numbers together: $(5)(4)(3)(3)(2)(1) = 360$.

24. B

The best way to deal with an equation containing fractions is to multiply every term by the least common denominator. Here, when we multiply every term by m, we are left with $5m^2 + 4 - 2m^2 = n$. This simplifies to $n = 3m^2 + 4$.

25. E

The question itself contains an inequality: Is $x > 0$? Both statements are in the form of inequalities, making this question a little tricky. In each case, the expression enclosed by the absolute value sign could represent a positive or a negative number. For instance, the inequality $|a| > 6$ could mean that $a > 6$. But it would also be true if a were less than –6. For example, $|-7| > 6$, because $|-7| = 7$. So for each statement, we must consider two possibilities.

Statement (1): insufficient. Remember that in general, if $h > 0$, then $|y| > h$ is equivalent to $y > h$ or $y < -h$. If $|x + 6| > 6$, then $x + 6 > 6$ or $x + 6 < -6$. If $x + 6 > 6$, then $x > 0$. If $x + 6 < -6$, then $x < -12$. Thus, $x > 0$ or $x < -12$. So the inequality in statement (1) is insufficient to answer the question, because it's true for $x > 0$ or for $x < -12$.

Statement (2): insufficient. The statement $|x - 6| > 6$ is true if $x - 6 > 6$ or if $x - 6 < -6$. That is, this statement is true if $x > 12$, or if $x < 0$, so this statement is insufficient.

Statements (1) and (2): insufficient. If we combine the two statements, x could be greater than 12 *or* less than –12; we still don't know whether x is positive or negative.

26. E

b and r are the original numbers of blue and red marbles, respectively. After adding 4 blue and 5 red, the total number of blue is $b + 4$ and the total number of red is $r + 5$. When all the outcomes are equally likely, the probability formula says that

$$\text{Probability} = \frac{\text{Number of favorable outcomes}}{\text{Number of possible outcomes}}.$$ So the probability of choosing a red marble is

$$\frac{r + 5}{r + 5 + b + 4} = \frac{r + 5}{r + b + 9}.$$

We could also answer this question by picking numbers. Let $r = 1$ and $b = 2$. After the marbles are added, there are 6 red and 6 blue. Therefore, the probability of choosing a red marble is $\frac{1}{2}$. Now substitute $b = 4$ and $r = 5$ into each answer choice. Any answer choice that does not equal $\frac{1}{2}$ when $b = 4$ and $r = 5$ can be eliminated. When using the picking numbers method, all 4 incorrect answer choices must be eliminated because sometimes an incorrect answer choice works for the particular values that we choose.

(A): $\dfrac{r}{b + r} = \dfrac{1}{2 + 1} = \dfrac{1}{3}$. This is not $\dfrac{1}{2}$. Incorrect.

(B): $\dfrac{r}{b + 4} = \dfrac{1}{2 + 4} = \dfrac{1}{6}$. Incorrect.

(C): $\dfrac{r + 5}{r + 9} = \dfrac{1 + 5}{1 + 9} = \dfrac{6}{10}$. Incorrect.

(D): $\dfrac{r + 5}{b + r + 5} = \dfrac{1 + 5}{2 + 1 + 5} = \dfrac{6}{8}$. Incorrect.

Now that all 4 incorrect answer choices have been eliminated, we know that choice (E) must be correct. Just to be sure, let's check.

(E): $\dfrac{r + 5}{b + r + 9} = \dfrac{1 + 5}{2 + 1 + 9} = \dfrac{6}{12} = \dfrac{1}{2}$.

27. C

This is a value question, so we need one and only one value for ab to have sufficiency. We can either find values for a and b or a value for ab itself.

Statement (1) relates a to b in percentage terms but doesn't give us any concrete numbers to go on, so it's not sufficient. Eliminate (A) and (D).

Statement 2 tells us that $b = 2$ (remember: 1 is not a prime number; 2 is the only prime less than 3), but nothing about a, so it's also insufficient. Eliminate (B).

Together, the statements are sufficient. We know that $b = 2$ and a is 200% more than b. With this information, we could calculate the value of a and then ab, although there is no need to do the math. For sufficiency, it's enough to know that we could find the exact values of a and b.

28. D

Look at statement (1). The left side of the equation $a^2 - b^2 = 32$, $a^2 - b^2$, is a difference of squares and can be factored. $a^2 - b^2 = (a - b)(a + b)$. So $(a - b)(a + b) = 32$. The question stem says that $a + b = 8$, so we can substitute 8 for $a + b$ in the equation $(a - b)(a + b) = 32$. Then $8(a - b) = 32$. Now we have the two different first-degree equations: $a + b = 8$ and $8(a - b) = 32$. So we know that statement (1) will lead to one value for a and one value for b, so statement (1) is sufficient. Although we do not have to solve the equations, let's see what the solution is. We have $a + b = 8$ and $8(a - b) = 32$. Dividing both sides of $8(a - b) = 32$ by 8, we have $a - b = 4$. Now let's add the corresponding sides of the equations $a + b = 8$ and $a - b = 4$. The b terms will cancel. We have $(a + b) + (a - b) = 8 + 4$, $a + b + a - b = 12$, $2a = 12$, and $a = 6$. Substitute 6 for a in the equation $a + b = 8$. Then $6 + b = 8$ and $b = 2$. Thus, $a = 6$ and $b = 2$. So $ab = (6)(2) = 12$. Thus $ab > 8$ and we can answer the question with a YES. Statement (1) is sufficient. Eliminate (B), (C), and (E).

Now let's look at statement (2). Here, $a^2 + b^2 = 40$. If we square the corresponding sides of the equation $a + b = 8$, we obtain $(a + b)^2 = 8^2$, and then $a^2 + 2ab + b^2 = 64$. Now let's subtract the corresponding sides of the equation $a^2 + b^2 = 40$ from the equation $a^2 + 2ab + b^2 = 64$. The a^2 and b^2 terms will cancel and we will be left with $2ab$ on the left side of the resulting equation. We have $(a^2 + 2ab + b^2) - (a^2 + b^2) = 64 - 40$, $a^2 + 2ab + b^2 - a^2 - b^2 = 24$, $2ab = 24$, and $ab = 12$. Thus $ab > 8$ and we can answer the question with a YES. Statement (2) is sufficient.

29. C

The stem tells us very little, so move on to the statements.

Statement (1): insufficient. This says that when n is divided by 4 there is a remainder of 3. That is, n must be 3 greater than a multiple of 4. We can determine the several integers that are greater than 100 and less than 120 that satisfy this condition. These integers are 103, 107, 111, 115, and 119. Since there is more than one possible value for n, statement (1) by itself is not sufficient. Eliminate (A) and (D).

Statement (2): insufficient. If there is no remainder when n is divided by 5, then n must be a multiple of 5. The multiples of 5 that are greater than 100 and less than 120 are 105, 110, and 115. Again, there

are several possible values for n, so statement (2) is insufficient. Eliminate (B).

Statements (1) and (2): sufficient. If we combine the statements, we can see that only one of the integers, 115, is a possible value of n under the conditions in statement (1) and statement (2), so (C) is correct.

30. A

Since this is a yes–no question, we'll have sufficiency only if $a + 1$ is always prime or never prime. We can't get much from the question stem, so we can go directly to the statements.

Statement (1): If a is a prime number greater than 3, a could be 5, 7, 11 and so on. All these values are odd, so $a + 1$ will always be an odd number plus 1. Thus, all the possible values of $a + 1$ will be even numbers greater than 2 (4, 6, 8, 10, and so on). None of these is prime, so $a + 1$ is never prime and the answer to the question "is $a + 1$ a prime number?" is "no". Statement (1) is sufficient and we can eliminate choices (B), (C), and (E).

Statement (2): if $a + 2$ is not prime, a could be 2, in which case $a + 1 = 3$, which is prime. But a could also be any negative integer, which means that a is an integer that is less than or equal to -1. So $a + 2$ will be less than or equal to $-1 + 2$, which is 1. Therefore $a + 2$ is not a prime number. So $a + 1$ will be less than or equal to zero; in any case, NOT prime. So, is $a + 1$ a prime number? The only answer we get from (2) is "maybe" and that's not sufficient. So (A) is the correct choice.

31. D

To find the perimeter of sector *OPMN*, we need the

lengths of radii *OP* and *ON* (which are equal since all

radii in any circle are equal), and the length of arc

PMN. The circumference C of a circle having a radius

r is given by the formula $C = 2\pi r$. Here the

circumference is 24π. So if r is the radius of this

circle, then $2\pi r = 24\pi$. Then $r = \dfrac{24\pi}{2\pi} = 12$. So OP and ON which are both radii of the circle each have a length of 12. We now have the lengths of OP and ON, and we still need the length of arc PMN.

Since $OP = NP$, sides OP, ON, and NP of triangle OPN all have the same length. So triangle OPN is an equilateral triangle, that is, all three of its sides are equal. In an equilateral triangle, all three interior angles measure 60 degrees. So the degree measure of central angle PON is 60 degrees. (A central angle is an angle formed by 2 radii.) The length of an arc having a corresponding central angle of measure n degrees in a circle with a radius r is $2\pi r \times \left(\dfrac{n}{360}\right)$. In this question we know that the circumference $2\pi r$ is equal to 24π. So the length of arc PMN is $24\pi \times \dfrac{60}{360} = 24\pi \times \dfrac{1}{6} = 4\pi$. Thus, the perimeter of sector $MNOP$ is $12 + 12 + 4\pi = 24 + 4\pi$.

32. C

We need to solve for a and b, and then substitute them into the expression given.

$a = 4$ and $b = \dfrac{3}{5}$, so $\dfrac{3a}{5a + 4b} = \dfrac{3(4)}{5(4) + 4\left(\frac{3}{5}\right)} =$

$\dfrac{3(4)}{4\left(5 + \frac{3}{5}\right)} = \dfrac{3}{5 + \frac{3}{5}\left(\frac{5}{5}\right)} =$

$\dfrac{3 \times 5}{\left(5 + \frac{3}{5}\right)} \times 5 = \dfrac{15}{25 + 3} = \dfrac{15}{28}$.

33. A

We need to think about many different types of numbers here. The question does not say that these need to be integers, or that they are positive, or even that they cannot be zero, so we should pick different types of numbers and see which statements must be true. Let $a = -5$, $b = \dfrac{1}{3}$, and $c = 4$. Now substitute these numbers into each statement. Statement I becomes $-5 < \dfrac{1}{9}$. This is true, but consider $a = \dfrac{1}{3}$ and $b = \dfrac{1}{2}$. Now statement I says $\dfrac{1}{3} < \dfrac{1}{4}$. This is not true, so statement I does not have to be true. With our original values $a = -5$, $b = \dfrac{1}{3}$, and $c = 4$, statement II becomes $\dfrac{1}{3} - (-5) < 4$ or $5\dfrac{1}{3} < 4$, which is not true. So statement II does not have to be true. Now we'll try our original values $a = -5$, $b = \dfrac{1}{3}$, and $c = 4$ in statement III, which will make the statement $25 < \dfrac{1}{9} < 16$. This is not true, so none of the statements must be true.

34. C

If x is ALWAYS greater than 4, that's sufficient. If x is NEVER greater than 4, that's also sufficient. Anything else is insufficient.

Statement (1): Let's pick numbers with exactly three distinct factors and see if they are greater than 4. The numbers 1, 2, and 3 won't work, since they have fewer than 3 different factors. But x could be 4; the factors are 1, 2, and 4. The next possibility is $x = 9$; the factors are 1, 3, and 9. So we have one value for x that is NOT greater than 4 and one that IS greater than 4. There is no definitive answer to the question, so statement (1) is insufficient. Eliminate (A) and (D).

Statement (2) will also be insufficient; x could be 1 or 3, which are less than 4, or x could be 5, 7, 9, etc., which are all greater than 4. Eliminate (B).

When we combine the statements, what are the possible values for *x*? From (1), we know that the smallest possible value for *x* is 4, but statement (2) rules out all even numbers; *x* can't be 4. The next possible value is 9, which satisfies both statements. Since 9 is greater than 4, and all other possible values of *x* will be greater than 9, *x* must be greater than 4. The two statements together are sufficient.

35. C

We must first determine how many seconds there are in an hour. There are 60 minutes in an hour. In a minute there are 60 seconds. So the number of seconds in an hour is 60×60, which is 3,600. Since the object travels 720,000 meters in 3,600 seconds, the object travels 720,000/3,600 = 200 meters per second.

36. E

When the product of a group of numbers is nonzero, none of the numbers can be 0. This is because if even one number is 0, the product is 0. For example, $7 \times 10 \times 12 \times 0 \times 4 \times 35 = 0$, because the fourth factor is a 0. Here, $(v + w)(x - y - z)(x + y + z)z = 3$, so $(v + w)(x - y - z)(x + y + z)z \neq 0$. So each factor of this product must be nonzero. That is,

$v + w \neq 0$

$x - y - z \neq 0$

$x + y + z \neq 0$

$z \neq 0$

The last inequality tells us that *z* can never equal 0. Choice (E) is correct.

The other variables may or may not be equal to zero. If $v = 0$, $w = -3$, $x = 0$ $y = 0$, and $z = 1$, then $(v + w)(x - y - z)(x + y + z)z = (-3)(-1)(1)(1) = 3$, and we can eliminate choices (A), (C), (D), because *v*, *x*, and *y* can each be 0. Or, if $v = -3$, $w = 0$, $x = 0$ $y = 0$, and $z = 1$, then $(v + w)(x - y - z)(x + y + z)z = 3$, and (B) can be eliminated, because *w* can be 0.

37. D

We must first calculate the speed of the car in the sixth interval. The car's speed in the sixth interval is equal to $\dfrac{d}{t} = \dfrac{4.8 \text{ miles}}{8 \text{ minutes}} \dfrac{(1 \text{ hour}}{60 \text{ minutes})} = 36$ miles per hour.

Therefore, the car's speed in the first interval is 36 miles per hour + 5 × (3 miles per hour) = 36 miles per hour + 15 miles per hour = 51 miles per hour. This is because in the sixth interval, the car has slowed down 5 times.

ANSWER KEY: VERBAL SECTION

1. B	15. A	29. B
2. A	16. B	30. D
3. C	17. D	31. E
4. D	18. A	32. E
5. E	19. E	33. D
6. C	20. C	34. B
7. C	21. B	35. C
8. D	22. C	36. B
9. A	23. D	37. D
10. D	24. A	38. C
11. A	25. E	39. C
12. A	26. C	40. B
13. C	27. D	41. B
14. B	28. E	

1. B

The conclusion that support groups and counseling help the body heal is based on evidence that patients who attended such groups experienced or received counseling experienced fewer side effects and shorter recovery times than did those who did not attend. We can identify one assumption here: the validity of using the experiences of a group of chemotherapy patients to generalize about psychological supports effect on the body's ability to heal. Choice (A)'s suggestion that survival rates are the same whether or not a patient receives support weakens, rather than strengthens, the argument. Choice (B) says that *patients who did not attend support groups chose not to do so, even though they were healthy enough to attend*—in other words, the sample of patients who *did* attend support groups was not simply the healthy patients. This information strengthens the argument by stressing that the conclusion drawn from these patients' experiences are indeed representative, i.e., the group was made up of all patients, not just ones healthy enough to attend. Choice (C) is outside the scope of the

passage; we are concerned only with recovery from illness, not the cause and prevention of it. Choices (D) and (E) are irrelevant to the argument.

2. A

Three-quarters of the prisoners up for parole claimed they were remorseful. This number could be an overestimate if some of the prisoners lied; i.e., if they claimed they were remorseful, but they really were not. Choice (A) says this. Choices (B) and (E) are both outside the scope of the argument. We are not interested in the degree of remorse, or the prisoners not up for parole. Choices (C) and (D) basically say the same thing, and would cause the number to be underestimated, not overestimated.

3. C

The economist notes a correlation between stock market indices and the size of the federal deficit. She concludes that there was a causal relationship between a perception of bad economic conditions and the government's willingness to reduce the deficit. That connection cannot be made unless we know that the direction of the stock market is related to the government's assessment of economic conditions. Choice (C) establishes such a relationship, and so is correct.

Choice (A)'s vague reference to perceptions about the economy "over the years" is not clear enough to link the argument's evidence to its conclusion. Choice (B) discusses what *will always* happen—but as a prediction of the future, it is outside the scope of this argument, which deals with historical conditions. Choice (D) contains a subtle scope shift: discusses the government's *ability* to lower the deficit, while the economist's conclusion referred to *willingness*. Choice (E) incorrectly talks about actual economic conditions, rather than the government's perception of them (which is what the economist is concerned with)—another scope shift.

4. D

Grammatically, it is correct to say *ordered (person) to (action)*. The infinitive is the correct form of the verb to use here, so we can eliminate choices (A) and (B). Choice (D) uses the correct form of *to prepare* in this sentence. (C) and (E) both incorrectly use the infinitive of the verb *to be* instead of *to prepare*.

5. E

The stem tells us that neuroscientists traditionally believed that verbal cursing was modulated by the same part of the brain that modulated other forms of speech. If damage to the part of the brain that controls speech does not inhibit a speaker's ability to curse, as is stated in choice (E), then the neuroscientists' belief is contradicted. Choices (A), (B), and (C) do not even mention the brain's speech center, making them all out of scope. Choice (D) is out of scope; it mentions the physical mechanisms needed for speech, not the brain.

6. C

When an opening phrase is followed by a comma, the noun being modified needs to come after the comma. Choices (A) and (B) both illogically compare *people* with *importance*. (D) erroneously compares unlike actions with the conjunction *also*. (E) incorrectly changes the meaning of the sentence.

7. C

This sentence presents a series which consists of *communicating effectively, anticipation of customer needs,* and *learning from mistakes.* They are not parallel in the original sentence, nor are they parallel in (B) or (E). (D) is parallel, but it changes the plural verb *are* to the singular *is.* All three of the items in the series are subjects of the sentence. Thus, the verb must be plural. Choice (C) is both parallel and has the correct subject/verb agreement.

Passage Analysis

Topic: Intelligence testing
Scope: The usefulness of such testing
Purpose: To review the limitations and benefits of intelligence testing, while favoring the benefits
Paragraph 1: Reviews limitations and flaws of intelligence testing
Paragraph 2: Discusses the benefits of intelligence testing

8. D

The passage begins with a discussion of the controversy over intelligence testing and focuses on the arguments of testing opponents. The author then cites evidence in favor of testing and concludes that intelligence testing is essential, as paraphrased in choice (D). Choice (B) is tempting because the passage does discuss two competing schools of thought. However, this is a half-right/half-wrong trap since the author advocates testing in paragraph 2, never attempting to unify the competing points of view. Despite the imposing language in choices (A), (C), and (E), these are all off target. At no time does the passage discuss a phenomenon, hypothesis, or paradox.

9. A

The author says that opponents of testing feel the tests fail to assess social abilities or practical skills required for daily life. Therefore they would agree that testing should assess these abilities, as in choice (A). The word "never" is a tip off that choice (B) is too extreme to be correct. Opponents of testing feel the tests are flawed—not that they should never be used. Choice (C) distorts the author's wording. Opponents of testing are concerned that creative answers may not receive deserved points because they are not in the standardized scoring guide. We can infer that opponents of testing feel these answers should receive points—but not necessarily that they should receive *more* points. Choice (D) is outside the scope of the question. Choice (E) is again too extreme. Although the passage states that test administrators must be qualified, there is no suggestion that "most" administrators are unreliable.

10. D

The author's purpose in mentioning hearing, vision, and speech problems is two-fold. He wants to illustrate the multitude of dimensions that may affect IQ scores and also to provide a concrete example of poor test interpretation. Statement III is incorrect because the author does not mention labeling or psychological damage.

11. A

The original sentence is a correct comparison as written. Choice (B) incorrectly uses the non-restrictive *which* rather than the restrictive *that* necessary in this instance, and replaces *for* with *on*, which changes the meaning. (C) and (D), by using *earning* and *who,* respectively, create sentence fragments, not complete sentences. Additionally, (C) changes the meaning of the sentence by shifting the placement of *about*. (E) is needlessly wordy.

12. A

The university's decision to stop offering reduced-cost bus passes to students caused the bus company to lose a sizable portion of its revenue. For this to be true, the number of students using the bus must have decreased, as choice (A) states. Otherwise, the revenue for the bus company would have remained the same. Choice (B) is not supported by the passage since we do not know about other transportation options in the city. Choice (C) is outside of scope of the argument. Choice (D) is incorrect. We know only that the bus company lost a "sizable amount of revenue"; we don't know whether students are a large portion of population. Choice (E) cannot be inferred since students may have used other modes of transportation besides walking and buses.

13. C

This argument suggests a causal relationship between the broadcast of the execution and the decrease in the number of death sentences issued by State X's court system. Because of the correlation between these events, the legislators believe that the broadcast has caused people to commit fewer capital crimes. An alternate cause for the decrease in death sentences would weaken the causal argument. Choice (C) does this, by stating that the decrease is due to the fact that many capital offenses are now being handled by the federal courts.

Choice (A) is incorrect since the stimulus is not comparing State X with any other state. Choice (B) has no relevance to the strength or weakness of the argument (the overall ratings of the broadcast are not relevant to whether it served as a deterrent). The fact that the broadcast may have been illegal, as suggested in Choice (D), is completely tangential to the issue of whether or not it had a deterrent effect. Choice (E) gives no information about the crucial issue of causality.

14. B

This sentence requires parallel structure, which is missing in the original. *There is one when it is not* is an awkward construction not parallel with a fever; eliminate (A) and (C). The thermometers have two defects: they fail to register real fevers and they indicate false fevers. (B) states this in a parallel and concise way. It also correctly refers back to *fever* with the pronoun *it*. (C) and (D) change the meaning by using *when*; the implication is that the thermometers fail to register any temperature *at all* when a fever is present. (D) also uses the singular verb *indicates*, which does not agree with the plural noun *thermometers*. (E) repeats this mistake and is needlessly wordy.

15. A

In order to be linked by a semicolon, the two independent clauses need to be closely related. The second clause gives examples of *severe bankruptcy laws,* so it is appropriate to separate the clauses with a semicolon. Choice (A) is correct. Choice (B) neglects to separate the clause beginning with *including* with a comma. Choice (C) is unnecessarily wordy. Choice (D) incorrectly uses *being* instead of *be*. (E), by omitting *for example*, changes the meaning by implying that there were no other effects of the laws, in contrast to the original sentence.

16. B

The sentence contains a noun/pronoun agreement error: we need a plural subject in the clause to match *their minds*. (B) corrects this mistake. The construction *one result...was* requires a noun that represents a *result*. Choices (C), (D), and (E) all replace the noun *appreciation* with verb forms.

17. D

Instead of the typical causal argument "*X* causes *Y*," this question asks whether the causal chain extends one link further: "*X* causes *Y*, which causes *Z*," where *X* is nap rooms, *Y* is employee morale, and *Z* is productivity. In order to strengthen this argument, then, we'll look for an answer choice that supports the causal connection between naps, employee morale, and productivity. Choice (A) is outside the scope of the passage, which doesn't mention profits. Choice (B) is outside scope as well. Choice (C) would tend to weaken the argument rather than strengthen it. Choice (D) works: it provides evidence that naps do indeed lead to increased productivity. Choice (E) is concerned with analysts, who are outside the passage's scope.

18. A

The prediction made in this argument is that the diner will not be able to handle the additional orders, and that its poor service will drive customers away. The evidence is that the restaurant is expanding its dining area but not its kitchen. So a necessary assumption is that the orders from patrons in the new dining area will place additional burdens on the kitchen. But if the new dining room does not require the services of the kitchen, then the prediction will be weakened. Choice (A) suggests that the new dining area will only serve counter drinks and pre-cooked pastries. So (A) is the correct answer.

Choice (B) suggests that the kitchen is struggling to meet even current demands; this would strengthen the argument that expansion is a bad idea. Choice (C) also seems likely to strengthen the prediction, because it suggests that far more patrons will fill the dining room. Choice (D) is wrong because the presence of other diners in the neighborhood is outside the scope of the argument. Choice (E) is wrong because hiring new wait staff does not address the problem created by expanding the dining area without expanding the kitchen.

19. E

You can eliminate (A) and (C) because they use *you* to refer to the pronoun *one*; this is not parallel. You can eliminate (B) and (D) because they use *do it* to refer to operate a motor vehicle when *do so* is correct; a pronoun can never refer to a verb. Additionally, (D) contains *one have*, a plural verb with a singular subject. Only (E) is error-free. Note that the pronoun *one* does not require an antecedent.

20. C

Here we are comparing *tornadoes* to all the other *possible weather conditions.* Since we are comparing more than two things, we need the superlative form, *most,* instead of *more.* Eliminate choices (A), (B), and (E). Additionally, *difficult* requires the infinitive form of the verb. Choice (C)'s *difficult to predict* is correct, while *difficult for prediction* is incorrect.

Passage Analysis

Topic: Wage levels

Scope: Differential between women's and men's wage levels

Purpose: To argue that the solution for remedying this differential is for women to organize

Paragraph 1: Describes ways to address the under-valuation of women's work

Paragraph 2: Explains the difficulty in bringing about the collective action mentioned in paragraph 1.

KAPLAN

Paragraph 3: Encourages women to try to reshape their work situations themselves rather than hope that laws will remedy the problem

21. B

In paragraph 1, the author presents two methods of correcting the wage discrepancy, both of which require women to organize themselves into groups. This points us to choice (B) as the credited answer. Choice (A) doesn't work; one of the methods the author suggests "lobby for a change in the differing pay scales that persist in predominantly female industries and those...up largely by males," rather than in *a single industry*, as this choice suggests. Choice (C) is a distortion of the passage's reference to collective bargaining; the passage makes no suggestion that collective bargaining should be changed in any way. Choice (D) is a 180; in the last paragraph, the author makes clear her belief that "women workers should try to reshape or otherwise influence their work situations themselves rather than simply hoping that laws...will remedy the problem for them." Likewise, choice (E) contradicts the passage. The author does not suggest that women reduce unionization, she suggests the opposite.

22. C

This detail question asks about unionization and collective bargaining, concepts whose aims—namely, as means of addressing the under-valuation of women's work—are discussed in the passage's first paragraph. Choices (A) and (B) are out of scope; the passage makes no reference to either *overcoming market pressures that keep wages in some industries lower than in others* or *encouraging worker flexibility in adjusting a new pay scale to economic conditions*. Choice (C), *helping workers to apply group pressure on their employers*, is supported by the passage, specifically lines 4–8, "one method is for women to organize into unions, and then collectively bargain with—or exert pressure on—management to commit to increases in wage levels." Like (A) and (B), choices (D) and (E) are outside the passage's scope.

23. D

The correct answer to this inference question must follow directly from the information contained in the passage. Which of the answer choices fits this criterion? Choice (A) looks tempting; we recall that the passage mentions *pay inequity for women and the lack of unionization in traditionally female occupations*. But let's look closely at the contexts in which these references appear. In the first paragraph, unionization is proposed as a means of remedying, rather than a cause of, the wage differential. (A) distorts this reference by presenting it as a cause-effect relationship. We cannot infer choice (B) from the passage's sole reference to government in the third paragraph: "women workers should try to reshape or otherwise influence their work situations themselves rather than simply hoping that laws and other external means will remedy the problem for them." (C) is extreme; the passage claims only that unionization may remedy the problem of the under-valuation of women's work.

Choice (D). is the credited answer. The author states in paragraph 3 that "women workers should try to reshape...their work situations themselves rather than simply hoping that laws...will remedy the problem for them." In other words, women should *first* try changing their situation themselves. But once women have attempted to remedy the problem by means of collective bargaining, for example, as choice (D) suggests, and failed, we can infer that the author agrees that another method, such as government regulation, may then play a role. Choice (E) is outside the passage's scope; we learn nothing about the author's opinion of men's access to economic resources.

24. A

The scientists' conclusion is that mild winters are a result of the conversion of commercial areas to industrial areas—not a result of vehicle exhaust. For this to be true, the scientists must assume that industrial areas contribute more pollution than either commercial areas or vehicles. Choice (A) confirms this assumption, and strengthens the argument; therefore, it is the best answer.

Choice (B) suggests that commercial areas have high levels of vehicular traffic from people driving to work each day. However, we don't have any information about traffic in industrial areas to make a comparison, and thus can't judge what impact this statement would have on the scientists' argument. Choice (C) is outside the scope of this question; additionally, reduced pollution from industrial areas would weaken, rather than strengthen, the argument. Choice (D) is outside the scope of this question. Choice (E) is irrelevant—we are comparing total pollution levels.

25. E

The stem tells us that reducing serotonin deficit can be a successful treatment for clinical depression. It follows that Selective Serotonin Reuptake Inhibitors act to allow the normal flow of serotonin, i.e., reduce the deficit. It therefore follows that a Selective Serotonin Reuptake Inhibitor would be a successful remedy for depression, as stated in (E).

We cannot assume that too much serotonin will cause euphoria, just because too little serotonin causes depression, making (A) incorrect. We also do not know whether Selective Serotonin Reuptake Inhibitors are the only remedies for depression. Nor do we know whether a serotonin deficit is the only cause of depression; choices (B) and (C) are incorrect. The stem says depressed individuals have a deficit of serotonin, but it does not indicate that the serotonin levels can be depleted, as stated in (D).

Passage Analysis

Topic: Gulf of Mexico

Scope: The formation of a dead zone in the Gulf of Mexico

Purpose: To discuss the causes and possible solutions for the dead zone in the Gulf of Mexico.

Paragraph 1: Introduces and definition of the dead zone

Paragraph 2: Explains of the process that causes and expands the zone seasonally

Paragraph 3: Describes the sources of the pollution that causes the zone

Paragraph 4: Discusses possible solutions

26. C

The question stem directs us to this sentence in the passage: "The pollution that finds its way to the Gulf is traceable in large part to farmers upstream on the Mississippi." Two sentences later, the passage tells us, "...farming methods poured by-products of fertilizers and chemicals into the river." Based on these two quotes, (C) is the best answer choice. The second paragraph, in discussing the dead zone cycle, makes clear the importance of nitrogen to the process; both the first and second sentences of paragraph 2 mention nitrogen-rich water. Also, the final paragraph, while discussing possible solutions, mentions "agricultural sources of nitrogen." Choice (A) is too general. As stated above, the specific reference to "the pollution that finds its way to the Gulf" ends with "farmers upstream on the Mississippi." Industrial and urban wastes are mentioned elsewhere, but not in this context. Choice (B) is specific, but the context is wrong. Phosphorus from wastewater is mentioned in the last sentence of the passage, far from the very specific context of the quotation in the question. Choice (D) is also out of context, referring instead to paragraph 2 and the specifics of the dead zone cycle. Choice (E), like choice (D), belongs to the context of paragraph 2 and the dead zone cycle.

27. D

The word *assumption* reveals that this is an inference question. The correct answer will be implied by the passage, but will not appear explicitly. We'll go through each answer, eliminating the ones that don't work.

The final paragraph mentions possible solutions, but no definite expectation that the problem will be corrected. The author does not assume that farmers will do anything, so choice (A) does not work. Fishermen only appear in the first paragraph as one source for the name of the dead zone. They are otherwise out of the scope of the passage, so choice

(B) also does not work. The possible relationship of the dead zone to other environmental problems in the Gulf is outside the scope of the passage; choice (C) doesn't work. Paragraph 1 and paragraph 3 both discuss the growth of the dead zone. The first paragraph also states that the dead zone was discovered in 1974, implying that prior to 1974 the zone either did not exist or was too small to be noticed. Further, the argument in paragraph 3 that farming waste has increased along with the increase of the dead zone implies that before farming there was little or no dead zone. Therefore, the implication is that the dead zone has not always been the same size as choice (D) says. Choice (E) contradicts the passage, particularly the discussion in paragraph 2, which tells us that an increased algae population promotes the dead zone.

28. E

We're looking for the answer that does not appear in the passage. The question involves the elimination of environmental hazards, that is, solutions to the dead zone problem, which appear in paragraph 4. Choice (A) appears in the last sentence; "the removal of nitrogen and phosphorus from wastewater" constitutes treatment of wastewater, which would limit the amount of untreated wastewater in the river. Choice (B) appears in the first sentence of paragraph 4; an investigation of nitrogen run-off from farms would be included in the "intensive research on all farms bordering the Mississippi." Choice (C) appears in the second sentence of paragraph 4, which mentions the "reduction of agricultural sources of nitrogen" (reduction implies control). Choice (D) appears in the third sentence of paragraph 4 almost verbatim. That leaves choice (E). The word "sediment" appears only once in the passage, in paragraph 3, sentence 4, where reference is made to "sediment samples of the land before European settlement...." No mention is made of sediment levels in the area surrounding the dead zone.

29. B

For the purpose of the passage, we predicted "to discuss the causes and possible solutions for the dead zone in the Gulf of Mexico." Which of the answer possibilities is most in line with our prediction? Choice (A) isn't correct; the passage does not refer to nor resolve a *debate*. One of the verbs in (B), *discuss*, matches our prediction; the rest of the choice jibes well with our prediction of "causes and...solutions for the dead zone," which, as described throughout the passage, is certainly a *problem*, as this choice suggests. Our predicted verb does not match choice (C)'s *criticize and discredit* or choice (D)'s *explain and criticize*. Choice (E) doesn't work; the passage discusses causes and solutions, not a particular position.

30. D

Each answer choice suggests a way in which a problem can be treated. Choice (A) says that the passage compares and contrasts solutions to a problem. Although paragraph 4 mentions several possible solutions, they are in no way compared or contrasted. Eliminate choice (A). Choice (B) mentions the exploration of *historical roots and consequences of a problem*. Although some history pops up in paragraph 3 in order to illustrate the causes of the dead zone, a single paragraph does not constitute this entire passage. Eliminate (B) as well.

Paragraph 2 might be considered a dissection of the mechanism of the dead zone problem, as choice (C) phrases it, but no part of the passage discusses *societal implications* of the problem. (C) can be eliminated. Choice (D) proposes that *the source and mechanism of a problem are identified and solutions are proposed*. As stated above, paragraph 2 discusses the mechanism of the dead zone cycle. Paragraph 3 identifies sources of the problem and paragraph 4 proposes possible solutions. The best choice is (D). Choice (E) does not work because the author only proposes a solution without demanding that any particular action be taken.

31. E

The environmentalists want to stop Corporation Y's logging actions. They are considering holding a demonstration at Corporation Y's other facility, which just happens to be a plastics production facility. Therefore, it is not directly relevant to know if other logging corporations own plastic facilities, as (E) suggests.

Each of the other answers is directly relevant. (A) and (B) are relevant to whether the demonstration would have a desired negative effect on Corporation Y's income or production. (C) and (D) are relevant as to whether demonstrations of this type have proven to be successful in the past.

32. E

The conclusion of this argument is that the pet store is endangering the safety of children. The evidence is that certain pets can be dangerous if their handlers do not receive proper training. In order for this argument to hold water, it must be true that the pet store is not providing proper training for those who purchase these dangerous pets. Choice (E), which matches this prediction, is the correct answer.

Choice (A) is wrong because the government is outside the scope of the argument. Choice (B) incorrectly focuses on snakes (which may or may not be included among the "dangerous pets" in question), and on selling them to people without training (which has no bearing on whether the pet store is endangering children). Choice (C) is wrong because it does not matter who is more skilled in caring for dangerous pets. Again, the point in contention is whether the pet store, which sold dangerous pets to children, endangered their safety. Choice (D) is wrong, because the needs of the community are outside the scope of this argument.

33. D

Color blindness appears <u>in</u> people, not <u>between</u> them. Choice (A) seemingly says that color blindness is more common in people situated between two white males than those otherwise

situated; in (B) it's those situated between a white male and either a woman or a member of another race. (C) creates an improper comparison by removing the *than* necessary after *more* or *less*. (D) is best, because the *it is* in (E) is not needed.

34. B

In the situation described, the benefit of cooperation among political parties is "legislation important to the general welfare...that might have foundered...can effectively be enacted." The benefit described in choice (A) is considerably less high minded; the minister chooses compromise over "the risk of not having legislation that we propose pass." Choice (B) gets it right; the minister chooses cooperation so that "issues important to our constituents" will be addressed. Choice (C) incorrectly suggests that cooperation is the aim. Choice (D) doesn't work; the passage makes no claim to support the notion that *parties would rather have other parties join in support of our legislation than join in supporting the proposals of other parties*. Choice (E) mentions "the welfare of our country," but only in comparison to becoming "engaged in the agendas of other parties," a connection the passage does not make.

35. C

The stem states in the first line that "Multi-partisan initiatives are becoming increasingly popular..." We can infer from this that these initiatives were less common in the past, which makes (C) correct.

36. B

The use of *the higher...* calls for another comparative adjective. In this case, the correct construction is *the higher...the greater...* No other answer choice uses a second comparative adjective.

37. D

When we see an introductory phrase set off with a comma, we should look for possible modification mistakes. Who or what is *using sophisticated technology?* Possibly weather experts or meteorologists. We know hurricanes are not using the technology, so (A) is incorrect. Choices (A), (B), and (C) all use the passive voice, which the GMAT considers inferior to the active voice. (D) correctly uses the modifying phrase to modify *meteorologist* and uses the active voice. (E) changes the tense of the sentence, thereby altering its meaning. The sentence says meteorologists *can detect*, not that they *are detecting*.

38. C

The underlined portion as written is nearly correct. The only mistake is a misuse of idiom: Virgil could be "credited as" something ("the inventor of her encounter with Aeneas," for example), or he could be "credited with" *doing* something, but he can't be "credited as" doing something. In other words, "credited *as*" should be used with a noun, and "credited *with*" should be used with a verb. (C) correctly does this. (D) uses the idiom correctly, but is unnecessarily wordy. The others choices are all unidiomatic.

39. C

In order to be connected by a semicolon, both clauses need a subject and a verb. In the original sentence, the second part is missing a verb. (C) eliminates the semicolon and uses the correct form of *result* to join the phrase to the main clause. (B) is out because it isn't idiomatic to use the infinitive from of *result* here. (D) incorrectly uses *and* with the semicolon, and (E) is a run-on sentence.

40. B

The underlined portion of this sentence is wrong because of a redundancy. The correct answer will eliminate the redundancy by eliminating either *decline* or *decrease*. By scanning the answers, we can quickly eliminate (A) and (C) because they maintain the redundancy. (E) is also out because it uses the wrong tense of *decline*. (D) is idiomatically incorrect. The answer is (B) because it corrects the redundancy, uses the right verb tense, and is idiomatically correct.

41. B

This question tests rules of both parallelism and modification. Investors need to request three pieces of important information: *maturity date*, *interest rate*, and *credit rating*. These three items must be parallel, which is not the case in the original sentence. In addition, the information at the end of the sentence must clearly modify *credit rating*. Choice (B) presents the information in a clear and correct manner. In choice (C), it is not clear what *which* refers to. In choice (E), it is not clear what *them* refers to. In addition, (C), (D), and (E) all contain faulty parallel structures; (D) contains *in regards to* when the proper expression is *in regard to*, and (E) uses *if* where *whether* should be used.

Section Two

GMAT STUDY PLAN

CHAPTER THREE

Customize Your Study Plan

Now that you have completed the Diagnostic Exam, it is time to assess your results. By giving yourself an idea of how well you have performed, you will better be able to identify those areas in which you need help. Study time is limited, we know, so how you spend your time is crucial.

SCORE YOURSELF

There are many variables that go into how well you will perform on the real test, and as such, there is no way to predict your score with great precision. You can, however, get a ballpark idea of how you are now performing compared to the population taking the actual GMAT.

First, look at the **AWA**. The AWA score ranges **from 0–6 (best)**. This score is an average of the two essay scores, and is totally separate from the Verbal and Quantitative scores. You can get a good idea if your essay is on the right track by reading your finished essay and comparing it to the sample essays in this book. Then, use the scoring criteria included in the Diagnostic Test Answers and Explanations (pages 39–40) to see what elements you covered and what elements you missed. Be as objective as you can, and if you aren't sure, ask someone whose opinion you respect to read your essay as well.

Second, turn to the multiple-choice answers. Tally the number of questions you got right. Hopefully, you answered every question, since on the real CAT, you won't be able to skip a question. (You will be penalized for not finishing a section.) Then use the charts below to calculate your scaled subscores, and your scaled overall score. Use a calculator to make your work easier.

For these two sections, scores range from **200–800**. More than 60% of test takers score between 400 and 600.

GMAT SCORE CALCULATION

Number of questions answered correctly in each section	Quantitative		Verbal	
	Scaled Subscore	Subscore Percentile	Scaled Subscore	Subscore Percentile
0	9	1	0	0
1	11	1	0	0
2	12	2	0	0
3	14	3	0	0
4	15	4	0	0
5	16	4	0	0
6	18	6	0	0
7	19	7	0	0
8	20	8	2	0
9	22	10	4	0
10	24	14	6	0
11	25	15	7	0
12	26	18	8	0
13	27	20	9	1
14	28	23	10	1
15	30	29	11	2
16	31	31	13	4
17	32	35	14	6
18	33	39	15	7
19	34	41	17	12
20	35	43	18	15
21	36	48	19	16
22	37	52	21	24
23	39	57	22	28
24	40	62	23	30
25	42	67	25	38
26	43	71	26	43
27	45	78	26	43
28	47	83	27	45
29	48	87	28	51
30	49	91	29	56
31	50	96	31	59
32	51	99	32	61
33	53	99	34	72
34	55	99	35	76
35	56	99	36	81
36	57	99	37	83
37	58	99	39	89
38	na	na	40	90
39	na	na	43	97
40	na	na	44	97
41	na	na	45	99

KAPLAN

GMAT SCORE CONVERSION

200 to 800 points

Use this procedure to calculate your scaled score.

1. Write the number of correct answers in Section 2 (Quantitative): _____.

2. Multiply the number from (1) by 1.108 (using a calculator may help): _____.

3. Write the number of correct answers in Section 3 (Verbal): _____.

4. Sum the results of (2) and (3): _____.

5. Round off (4) to the nearest integer: _____.

6. Use (5) to determine your scaled score in the chart below.

Suppose you answered 21 questions correctly on the Quantitative section, and 23 questions correctly on Verbal. In (1), write 21. In (2), calculate (21)(1.108) = 23.628. In (3), write 23. In (4), calculate 23.628 + 23 = 46.628. In (5), round off 46.628 to 47. In (6), use the table below to determine that your score is 520, which is in the 44th percentile.

Result from (5), above	Scaled Score	Percentile
<=7	200	0
8	210	0
9	210	0
10	220	0
11	220	0
12	230	0
13	240	1
14	250	1
15	250	1
16	260	1
17	270	1
18	280	2
19	280	2
20	290	2
21	300	2
22	300	2
23	310	2
24	320	3
25	320	3
26	330	4
27	340	5
28	350	6
29	360	7
30	370	8
31	380	9
32	390	11
33	400	12
34	400	12

GMAT Score Conversion (Continued)

200 to 800 points

Result from (5), above	Scaled Score	Percentile
35	410	14
36	420	16
37	430	18
38	440	20
39	450	22
40	460	25
41	470	29
42	470	29
43	480	31
44	490	34
45	500	37
46	510	40
47	520	44
48	530	45
49	530	45
50	540	50
51	550	54
52	560	57
53	570	61
54	570	64
55	580	67
56	590	67
57	590	70
58	600	74
59	610	77
60	620	79
61	630	81
62	640	81
63	640	81
64	650	85
65	660	87
66	670	89
67	680	90
68	690	92
69	690	92
70	700	93
71	710	95
72	720	96
73	720	96
74	730	97
75	740	98
76	750	99
77	750	99
78	760	99
79	770	99
80	780	99
81	790	99
82	800	99

REVIEW EACH QUESTION TYPE AND IDENTIFY YOUR WEAK AREAS

Now it's time to review how well you did on each question type. By doing this, you will be able to build a customized study plan. You'll first have to go back and tally the number of questions by *type* of question.

Analytical Writing Assessment: 2 essays

There are many ways to turn a good essay into a great essay, but the best way is through focused practice with test-like prompts. To find appropriate prompt topics, turn to the op-ed page in your local newspaper and find an issue or an argument to write about. Before you write, keep in mind the following things:

1. If possible, type your essays into a computer. As you know, the GMAT is computer based, so you'll want to practice under the same circumstances.

2. When you sit down to write your essays, make sure you have an alarm clock on hand. Set it to ring after 30 minutes. Make sure to do both essays in the same sitting. These are the first tasks you will be required to do on test day.

3. Always spend a few minutes creating an outline for your essay. You'll be sorry if you jump in and just start typing.

4. When you complete your essay(s), put it away for a few days before you assess it. A fresh eye is key for proper evaluation. How convincing is your case? Is your discussion clear and do you see progression from start to end?

Try another prompt the following week to see how you have progressed. You're sure to improve if you dedicate time to practice writing a winning GMAT-style essay.

Problem-Solving: 23 questions

Problem-solving questions are the classic multiple-choice math problems found on many standardized tests. They consist of a question followed by 5 answer choices, one of which is correct. The math tested on these questions mainly consists of junior and senior high school level arithmetic, algebra and geometry. You can expect 22–23 questions, constituting approximately 60 percent of the Quantitative section.

If you answered 17–23 questions correctly:
You're a good problem solver. Skim over the questions you missed and try to understand why.

If you answered 7–16 questions correctly:
You need a more focused and careful review of problem-solving. Look at the questions you answered correctly and review how you came up with the right answer. Did you simply know the answer offhand? Did you make an educated guess?

If you answered 0–6 questions correctly:
Your problem-solving skills need work. Go back and learn to develop a systematic approach to Problem Solving. Learn to decipher question stems quickly. Decide how much effort to put into each question. Learn to get comfortable using alternative methods, such as Picking Numbers or Backsolving, where you plug answer choices into the question to see which one works.

Data-Sufficiency: 14 questions

There are **14–16 Data Sufficiency questions**. Together, they account for 40 percent of your Quantitative score. All Data Sufficiency questions look the same. The basic task here is to determine whether you have enough information to make a decision or solve a problem. You don't actually need to solve anything; you just need to know whether you could give an answer if you had to. You rarely need to do a great deal of calculation on a Data Sufficiency question.

The math tested on Data Sufficiency questions is the same as that tested on Problem-Solving questions: arithmetic, algebra, and geometry.

If you answered 11–14 questions correctly:
You're in great shape. Skim the questions you missed.

If you answered 7–10 questions correctly:
Review those questions that gave you the greatest difficulty. Maybe you just need a refresher in math, the focus of these kinds of questions: ratios/rates/percentages; algebra; number properties; and geometry. Get in the habit of thinking about the sufficiency of information from the question itself.

If you answered 0–6 questions correctly:
Data Sufficiency questions are difficult for you, but don't fret: You aren't alone. They're difficult for most students. Make this a high priority in your review. First, make sure you know the Data Sufficiency answer choices cold. They are always the same. Also, learn the two crucial questions for every Data Sufficiency question: Can you answer the question using the information from statement (1) only? from statement (2) only? If the answer to both of these questions is no, then you ask yourself a third question: Can you answer the question if you combine the information from both statements?

Sentence Correction: 16 questions

You will see 15–16 Sentence Correction questions, which account for about 40 percent of your Verbal score. Sentence Correction questions test your knowledge of the rules of "standard written English," the rather formal rules of grammar used in textbooks and scholarly periodicals. In addition, these questions test whether you can eliminate redundancy and ambiguity in a sentence.

While there are many rules of standard written English, the GMAT most commonly concentrates on the following five:

- Verb usage (proper agreement and correct tense)
- Reference (proper use of pronouns and modifiers)
- Parallel structure (consistency among items in a list or comparison)
- Idioms (proper use of idiomatic expressions)
- Style (avoiding excess verbiage, using active verbs, etc.

If you answered 11–16 questions correctly:
You have a great understanding of the structure of sentences. Clearly, this is an area of strength for you. Skim over the few questions you did miss and try to grasp why. Check to see that you didn't make careless errors.

If you answered 7–10 questions correctly:
You're solid in this area but could use some review. Look at the questions you missed. Check the tense of all verbs. Is the sequence of events in the original sentence clear? Are similar elements parallel to each other?

If you answered 0–6 questions correctly:
Reviewing the fundamentals of English grammar and usage needs to be a top priority. Go back to the five basics: verb usage; use of pronouns and modifiers; parallel structure; idiomatic expressions; and style (wordiness, redundancy). These are the fundamentals you'll need to know for the test. Don't worry about spelling or capitalization. Those don't count here.

Critical Reasoning: 12 questions

Critical Reasoning will account for about 30 percent of your Verbal score. Critical Reasoning is all about arguments and your ability to evaluate them, recognize assumptions, and make deductions. Each question is based on a short argument, and you must be able to break the argument into its component parts and evaluate its strengths and weaknesses.

If you answered 9–12 questions correctly:
You're in great shape. Clearly, critical reasoning is a strength for you. Skim over the questions you missed and try to understand why.

If you answered 4–8 questions correctly:
You have some understanding of Critical Reasoning but need to move on to a higher level of understanding. Go back to the questions you missed and try to figure out what went wrong. Make sure you are able to distinguish evidence from a conclusion. If you're unsure, ask yourself whether a given sentence expresses what an author believes or whether it expresses *why* he believes it.

If you answered 0–3 questions correctly:

You need to go back to the fundamentals of logic: understanding the logic of an argument, evaluating its merits, and responding to its strengths and weaknesses. Go back and review the structure of an argument. Then, concentrate on the two key elements in critical reasoning: the evidence and the conclusion (the point that the author is trying to make)—and whether there's enough evidence to prove the conclusion. Learn clue words that signal a conclusion: *consequently, therefore, thus,* and *accordingly,* and those that signal evidence: *because, since,* and *as a result of.*

Reading Comprehension: 13 questions

Reading comprehension is the most time-consuming question type, and for many test-takers, the most intimidating part of the Verbal section. This doesn't have to be the case.

Despite what many test-takers seem to believe, Reading Comprehension questions do not test your ability to comprehend a passage so thoroughly that you practically memorize what you read. Nor do they test your ability to relate what you read to outside knowledge. What they demonstrate is test your ability to understand the substance of the passage and, where necessary, to research the passage for specific information.

If you answered 10–13 questions correctly:

You're in great shape. You are masterful at being able to understand the substance of a passage and to research a passage for specific information. Clearly, you have a talent for understanding reading texts. Skim over the questions you missed, and try to understand why.

If you answered 6–9 questions correctly:

You need some work in this area. Review the questions you missed, going back to the original reading passage as needed. Maybe you misread something. Maybe you skipped an important detail. Being able to distinguish opinions or interpretations from factual assertions is important in Reading Comprehension.

If you answered 0–5 questions correctly:

You'll need to learn to home in on the "why" and the "how" of a text. Those two things make GMAT reading different from everyday reading. Re-read the passages on the questions you missed. Start off focusing on the author's views. What is the main idea? Examine how each paragraph fits in to the overall scope of the passage. Then, practice making a road map—handwritten notes at the side of each paragraph indicating the general idea. Don't sweat the details in the passage.

BUILD YOUR STUDY PLAN

Now that you have reviewed all the question types and assessed your skill set, it's time to implement your study plan. To do this, you'll need to map out your objectives in a calendar.

CHAPTER FOUR

Customize Your Study Schedule

Maybe you have plenty of time to devote to studying for the GMAT. Maybe you're such a whiz with data sufficiency that you barely need to review. Maybe, though, you're like most people, and you need to make a study plan.

The key to effective test preparation goes beyond practice quizzes; it starts with planning. To get you from today to test day, we're going to work with your diagnostic test results and come up with a study plan that works for you—tailored to your skills and timetable.

STEP 1: HOW MANY MONTHS UNTIL THE GMAT?

On the following page, you'll find a blank calendar. The page shows only one month, so if you have more time than that, photocopy it for every month you have. Ideally, you should have three full months to study. If you have less than two months to prepare, however, don't despair; just get going on your study plan today.

STUDY CALENDAR

Make a copy of this page for every month of study. Fill it out. Stick to it!

Month: _____

Sunday	Monday	Tuesday	Wednesday	Thursday	Friday	Saturday

KAPLAN

STEP 2: HOW MUCH REAL TIME DO I HAVE TO STUDY?

It's easy to think that if you have three months to study, you're all set. That's all the time in the world, right? Not likely. You probably have a job or school to factor in, as well as other time-consuming obligations. And don't forget your social life!

That said, let's give your calendar a good look. Block out the time you are at work or school. Next, block out any weekly meetings you have, remembering to include volunteer work, club activities, religious observances, sessions at the gym, and so on. Go ahead and write in your calendar. Carve it up and make it your own.

If you're like most busy business school candidates, you'll see that you may not have as much time to devote to GMAT prep as you thought. That might be the bad news. The good news is that you now know exactly how much study time you have to work with. Maybe it's an hour in the evening, plus four hours straight on Sunday for the next three months. Maybe it's less. Either way, you can now approach your study time more realistically.

STEP 3: HOW SHOULD I TARGET MY STUDY TIME?

Go back to your diagnostic results. Sort the question types in order of difficulty; that is, the order of difficulty that *you* experienced. Focus first on the types that gave you the most trouble. Then, focus on the subsequent types as they appear on your list.

Of course the focus should be on the questions types you found challenging, but don't totally dismiss those on which you did well. When you need to break-up the intensity of the problem questions, put them on hold and review the questions you aced. The power of review goes a long way, even if you think you know the subject matter through and through.

In the chapters that follow, you will find practice quizzes for each GMAT question type. Go right to the question type that gave you the most trouble. (For many students, it's Data Sufficiency. For many others, it's Critical Reasoning.) Complete the skill-building quiz for that topic in Week 1. Analyze your results. Compare your results with how you performed on the Diagnostic. Did you improve? We hope so. If you still need more practice, Kaplan offers a comprehensive preparation guide to the GMAT, available at Borders. Check out your local store.

Also in Week 1, consider all the broader topics areas you may see on the Quantitative and Verbal sections of the test. You may be shaky on geometry and logic. Make flashcards to drill yourself on math rules, word roots, and vocabulary to help you refresh your skills. (Check out other Kaplan test-prep books available at your local Borders.) We provide a tear-out reference sheet with some of these in the front of this book: Tear it out and carry it with you for studying on the go. Five-minute capsule reviews here and there can add up to a bonus study section.

In Week 2, start by reviewing what you studied in Week 1. Add some flashcard practice, then tackle another practice chapter—this time on your second weakest section.

For Week 3, you guessed it: Review Weeks 1 and 2, build on the skills you developed by practicing with flashcards, and then plow through another practice chapter. At this point, you're well on your way to a systemic approach to conquering the GMAT.

For each of the remaining weeks until test day, take on another chapter from this book. If you don't make it through the whole way, that's okay—you've already tackled your weakest areas. Don't wait until the last month to try the Analytical Writing prompts, though. It takes time to develop the skills required for these. Fine-tuning them for the needs of the GMAT will take practice. Take a stab at the AWA prompts we include here, and then review your essay based on the grading rubric provided.

It's a good idea to take another practice test before the real exam—ideally, just one week before. Try out the official test prep from GMAC, the maker of the GMAT. Log onto mba.com to see what study tools are available.

Use the weeks up to test day to continue reviewing the topics that still give you trouble: Go over math topics you learned in school and word roots that are the fundamentals of most words. And keep reading—there's no better way to build vocabulary!

STEP 4: WHERE'S THE BEST PLACE TO STUDY?

OK, so you know when you can study, but what about where? Some people require silence, others prefer white noise. Go where you will optimize your study time. Bear in mind, though, if it takes 20 minutes to get to your favorite study location, you're cutting into valuable study time. Pick a location that's close by.

STEP 5: AM I READY FOR THE TEST?

First of all, the fact that you have set up a study schedule and stuck to it deserves praising. That's more than most students do, and the discipline you applied here will prove to be invaluable on test day. If you suffer a lapse of focus, remember your goals. Your hard work is going to pay off one day when you are accepted into business school.

Many of us feel unsure of our test-taking abilities. We all know the feeling of walking confidently into an exam only to blank out at the start of the test. Expectations tend to be fulfilled. Be positive! Think about the progress you have made. You surely will have strengthened your skills after working through this book.

One last thing: Don't cram the night before the test. Get a good night's sleep. You'll wake up prepared and ready to succeed on the GMAT. Good luck!

CHAPTER FIVE

Countdown to the Test

COUNTDOWN TO THE TEST

It's no secret that preparation plays a huge role in test success. If you're aiming to ace any sort of exam, you'll undoubtedly invest time in learning the test layout, familiarizing yourself with question types, and reviewing important content. A critical part of effective preparation, too, is knowing the environmental set-up ahead of time. You must manage natural test-day jitters, and you have to be able to overcome challenges presented by factors that are out of your control—noise, temperature, security issues, and, in the case of the GMAT, the particular hurdles presented by the computer adaptive format, among other things.

You will be taking the GMAT at a Prometric computer center. There, you'll be assigned a private computer work station. You can expect to be there for approximately four hours.

COME PREPARED

Make sure to arrive 20–30 minutes before your scheduled test time for check-in procedures. You'll need to present valid ID at the test center. Your ID must be current and contain the following:

- Your name exactly as provided when you made your test appointment
- A recent, recognizable photograph
- Your signature

If the name on your ID doesn't match the name on your test appointment, the test administrator will have the right to turn you away. So when you register to take your exam, be sure that you give the name is consistent in both places.

Additionally, you will be asked to sign a confidentiality statement. Your signature is required. If you do not sign the statement, you will not be permitted to take the test and you will forfeit your test fee.

Remember to bring your authorization voucher if you registered by mail.

WHAT NOT TO BRING

You will not be permitted to use "testing aids" during the test session or during breaks. So leave the following at home:

- notes
- scratch paper
- a calculator
- a stop watch or watch alarm
- cell phone
- pens or other writing utensils (they're provided at the test center)
- a ruler
- a dictionary

WHAT NOT TO DO

Test conditions are strict. The test administrator is authorized to dismiss you for:

- Attempting to take the test for someone else
- Failing to provide acceptable identification
- Creating a disturbance
- Giving or receiving unauthorized help
- Eating or drinking during the test
- Using test aids of any kind
- Accessing your locker during the exam
- Exceeding the time permitted for scheduled breaks
- Leaving the test center
- Attempting to remove scratch paper from the testing room
- Attempting to tamper with the operation of the computer
- Attempting to remove test questions from the testing room
- Refusing to follow directions

THE SCOOP ON SCRATCH PAPER

You may not bring your own scratch paper into the testing room. You will be provided with six sheets of scratch paper at the test center, and if you need more, it will be available. All scratch paper must be returned at the end of the test session.

IMPORTANT FACTS ABOUT COMPUTERIZED TESTING

- You cannot skip a question. What that means is that even if you're having trouble figuring something out, you'll have to guess and move on. Also, you cannot go back and check earlier answers, so choose your answers quickly and carefully.

- *CAT* stands for computer-adaptive test. In a computer-adaptive test, the computer determines whether to increase or decrease the level of questions based on how well you are doing within each section. In other words, if you answer a question correctly, you will be given a harder question next. For this reason, early questions are vital for a good score. Hard questions are worth more than easy questions.

- You may be penalized more heavily for not getting to a question at all than for answering it incorrectly. So even if you only have a minute or two left in a section, you should guess at random rather than leave questions unanswered.

- Earlier questions in a section are worth more points than the later questions. The value of each question decreases as you progress in a section.

Section Three

GMAT SKILL-BUILDING QUIZZES

CHAPTER SIX
Critical Reasoning

1. The earliest known records of wartime activities detail the use of carrier pigeons to communicate classified military information. Many people are not aware that the birds were also used extensively in the world wars of the 20th Century. Even today, their uncanny ability to fly home over great distances makes them valuable to military units that need to deliver messages without the use of portable electronic devices, whose signals can be intercepted.

    The statements above, if true, best support which of the following conclusions?

    (A) The use of carrier pigeons is usually preferable to the use of portable electronic devices when a military unit needs a way to send classified military information.
    (B) The messages that carrier pigeons carry cannot be intercepted.
    (C) The use of carrier pigeons decreased once portable electronic devices became practical in warfare.
    (D) Carrier pigeons were used in warfare prior to the date of the earliest known record of wartime activity.
    (E) Carrier pigeons are still used extensively by modern military units.

2. The *Mona Lisa*, arguably the world's most famous painting, may be a masterpiece, but it is neither flawless nor incomparable. The hands are badly matched, the background is dull, and other portraits from the same period evince equally enigmatic expressions. The undue focus on this painting, along with the popularity of a few other pieces, prevents most people not only from seeing the painting for what it really is, but also from understanding the true scope of 15th and 16th century European painting.

    Which of the following, if true, provides the strongest support for the argument's conclusion?

    (A) Most people do not believe that the *Mona Lisa* has any evident flaws.
    (B) The creator of the *Mona Lisa*, Leonardo DaVinci, did not regard the painting as his finest work.
    (C) It is possible for most people to understand the true scope of 15th and 16th century European painting.
    (D) Other European paintings of the 15th and 16th century were once better known than the *Mona Lisa*.
    (E) Most art scholars feel that *The Last Supper* is a superior painting to the Mona Lisa.

3. Nearly all the music heard at an orchestral performance today contains pitch relationships that do not precisely match those that musical instruments naturally produce. This is because the members of a modern orchestra read musical notation that, more than 99% of the time, represents a tempered system of tuning. In the tempered system, certain pitch relationships are slightly altered from those that naturally occur in vibrating bodies such as musical instruments. In non-tempered tuning systems, these relationships are not altered.

Which of the following, if true, most strengthens the argument?

(A) Because of lifelong exposure to tempered tuning systems, most people perceive music written using non-tempered tuning systems as being out-of-tune.

(B) Orchestra musicians always play music exactly as it is notated.

(C) The tempered tuning system is used by the vast majority of jazz and rock musicians.

(D) The standard orchestral repertoire is drawn from music written during the last three centuries, during which time composers have almost always used musical notation that represents the tempered system of tuning.

(E) The tempered system of tuning allows musicians to make key changes more easily than does the non-tempered.

4. Doctors conducted studies on two distinct groups of children between ages 3 and 13 who suffer from allergic reactions to wheat. Each group contained 1,000 children. One group was given weekly doses of Allerease for 3 months. The other group was given weekly doses of Innalex for 3 months. At the end of the study, 77% of the children taking Allerease showed milder than usual allergic reactions after consuming small amounts of wheat products. Only 19% of the children taking Innalex showed milder than usual allergic reactions to wheat products at the end of the study. Knowing the results of the studies, Dr. Lucas has recommended that Barry, a 4-year old, be given Innalex, not Allerease, as a way of treating his wheat allergy.

Which of the following, if true, most helps to explain Dr. Lucas' choice of treatment for Barry?

(A) Innalex has been shown to be effective in relieving other food allergies.

(B) The relative effectiveness of Innalex is inversely proportional to the age of the person being treated.

(C) Dr. Lucas was told of the results of the experiment by a colleague, and hadn't read them himself.

(D) Barry was not one of the 2000 children involved in the studies.

(E) Allergies to wheat are less common in children between ages of 3 and 13 than are allergies to animal dander.

5. The word *hue* is sometimes used interchangeably with the word *color*. However, the latter refers to an object's brightness and saturation as well as to its hue, whereas hue refers only to an object's dominant wavelengths. When most people use the word *color*, they are actually referring just to an object's hue.

   Which of the following, if true, would weaken the argument above?

   (A) Most people are aware of the distinction between color and hue.

   (B) Most people take into account an object's brightness when describing what they refer to as its *color*.

   (C) Most people use the word *hue* to refer to an object's dominant wavelengths.

   (D) The words *color* and *hue* are used correctly by thousands of people.

   (E) In most non-technical discussions, there is no significant reason to distinguish between the terms *color* and *hue*.

6. Those who feel that fewer and fewer people in this country have a genuine interest in the fine arts are absolutely correct. This is true despite the oft-mentioned record levels of attendance at art museums.

   The argument above would be most strengthened if which of the following statements were true?

   (A) The increase in the number of people who visit art museums more than once has been greater than the increase in the number of visits to these museums.

   (B) An interest in the fine arts cannot be determined by examining levels of museum attendance.

   (C) A substantial and relatively consistent portion of the visitors to this country's art museums are, and always have been, international tourists.

   (D) Sales of art books have declined sharply.

   (E) Art museums in this country now display a much wider range of exhibits than was once the case.

7. *Grimm's Fairy Tales* is a collection of 200 folktales, mostly taken from oral sources. Some of these stories, as told to the Grimm brothers, who jointly wrote the collection, were quite grotesque and filled with horrific violence. In putting the stories down on paper, the Grimms lessened some of this violence, which was reduced still further by American movie-makers who used some of the tales as the bases for popular films. What children who saw these films experienced was a diluted version of the powerful, if raw, original stories, and thus the impact of the moral lessons embodied in the folktales was lost.

   The conclusion above depends on which of the following assumptions?

   (A) Some violence is needed in stories that attempt to embody moral lessons.

   (B) Children who view the films based on Grimm's Fairy Tales are capable of being exposed to the violence of the original tales without becoming unduly upset.

   (C) Morality has remained basically unchanged since the time when the folktales were first recorded by the Grimm brothers.

   (D) The Grimm brothers' aim in lessening the violence of the stories they recorded was not to lose the impact of the moral lessons embodied in the stories.

   (E) The force of the moral lessons of the folktales depends on the tales containing a certain level of violence.

8. Some say that an asteroid colliding with Earth was responsible for the extinction of the dinosaurs. It is indeed likely that such a collision occurred and that it caused the death of the vast majority of dinosaurs. However, new evidence suggests that perhaps tens of thousands of dinosaurs lived far enough from the point of collision that they were not directly killed by the impact or by the drastic change in temperature when immense dust clouds, created by the impact, blocked the sun. Some other force must have been responsible for the death of these remaining dinosaurs.

   Which of the following, if true, is an assumption made by the author of the above argument?

   (A) The water supply used by the dinosaurs who survived the asteroid collision and subsequent change in global temperature had not become contaminated by lethal fallout from the collision.

   (B) A second asteroid impact or some other cosmic event is likely to have killed off the dinosaurs that survived the asteroid impact and global temperature change.

   (C) At least a few dinosaurs continued to exist for some years after the asteroid collided with Earth.

   (D) There is another existing theory that does a better job of explaining the extinction of the dinosaurs than the theory involving an asteroid collision with Earth.

   (E) The change in temperature caused when dust clouds from the asteroid impact blocked the sun could not have lasted for several years.

9. Some scientists have decided that Pluto should no longer be classified as a planet. The plain facts of the matter, however, say otherwise. Pluto is a relatively large body that orbits the sun and has a moon of its own. This is true for the other 8 bodies for which the designation "planet" is not in question, and for no other bodies in the universe but these. Clearly, Pluto should be classified as a planet.

   Which of the following indicates a flaw in the reasoning above?

   (A) The author attempts to prove that an object belongs in a classification by showing that it has no characteristics in common with objects outside that classification.

   (B) The author presents a list of characteristics shared by members of a classification, rather than the defining attributes of membership in that classification.

   (C) The author assumes that membership in one classification excludes membership in another.

   (D) The author does not support his conclusion with corroborative evidence from scientific authorities.

   (E) The strength of the author's argument depends on an imprecise use of the term "relatively."

10. Five years ago, the government approved a new drug for the treatment of lung cancer. The researchers who developed the drug had shown that it reliably yielded a cure rate of 95%, in contrast to the cure rate of 50% obtained through earlier treatments. Despite widespread use of the drug, however, a greater percentage of lung cancer patients have died from the disease over the past five years than died from the disease during the previous five-year period.

    Which one of the following, if true, most helps to resolve the apparent discrepancy in the information above?

    (A) More people have developed lung cancer during the past five years than during the previous five-year period.

    (B) The new drug costs more than any other treatment currently available.

    (C) In light of the new drug, many people at risk of developing lung cancer no longer feel pressure to monitor their health and thus do not discover their illness until it has reached an untreatable stage.

    (D) The government has also recently approved other, less effective treatments for lung cancer.

    (E) Many people with lung cancer also suffer from other cancers.

11. A new species of fish has just been discovered living in great numbers in the waters off Papua New Guinea. The fish exhibits some characteristics belonging to sharks, such as a cartilaginous skeleton. However, the fish also exhibits characteristics belonging to eels, such as a long, snake-like body. Because of the habitat where it was found and its obviously eel-like body, almost all scientists believe that the fish is an eel. But the cartilaginous skeleton puzzles them, since no known eel possesses one. So scientists are still unsure as to the fish's precise classification, but they agreed immediately that the most logical classification would be as either a shark or an eel.

    The statements above, if true, most strongly support which of the following?

    (A) To be placed into a certain classification, a fish must possess all the characteristics of that classification.

    (B) Physical characteristics, such as skeletons, are scientists' primary means of classifying new species.

    (C) Some fish with cartilaginous skeletons are not sharks.

    (D) The waters off Papua New Guinea are generally hospitable to eels.

    (E) A fish cannot be both a shark and an eel.

12. In the Middle Ages, monks possessed the only copies of many of the great works of Antiquity. They maintained these works in their libraries and spent many hours transcribing them for distribution to other monasteries. However, last week a Classics scholar discovered that a monk had consistently miscopied a word while transcribing Plato's *Republic*, thereby altering the meaning of the entire text. All subsequent copies of Plato's *Republic* will now have to be corrected.

The conclusion above would be more reasonably drawn if which of the following were inserted into the argument as an additional premise?

(A) No copy of Plato's Republic predates the Middle Ages.

(B) Only Plato's Republic needs to be corrected.

(C) A single word can alter the meaning of an entire text.

(D) No one had ever noticed the mistake before last week.

(E) All subsequent copies of Plato's Republic can be traced back to the flawed copy.

13. A complete ban on the sale of semi-automatic machine guns will not reduce the incidence of violent crime committed with these guns. People who want to commit violent crimes with these guns will still get them even if they are banned.

The argument above would be most weakened if which of the following statements were true?

(A) Banning semi-automatic machine guns will result in an increase in the number of other dangerous weapons purchased.

(B) People who do not want to break the law will not buy guns illegally.

(C) Fully-automatic machine guns, presently banned, are much more difficult to obtain than other banned weapons, such as switchblade knives.

(D) Seeing semi-automatic machine guns legally displayed for sale tends to increase people's inclination to use those weapons to commit violent crimes.

(E) The number of accidental gun deaths is lowest in those states with the most restrictive gun control laws.

14. The sanitation chief, hailing the success of her voluntary conservation program, reported that the amount of garbage produced per capita in the city decreased dramatically last year. But that statistic is deceptive. Last year the city incorporated three villages from the surrounding suburban area, increasing its population by almost 30 percent. It is this increase, rather than the conservation program, that explains the statistical drop.

Which of the following, if true, would seriously weaken the author's objection to the sanitation chief's claim?

(A) Because of differences between urban and suburban life, most suburban areas produce less garbage per capita than do urban areas.

(B) The voluntary conservation program was not implemented in the three incorporated villages until very late last year.

(C) The year before last, the three villages produced as many pounds of garbage per capita as did the city.

(D) The statistics cited by the sanitation chief do not include commercial waste or garbage collected by private carters.

(E) Due to a three-week strike, some of the garbage produced in the city during the year before last year was not counted in the statistics.

15. The dollar amount of federal tax revenues gained from personal income tax has increased markedly in recent years. Clearly, people are being more honest in declaring their annual earnings than they used to be.

The argument above would be greatly weakened by each of the following EXCEPT:

(A) Fewer income tax deductions are allowed now than in the past.

(B) The nation's population has increased.

(C) Tax revenue from the corporate sector has decreased.

(D) The average yearly income of the nation's resident has increased.

(E) The rate of personal income taxation has increased.

16. A number of law schools are offering their first-year students an opportunity to prepay, at the current rates, the cost of any of the commercially offered courses that prepare them for the bar exam. The school then pays the cost of the course that the student selects upon graduation. Students should participate in the program as a means of reducing the cost of preparation for the bar.

Which of the following, if true, is the most appropriate reason for students NOT to participate in the program?

(A) The students are unsure which course they will take.

(B) The prepayment funds, invested in an interest-bearing account until graduation, will grow to more than the total cost of any of the bar exam preparation courses.

(C) The cost of the bar exam preparation courses is expected to increase at a rate faster than the annual increase in the cost of living.

(D) Some of the bar exam preparation courses are contemplating large price increases next year.

(E) The prepayment plan would not cover the cost of the bar exam itself.

17. A public health official reported that 60 percent of the children at summer school have never had the measles or chicken pox, and that of this 60 percent, not one child has ever been observed to eat the cheese served in the school lunches. From this he concluded that children who abstain from cheese products will protect themselves from most childhood diseases.

Each of the following, if true, would strengthen the official's argument EXCEPT:

(A) Medically speaking, whatever serves to inhibit measles and chicken pox will generally inhibit the entire spectrum of childhood diseases.

(B) The observations the official carried out were extremely accurate, and all those observed to abstain from cheese products at school did, in fact, abstain.

(C) Children's eating habits are the same at school as anywhere else, and those who abstain form cheese products at school do so in general.

(D) Recent research has pointed to a deficiency in cheese products as one of the major causes of measles and chicken pox infections.

(E) Most cheeses and cheese products harbor bacteria that are known to be causative agents for many childhood diseases, such as measles and chicken pox.

18. In a nature reserve in India, people are sometimes attacked by tigers. It is believed that the tigers will only attack people from behind. So for the last few years many workers in the reserve have started wearing masks depicting a human face on the back of their heads. While many area residents remain skeptical, no worker wearing one of these masks has yet been attacked by a tiger.

Which of statements below, if true, would best support the argument of those who advocate the use of the mask?

(A) Many workers in the nature reserve who do not wear the masks have been attacked by tigers.

(B) Workers in other nature reserves who wear similar masks have not been attacked recently by tigers.

(C) No tigers have been spotted on the nature reserve in recent years.

(D) Many of the workers who wear the masks also sing while they work in order to frighten away any tigers in the area.

(E) The tigers have often been observed attacking small deer from in front rather than from behind.

19. Since Arlene Hodges was installed as president of the Caralis corporation, profits have increased by an average of 11 percent per year. During the tenure of her predecessor, the corporation's profits averaged a yearly increase of only 7 percent. Obviously, Ms. Hodges' aggressive marketing efforts have caused the acceleration in the growth of Caralis' profits.

    Which of the following, if true, would most weaken the conclusion drawn above?

    (A) The corporation's new manufacturing plant, constructed in the past year, has resulted in a 15 percent increase in production capacity.

    (B) For each year of Ms. Hodges' presidency, the corporation's financial records show an increase in profits over the previous year.

    (C) During the tenure of Ms. Hodges' predecessor, the corporation began an advertising campaign aimed at capturing consumers between the ages of 24 and 35.

    (D) Since Ms. Hodges became president, the corporation has switched the primary focus of its advertising from print ads to radio and television commercials.

    (E) Just before he was replaced, Ms. Hodges' predecessor directed the acquisition of a rival corporation, which has nearly doubled the corporation's yearly revenues.

20. Chef: An ordinance ought to be passed banning midtown street vendors from selling food within a certain proximity to restaurants. With their high rents and costs, restaurants cannot be expected to compete with the vendors. Even in cases where these vendors sell food completely different from the restaurant's bill of fare, the price differential is enough to attract to the vendors customers who would otherwise have eaten in the restaurants.

    Which of the following, if true, would most weaken the argument above?

    (A) The food served in midtown restaurants is better than that sold by street vendors.

    (B) Most street vendors who sell food would suffer losses from being forced to move to other locations.

    (C) Most customers who eat in midtown do so on expense accounts, and do not pay for their own meals.

    (D) There are not enough police officers to enforce regulations requiring street vendors to move a certain distance from restaurants.

    (E) The average profit on food sold by a street vendor is roughly the same percentage as that on food served in restaurants.

21. A recent study reported that, ten years after graduation, the average college graduate in country X has saved the equivalent of $40,000. Therefore, if a college graduate has saved only $36,000 ten years after graduation, that graduate's savings growth has been below the average in country X.

Which of the following indicates a flaw in the reasoning above?

(A) Savings is only one measure of a college graduate's success.

(B) Some graduates ten years out of college have saved as much as $65,000.

(C) It is possible to save $36,000 before graduating from college.

(D) The phrase "below average" does not necessarily mean insufficient.

(E) Average savings growth is not the same as average savings.

22. The local high school students have been clamoring for the freedom to design their own curricula. Allowing this would be as disastrous as allowing three-year-olds to choose their own diets. These students have neither the maturity nor the experience to equal that of the professional educators now doing the job.

Which of the following statements, if true, would most strengthen the above argument?

(A) High school students have less formal education than those who currently design the curricula.

(B) Three-year-olds do not, if left to their own devices, choose healthful diets.

(C) The local high school students are less intelligent than the average teenager.

(D) Individualized curricula are more beneficial to high school students than are the standard curricula, which are rigid and unresponsive to their particular strengths and weaknesses.

(E) The ability to design good curricula develops only after years of familiarity with educational life.

23. European nations are starting to decrease the percentage of their foreign aid that is "tied" — that is, given only on the condition that it be spent to obtain goods and materials produced by the country from which the aid originates. By doing so, European nations hope to avoid the ethical criticism that has been recently leveled at some foreign aid donors, notably Japan.

Which of the following can most reasonably be inferred from the passage?

(A) Many non-European nations give foreign aid solely for the purpose of benefiting their domestic economies.

(B) Only ethical considerations, and not those of self-interest, should be considered when foreign aid decisions are made.

(C) Many of the problems faced by underdeveloped countries could be eliminated if a smaller percentage of the foreign aid they obtain were "tied" to specific purchases and uses.

(D) Much of Japan's foreign aid returns to Japan in the form of purchase orders for Japanese products and equipment.

(E) Non-European nations are unwilling to offer foreign aid that is not "tied" to the purchase of their own manufactures.

24. For healthy individuals who wish to improve their overall fitness, cross-training in several sports is more beneficial than training in a single activity. Cross-training develops a wide range of muscle groups, while single sport training tends to isolate a select few muscles. Single sport activities, especially those that target slow-twitch muscles, tend to increase the tonic muscle fibers in the body. Cross-training works instead to increase the body's phasic muscle fibers, which burn more calories than tonic muscle fibers.

    Which one of the following, if true, best supports the argument above?

    (A) In healthy persons, overall fitness increases in proportion to the number of calories burned by the body.

    (B) Overall fitness is most effectively improved through athletic training.

    (C) Tonic muscle fibers are of greater value to overall fitness than are phasic muscle fibers.

    (D) Strenuous physical exertion on a single sport is not recommended for those recovering from a serious illness.

    (E) Some slow-twitch muscles contain many phasic muscle fibers.

25. This editorial cannot be a good argument because it is barely literate. Run-on sentences, slang, and perfectly dreadful grammar appear regularly throughout. Anything that poorly written cannot be making very much sense.

    Which of the following identifies an assumption in the argument above?

    (A) This editorial was written by someone other than the usual editor.

    (B) Generally speaking, very few editorials are poor in style or grammar.

    (C) The language of an argument is indicative of its validity.

    (D) Generally speaking, the majority of editorials are poor in style and grammar.

    (E) The author of the editorial purposely uses poor grammar to disguise what he knows is a bad argument.

26. Citing the legal precedent set by asbestos exposure cases, a state judge agreed to combine a series of workplace disability cases involving repetitive stress injuries to the hands and wrists. The judge's decision to consolidate hundreds of suits by data entry workers, word processors, newspaper employees, and other workers who use computers into one case is likely to prove detrimental for the computer manufacturing companies being sued, notwithstanding the defense's argument that the cases should not be combined because of the different individuals and workplaces involved.

    The statements above best support which of the following conclusions?

    (A) The judge's decision to consolidate the suits implies a commonality among the situations, thereby strengthening the plaintiffs' claim that the manufacturers are liable.

    (B) Individual rulings in repetitive injury suits often enable manufacturers to escape liability on technical grounds.

    (C) The plaintiffs bringing suit against the computer manufacturers have similar employment histories and used similar equipment at their jobs.

    (D) The parties accused of liability in workplace injury cases are more likely to settle if the suits are consolidated into one case.

    (E) Because consolidated cases tend to receive more publicity than individual rulings, they often result in further lawsuits against manufacturers.

27. The city is required by federal environmental regulations to build a new water treatment plant. If this plant is built inside the city limits it will disrupt the lives of many more citizens than if it is built on vacant land near the city. However, despite the availability of the vacant land, the plant should be built inside city limits because of the increased economic benefits its construction would provide to the city in the form of jobs.

Which one of the following, if true, most weakens the argument above?

(A) The available land outside of the city is privately owned, whereas there is an adequate site within the city that is city-owned.

(B) Regardless of the site location, most of the jobs created by the plant's construction will go to residents of the city.

(C) A municipal plant like the water treatment plant will pay no taxes to city government regardless of its location.

(D) Most citizens of the city will tolerate brief disruptions in their daily lives if such disruptions will secure better water quality in the future.

(E) The amount of taxes paid by workers depends both on where they work and where they live.

28. Time and time again it has been shown that students who attend colleges with low faculty/student ratios get the most well-rounded education. As a result, when my children are ready for college, I'll be sure they attend a school with a very small student population.

Which of the following, if true, identifies the greatest flaw in the reasoning above?

(A) A low faculty/student ratio is the effect of a well-rounded education, not its source.

(B) Intelligence should be considered the result of childhood environment, not advanced education.

(C) A very small student population does not, by itself, ensure a low faculty/student ratio.

(D) Parental desires and preferences rarely determine a child's choice of a college or university.

(E) Students must take advantage of the low faculty/student ratio by intentionally choosing small classes.

29. The overall rate of emphysema has declined 15 percent over the last 15 years in region A. During that period, the total cost of care for emphysema sufferers in region A, after accounting for inflation, declined by two percent per year until eight years ago, at which time it began increasing by approximately two percent per year. Now the total health care cost for treating emphysema is approximately equal to what it was 15 years ago.

Which one of the following best resolves the apparent discrepancy between the incidence of emphysema in region A and the cost of caring for emphysema sufferers?

(A) The overall cost of health care in region A has increased by seven percent in the last 15 years, after accounting for inflation.

(B) Improvements in technology have significantly increased both the cost per patient and the success rate of emphysema care in the past 15 years.

(C) About seven years ago, the widespread switch to health maintenance organizations halted overall increases in health care costs in region A after accounting for inflation.

(D) The money made available for research into cures for emphysema had been declining for many years until approximately eight years ago, since which time it has shown a modest increase.

(E) Beginning about nine years ago, the most expensive-to-treat advanced cases of emphysema have been decreasing in region A at a rate of about five percent per year.

30. Recently, the research and development departments at major pharmaceutical companies have been experimenting with new injections that provide the boost in iron that anemic children need to reverse their condition. These companies have expressed confidence that children who are suffering from anemia will be cured relatively simply through the use of such biochemical supplements.

In concluding that the biochemical remedy being developed will have its desired effect, the pharmaceutical companies assume that

(A) major pharmaceutical companies have the primary responsibility to cure childhood anemia

(B) a low iron level in the body is the major factor influencing the incidence of anemia in children

(C) a diet rich in iron cannot improve the conditions of children suffering from anemia to the point that biochemical supplements would become unnecessary

(D) children afflicted with anemia will find out about and submit to injections that can reverse their conditions

(E) the use of biochemical supplements is the safest way to cure anemia in children

31. Cross-species studies of animal groups indicate that offspring who are separated from their mothers during the first months of life frequently develop aggression disorders. During group feedings, for example, separated offspring exert excessive force in the struggle over food, and continue to strike at other offspring long after the others have submitted. The best explanation for this observed behavior is the hypothesis that aggression disorders are caused by lack of proper parent-led socialization during the first stage of an offspring's development.

    Which one of the following, if true, provides the most support for the hypothesis above?

    (A) Some wildebeests who are not separated from their mothers during infancy display excessive aggression in conflicts that establish their place in the dominance hierarchy.

    (B) Human babies adopted in the first three months of life often display aggressive behavior disorders during early childhood.

    (C) Chimps raised in captivity in environments simulating traditional parent-led socialization display far less aggression in mating-related conflicts than do chimps raised without such social interaction.

    (D) Many polar bears display more aggression in conflicts over food and social dominance than they do in mating-related conflicts.

    (E) Elephants who are separated from their mothers during the first months of life do not display excessive aggression in food or social dominance struggles.

32. Four out of five people who filled out our questionnaire about solar energy indicated that they would strongly support any decision to direct more federal resources toward solar energy research, even if it involved cutting funds to synthetic fuel research. How, then, can the Administration claim that interest in solar energy is waning? The direction of public opinion is clear.

    The argument above would be most conclusively weakened if it could be demonstrated that

    (A) people who oppose solar energy research are far less likely to fill out a questionnaire than are people who support it

    (B) synthetic fuel is a cheaper and cleaner source of energy than is solar power

    (C) those who filled out questionnaires were not knowledgeable about energy issues

    (D) the Administration has never been known in the past to willfully mislead the public

    (E) the need for alternative energy sources will increase significantly in the future

33. Betty: My opponent for the office of scout superintendent opposes a rule that would require all Wilderness Scout troop leaders to lead their scouts in the loyalty pledge before all meetings. How can my opponent claim she will represent the high moral standards of the Wilderness Scouts when she would forbid troop leaders from leading the pledge that proclaims our most important virtue?

    Which one of the following points would be most useful to a person disputing the reasoning of the argument above?

    (A) Some Wilderness Scouts also oppose the loyalty pledge rule.
    (B) Loyalty is only one of many virtues espoused by the Wilderness Scouts.
    (C) The opponent's position on the loyalty pledge rule may be atypical of her positions in general.
    (D) Refusing to require an activity like the loyalty pledge is not the same thing as forbidding it.
    (E) Opposing loyalty to an organization does not necessarily mean that one is disloyal to that organization.

34. The Board of Directors of the Lejon Etymological Museum imposed a 50-cent admission charge in order to reduce the Museum's deficit. Attendance remained stable and there was no protest from the public, so, six months later, the Museum announced that the admission price would go up to $1.50.

    It can be inferred that, in increasing the admission charge to $1.50, the Board of Directors assumed that:

    (A) People did not protest the initial charge because they felt it was necessary to keep the Museum in operation.
    (B) Since people did not protest the initial charge, they will also accept the raised price.
    (C) Since $1.50 is three times the original charge, it is probable that attendance will drop as the public protests the increase.
    (D) The increased revenue from admissions will enable the Museum to expand its operations.
    (E) Tripling the admission cost every six months will not cause a drop in attendance.

35. Ernesto: Sales of VCRs—videocassette recorders— will decline in the next few years because the saturation level among U.S. households has virtually been reached.

Milton: Every year a greater number of popular feature films is released on cassette— at least 6 per month. Clearly VCR sales will remain constant, if not rise.

Which of the following is the best logical evaluation of Milton's response to Ernesto's argument? `

(A) He cites evidence that, if true, disproves the evidence cited by Ernesto in drawing his conclusion.

(B) He points out a gap in the logic followed by Ernesto in drawing his conclusion.

(C) He cites an issue ignored by Ernesto and which outweighs the issues raised by Ernesto.

(D) He does not speak to Ernesto's point because he fails to raise the issue of whether VCR sales may be linked to sales of other leisure-related products.

(E) He fails to respond to Ernesto's argument because he assumes that nothing will significantly retard the sale of VCRs, which was the issue that Ernesto raised.

36. Manager: The success ratio for new businesses is lower than ever, with only 12 percent surviving the first two years. Furthermore, many businesses already operating are doing so at a loss, or with their lowest profit margin in decades. The blame must fall on the excessive demands of the workers. Profits drop in order to pay for new paint, radios, and artwork. We have lost sight of the fact that work is intended to be productive, not enjoyable.

Which of the following, if true, would most weaken the manager's argument?

(A) Workers, whether they are performing productively or not, often have very difficult and highly taxing duties.

(B) In most cases, improvements in the work environment increase productivity by increasing worker satisfaction.

(C) The failure of many businesses in the past was due to exorbitant taxation rather than excessive demands of the workers.

(D) The failure of a new business is not necessarily the same thing as the failure of an already existing business.

(E) The failure of a new business is not necessarily the same thing as operating an already existing business without a profit.

37. Through their selective funding of research projects, pharmaceutical companies exert too much influence upon medical research in universities. Only research proposals promising lucrative results are given serious consideration, and funding is usually awarded to scientists at large institutions who already have vast research experience. As a result, only larger universities will be able to continue developing adequate research facilities, and graduate students will learn that their future research must conform to the expectations of the corporation. Research will continue to be conducted at the expense of human welfare.

    Which of the following reactions by a pharmaceutical company representative would provide the strongest rebuttal to the comments above?

    (A) Many of the research projects funded by pharmaceutical companies do not end up being lucrative.

    (B) Much of the funding provided by pharmaceutical companies goes to fellowships that help pay for the educations of graduate students.

    (C) If it were not for the funds which pharmaceutical companies provide, very little medical research could be conducted at all.

    (D) The committee members fail to discuss other methods of funding research projects.

    (E) Larger universities are the only ones equipped to conduct the kind of research sponsored by pharmaceutical companies.

38. Elderly women who have suffered heart attacks are five times more likely to develop a dementia than are other elderly women. **Therefore, steps taken to prevent heart attacks, such as dieting, may also prevent dementia.** Other studies have shown vision loss to be more common among elderly women who have suffered heart attacks. Thus, demented elderly women are much more likely to suffer from vision loss than are other elderly women.

    The statement highlighted in boldface plays which of the following roles in the argument?

    (A) It is an assumption made by the author in constructing the argument.

    (B) It contradicts part of the author's conclusion.

    (C) It is the main conclusion to which the author is proceeding

    (D) It acts as the principal piece of evidence for the conclusion that the author draws.

    (E) It is a conclusion drawn by the author but not relevant to the main point.

39. Politician: An investigation must be launched into the operations of the private group that is training recruits to fight against Country Z. The Neutrality Act plainly forbids citizens from engaging in military campaigns against any nation with which we are not at war. Since no war has been declared between us and Country Z, we should bring charges against these fanatics, who are in open defiance of the law.

Which of the following, if true, would cast the most serious doubt on the politician's argument?

(A) Country Z is currently engaged in a bloody and escalating civil war.

(B) Diplomatic relations between the politician's country and Country Z were severed last year.

(C) The recruits are being trained to fight only in the event the politician's country goes to war against Country Z.

(D) The training of recruits is funded not by citizens of the politician's country, but rather by a consortium of individuals from abroad.

(E) Charges cannot be brought against the private group that is training the recruits unless an investigation is first launched.

40. In its report for the quarter just ending, Company X announces that in some of its manufacturing processes it plans to begin converting from conventional fuels like oil and natural gas, which are rapidly becoming scarce, to synthetic fuels currently under development in the company's laboratories in Europe and the American far west. Implementation of this plan will almost certainly increase the company's expenses, since even if the synthetic fuels are rendered practical for use they can be expected to cost considerably more than conventional fuels.

Which of the following, if true, casts the most doubt on the argument above?

(A) Company X's synthetic fuels will not be ready for use in its manufacturing processes for at least a decade.

(B) Whatever increased expenses accrue from the development and use of synthetic fuels can and will be passed on to consumers of Company X's products.

(C) Company X's manufacturing processes can be adapted to the use of synthetic fuels at little or no expense.

(D) In time, the raw materials used to produce Company X's synthetic fuels will become as scarce as oil and natural gas.

(E) Long-needed conservation procedures will become practical when synthetic fuels are introduced and will compensate for the higher cost of the fuels.

ANSWER KEY: CRITICAL REASONING

1. D	15. C	29. B
2. A	16. B	30. D
3. B	17. D	31. C
4. B	18. A	32. A
5. B	19. E	33. D
6. A	20. C	34. B
7. E	21. E	35. E
8. A	22. E	36. B
9. B	23. D	37. C
10. C	24. A	38. E
11. D	25. C	39. C
12. E	26. A	40. E
13. D	27. B	
14. C	28. C	

1. D

When asked for a conclusion, select the one answer choice that must be true strictly based on the evidence given in the argument. Since the earliest known records of wartime activities mention carrier pigeons, the birds must have been used prior to the time that the records were written (or else how could they have been written about?). Carrier pigeons are preferable in some cases, but we can't infer that they are usually preferable. What if speed is a more important factor than security? Thus, (A) does not have to be true. Pigeons can be shot out of the sky, and thus their messages intercepted, (B). There is no way, based only on the evidence we've been given, to determine whether the use of the pigeons has increased, decreased, or stayed the same, so (C) can be ruled out. The stimulus tells us that the birds are valuable to modern military units, but not that they're being used extensively, (E).

2. A

THE CONCLUSION: The fame of the *Mona Lisa* prevents most people from seeing it as it really is

and from understanding the true scope of 15th and 16th century European painting.

THE EVIDENCE: All we are told in the way of evidence is that the painting is the most famous in the world, but that it is not flawless or incomparable. This doesn't directly lead to the conclusion, so the correct answer choice must help connect this information to the conclusion.

We are told that the painting has flaws (and we have to accept that this, like all stated evidence, is true). So if most people don't agree that it has flaws, they're wrong, thus supporting the conclusion that most people don't see it as it really is: flawed.

DaVinci's opinion is irrelevant to the logic of this argument, (B), as is the opinion of art scholars, (E), and comparisons with other paintings, (D). Most people may be capable of understanding the scope of 15th and 16th century paintings, (C), but that doesn't support the notion that the attention given to the *Mona Lisa* currently prevents them from doing so.

3. B

THE CONCLUSION: Nearly all the music heard at an orchestral performance contains pitch relationships that differ from those that musical instruments naturally produce.

THE EVIDENCE: Practically all of this music is written using a system that represents slight alterations of natural pitch relationships.

The author is assuming that the way the music is played will be the way it was notated. If not, then the musicians might choose to play using a non-tempered system of tuning, and the audiences would hear natural pitch relationships, contrary to the argument's conclusion. However, if the musicians never play anything other than the music exactly as it is notated, they would—more than 99% of the time—use a tempered system of tuning, and almost all the music the audience hears is certain to contain pitch relationships that differ from the ones instruments naturally produce.

(A) tells us that audiences might prefer the "unnatural" sounds of the tempered system, but this does not tell us whether these unnatural sounds are what they hear at a performance. (C) brings us well outside the scope of the argument, which only deals with orchestral music. (D) does say that most orchestral music has been written with tempered music in mind, but the question is: How is it actually played, and thus heard? (E) gives us a reason why the tempered system has been used in the first place, but this is background information that doesn't relate to the logic of this argument.

4. B

THE CONCLUSION: Dr. Lucas concluded that Barry should be treated with Innalex, not Allerease.

THE EVIDENCE: Allerease performed BETTER overall than did Innalex in a studies involving 2,000 children. This seems to be a reason NOT to recommend Innalex over Allerease. So, we must explain this apparently paradoxical decision to recommend Innalex.

If the effectiveness of Innalex depends on the child's age, then it's possible that 4-year olds, like Barry, respond better to Innalex. (A)'s mention of other food allergies is outside the scope of the argument. The relevant issue is whether Innalex is the better treatment to administer to a 4-year old with a wheat allergy. It doesn't matter how Dr. Lucas found out about the study—just that he did, (C). Whether Barry was one of the 2,000 children involved in the studies, (D), is an issue that is outside the scope of the argument. Other allergies, (E), is out of scope.

5. B

THE CONCLUSION: Most people use the word *color* when referring just to an object's hue.

THE EVIDENCE: *Hue* is sometimes used interchangeably with the word *color*, though the latter refers to an object's brightness and saturation as well as its hue. Hue only refers to an object's dominant wavelengths. If most people take into account an object's brightness when they refer to its color, then they aren't "referring just to an

object's hue." They may be omitting the object's saturation, but they aren't referring just to hue. (B) directly contradicts the conclusion.

The argument isn't about people's awareness of the true meanings of these terms (A), but rather about how they use them. The conclusion is about the incorrect use of the term *color* not the term *hue*, (C). The argument allows for the correct use of the terms by thousands, (D), as long as most use the term *color* incorrectly. This doesn't weaken the conclusion. Whether there is any purpose in distinguishing the two, (E), is outside the scope of the argument.

6. A

THE CONCLUSION: Fewer and fewer people in this country have a genuine interest in the fine arts.

THE EVIDENCE: The evidence—record levels of attendance at art museums—seems to contradict the conclusion. The task is to reconcile this apparent discrepancy.

If the increase in the number of repeat visitors has been greater than the increase in the number of visits, then fewer people are going the museums, despite the increase in visits. This supports the author's conclusion that fewer people are interested in the arts. Imagine 1,000 visits in a week for one museum, 10 of which are by people who show up twice during that week. That's 990 individual people who have gone to the museum. Then imagine that the next week there are 1,200 visits (an increase of 200 visits), and the number of repeaters that week is 220, (an increase of 210 repeaters). That represents only 980 individuals going to the museum. If an interest in the arts cannot be determined by looking at museum attendance, then this would weaken the argument, (B). If tourist attendance is relatively consistent as a portion of total visitors, then this doesn't have any known impact on the argument, (C). (D) is out of scope, as is (E), unless we were told that fine art was not being displayed.

7. E

THE CONCLUSION: Children who saw films based on *Grimm's Fairy Tales* did not experience the full impact of the moral lessons embodied in the original folktales.

THE EVIDENCE: The violence of the original stories was lessened, first by the Grimm brothers, and then by the film-makers.

To draw the above conclusion, one first needs to assume that the violence of the original folktales is necessary to experience the full impact of the moral lessons. This ties the evidence securely to the conclusion. (A) is too general about *stories*; there's no need to assume that violence is always needed whenever a story contains a moral lesson. (B) isn't central to the logic of the argument. One doesn't need to assume that morality has remained unchanged, (C), only that some moral lessons of the past can still be imparted to today's children. (D) is out of scope.

8. A

THE CONCLUSION: Some force besides the asteroid collision must have been responsible for the death of the remaining dinosaurs.

THE EVIDENCE: Some dinosaurs were not killed by the impact or the lack of sunlight caused by the collision.

The author states that "some other force" killed the remaining dinosaurs without ruling out collateral damage caused by the collision (other than the dust clouds blocking the sun). If the collision created a contaminated water supply that killed the dinosaurs, this would weaken the conclusion. Therefore, the author must be assuming that this never happened, (A).

(B) is out because the author does not explain the "other force," nor how long it took for the remaining dinosaurs to be killed (C). The author does make it clear that the asteroid-collision theory is incomplete, but doesn't imply the existence of any other theory (D). There is no reason the author needs to assume that the temperature change couldn't have lasted for years (E).

9. B

THE CONCLUSION: Pluto is a planet.

THE EVIDENCE: It has certain characteristics in common with the other planets, and only those planets.

Pluto can be considered a planet if the author defines what is meant by "planet" and then shows how Pluto fits that definition. Shared characteristics do not guarantee membership in the same classification. Assuming that they do is the flaw in the argument. The author states that SOME of Pluto's characteristics are uniquely shared with the other 8 planets, but does not state that ALL of its characteristics are shared only with them, as stated in (A). There is no discussion of any classification besides "planet" (C). Evidence from scientific authorities has no bearing on the reasoning presented by the argument's evidence and conclusion, which is internally flawed. The same can be said for a discussion of the exact meaning of *relatively*—a more precise definition would not improve the reasoning (E).

10. C

THE CONCLUSION: A greater percentage of lung cancer patients have died from the disease over the past five years than have died from the disease during the previous five-year period.

THE EVIDENCE: A new drug for cancer was introduced five-years ago that produces a high and reliable cure rate. In addition, many patients have used the drug over the course of the past five years. This information seems to contradict the conclusion, so we have to choose an answer that shows why, despite this evidence, the conclusion holds true.

If patients who took the new, effective drug are still dying of lung cancer, then something must be interfering with or lessening the effect of the drug. We can't say that the patients are dying of something other than lung cancer since the stimulus tells us that lung cancer is the cause of death. (C) addresses the proper administration of the drug—since people aren't monitoring their health as closely, lung cancers are being diagnosed at later stages of development. The drug's effectiveness is compromised at later stages. (A) is out because if more people developed lung cancer, the effective new drug should still affect a smaller percentage of deaths (though the actual number of deaths may rise). (A) confuses the concept of number with the concept of percent. (B) is irrelevant since we know from the stimulus that use of the drug is widespread.

With (D), the usage rate of the effective drug can still be high even if other treatments for lung cancer have been approved. (D) invites us to assume that more patients are using the less-effective, newly-approved treatments relative to the fantastic new drug. But nothing in the stimulus or in this answer choice states this to be the case. And (E) is irrelevant since the argument only applies to patients who died of lung cancer.

11. D

THE CONCLUSION: This is an inference question that asks us to draw a conclusion from the information provided. What must also be true given the stimulus?

THE EVIDENCE: Since we need to draw our own conclusion, we can use all facts provided in the argument as evidence.

The first sentence states that the new fish was discovered off the waters of Papua New Guinea. In addition, the fourth sentence states that the new fish shares its habitat with the eel. In combination, these two sentences indicate that eels also live in the waters off Papua New Guinea. Therefore, this region must be hospitable to eels, as stated in (D).

With (A), the last sentence implies that the new fish could be classified as a shark even though it does not have a cartilaginous skeleton. So it is out. Also, watch out for language (all, every, never, always) that indicates extreme answer choices. With (B), the stimulus suggests that scientists use physical characteristics to classify, but it does not address the importance of physical characteristics relative to other characteristics for this purpose. With (C), if the new fish were to be classified as an eel, then we could conclude that at least one fish with a cartilaginous skeleton is not a shark. The stimulus, however, never says this. Furthermore, we are not told anything about other fishes' classifications. And

though (E) may seem "true," we are not given any information that would allow us to say for certain whether or not an animal can be both shark and eel.

12. E

THE CONCLUSION: All copies of Plato's Republic made after the monk's error will need to be corrected.

THE EVIDENCE: Monks were responsible for the production and distribution of literary works, and a monk consistently miscopied a word in Plato's Republic.

This question asks for an additional premise that would make the argument "more reasonably drawn." This means that we must look for an answer choice that strengthens the link between evidence and conclusion. The evidence states that a monk miscopied a word in Plato's Republic. The conclusion is that all copies of this work made after the monk's error will need to be corrected. The assumption that links the two is that all these copies contain the monk's error. The correct choice will support this assumption. (E) states that all copies of the Republic produced after the error was made can be traced back to the flawed copy. This supports the idea that these copies do contain the error.

(A) doesn't tell us how many copies of the Republic actually contain the monk's error. We need an answer choice that supports the error in all subsequent copies. (B) is irrelevant. We're asked only to consider copies of Plato's Republic, not any other work. (C) is contained in the stimulus; we're told that a single word did in fact alter the meaning of the text. (D) doesn't support the idea that all subsequent copies of the Republic contained the monk's error; it simply states that no one noticed the error. We aren't given any information on the number of copies affected.

13. D

THE CONCLUSION: A ban on semi-automatic machine guns will not reduce the incidence of violent crime committed with these guns.

THE EVIDENCE: People who want to commit violent crimes with these guns will still get them.

There's not a whole lot of evidence here, just a couple of claims. To weaken the argument, we want to show that banning the guns will result in less criminal use of the guns. If much of the use is not truly premeditated, but occurs to the criminals when they see the guns displayed, then banning the guns (and their display) will result in less criminal use. So (D) is correct.

We don't know what the effect of the increased purchase of other dangerous weapons would be on the crime rate, so (A) does not weaken the argument. (B) talks about law-abiding people, who aren't a part of the argument. (C) is outside the scope because the argument is about semi-automatic guns, not fully-automatic guns. Accidental deaths (E) are also outside the scope.

14. C

THE CONCLUSION: The drop in per capita garbage is not due to the chief's conservation program.

THE EVIDENCE: The city incorporated three villages, whose extra residents accounted for the per capita drop.

Well, the author plainly believes (assumes) that the suburban villagers are deflating the per capita garbage figure, so he assumes that suburbanites produce less garbage. If, though, they produce every bit as much (or more) garbage, then the drop can't have been due to their incorporation into the city and the statistics.

The author assumes (A) so it strengthens rather than weakens his argument. (B) makes it less likely that the conservation program is responsible for the drop, which also strengthens his argument. As long as the same type of garbage is eliminated from both year's statistics (D), the effect of this on the different arguments is anyone's guess—a clear sign of a wrong answer. More garbage the year before last year (E) just increases the drop; it does not, however, affect the author's attempt to explain this drop.

15. C

THE CONCLUSION: People aren't cheating on their taxes as much as they used to.

THE EVIDENCE: The amount, in dollars, of taxes collected from personal income tax has gone up appreciably in recent years.

We're only concerned with revenue from the personal income tax, so any information about corporate taxes, (C), is outside the realm of our interest.

All the wrong choices provide alternate explanations—explanations as to how we can have more tax dollars collected without people being more honest in reporting their incomes. Fewer deductions (A) would probably cause people to pay more in taxes. A population increase (B) would produce more taxpayers. If average income went up (D), then average tax paid would go up as well. And if the tax rate rose (E), the government would very likely collect more money.

16. B

The passage recommends that students participate in a course-fee prepayment program to save money. If (B) were true, placing the funds in an interest-bearing account would save more than participating in the prepayment program, so the students should not participate. (A) is irrelevant, since the program will pay for whatever course the student selects. (C) and (D) support the argument that students should participate in the program. The costs mentioned in (E) are not covered whether or not the student participates in the program.

17. D

THE CONCLUSION: Not eating cheese protects children from childhood diseases.

THE EVIDENCE: All the children at summer school who have never had measles or chicken pox have also never eaten the cheese served in the school lunches.

The author deduces a causal relationship: not eating cheese leads to protection from childhood diseases. This argument has numerous holes. Four of the choices help to fill those holes; the fifth does not. That fifth choice is (D). If research shows that abstaining from cheese products is a major cause of some childhood diseases, then the health official's claim that children can protect themselves from disease by not eating cheese is flat-out wrong. It's important that the author be able (A) to infer from measles and chicken pox (in the evidence) to other childhood diseases. Also necessary is that the observations be accurate (B) and the students' behavior at home mirror their behavior at school (C). Each of those speaks to the legitimacy of the correlation. Most important, though, is that there really be (E), a causal connection, rather than just a correlation, between cheese eating and childhood illness.

18. A

THE CONCLUSION: The masks prevent the tigers from attacking the people who wear them.

THE EVIDENCE: For the past few years many workers have worn these masks and none of them has been attacked by a tiger.

We can't be sure that the masks are responsible for this situation. The tigers might no longer be attacking people at all. To strengthen the case for the masks we need evidence that the tigers are still attacking humans, though not attacking humans wearing masks. (B) can't help us—it's just more of the same. Perhaps there were no tigers spotted (C) because they are no longer on the reserve. In that case masks have nothing to do with worker safety. And maybe it's the singing (D), and not the masks, that has prevented the tiger attacks. Both (C) and (D) are 180 choices. Tigers attacking deer (E) doesn't tell us anything about the tigers' behavior with regard to humans, much less humans with masks.

19. E

THE CONCLUSION: Hodges's aggressive marketing efforts were responsible for the growth in profits.

THE EVIDENCE: Profits have increased under Hodges.

The author is assuming first, that Hodges is in fact responsible for the increase, and second, that it's her marketing efforts in particular that are responsible. If Hodges's predecessor was responsible for acquiring a rival company, and if this has nearly doubled the yearly revenues, then we have no reason to believe that Hodges is responsible for the increase in profits. (A) is off the point, since higher production capacity need not mean greater profits. Yes, profits have risen under Hodges (B), but the argument concerns why this is so. With (C), we don't know whether the campaign spoken of was successful. Since there's no evidence that the new

strategy (D) has not been profitable, it's possible that this switch was in fact the aggressive marketing strategy and is responsible for the increased profits. That would make (D) a strengthener.

20. C

THE CONCLUSION: Street vendors should be banned near restaurants.

THE EVIDENCE: Restaurants can't compete with the vendors because vendors have lower expenses and fewer costs to pass on to customers.

The assumption here is that the cheaper cost of vendor food attracts customers. But if most midtown customers don't pay for their own meals, then the higher prices that restaurants charge aren't an issue. Even if restaurant food is better (A), the price difference may still draw customers to the vendors. The author doesn't claim that moving won't hurt the vendors (B); it's the restaurants she's concerned about. The argument is that a ban should be enacted, not that it can be enforced (D). And that the percentage of food sales that is profit is the same for restaurants and vendors (E) doesn't have any effect on the argument. The vendors' advantage isn't due to a higher mark-up.

21. E

We are only given evidence about average savings, but the conclusion involves average savings growth. There is no connection between the absolute measurement, savings, and the rate of increase, savings growth. This reasoning error is described best in the last choice. Neither (A) nor (D) identifies a reasoning error in the passage, since no claim is made in the passage about savings being the only measure of success (A) or about sufficiency (D). (B) and (C) aren't inconsistent with the claims in the passage, which only deals with the average savings.

22. E

The author concludes that it would be a disaster to let students design their own curricula. The evidence is they don't have the maturity or the experience to do so. The assumption here is that it takes maturity and experience to design good curricula, which links the evidence and conclusion. (E) provides this link by saying that to design good curricula you need years of familiarity with educational life—in other words, experience. (A) and (C) are incorrect because the author's evidence deals with maturity and experience, not "formal education" or "intelligence." (B) doesn't strengthen the author's conclusion; it just adds detail to the analogy he uses. (D) isn't relevant, and even if it were, saying that individualized curricula are more beneficial to students would weaken, not strengthen, the author's argument.

23. D

According to the passage, when foreign aid money is tied, nation A gives money to nation B with the understanding that B will use the money only to buy A's products. That way, nation A makes most of its money back. The author says that European nations are phasing out this practice in order to avoid criticism that has been leveled at other donors, "notably Japan." The inference to be drawn is that Japan has been criticized for tying its foreign aid, so (D) is the inference we're looking for. (A) isn't inferable because the passage discusses only one non-European nation, Japan, and its foreign aid policy. You can't infer what many non-European nations are doing. (E) does essentially the same thing; one comment about Japan doesn't allow you to make sweeping inferences about non-European nations. (B) and (C) make statements of opinion—(B) about the role of ethical considerations and (C) about how to help underdeveloped countries. The author doesn't make any policy recommendations so (B) and (C) are wrong.

24. A

The author begins by concluding that cross-training is more beneficial than single sport training for those who wish to improve their overall fitness. The author presents two pieces of evidence to support this opinion: First, cross-training develops a wider range of muscle groups. Second, it increases phasic muscle fibers that burn more calories. Can you see any gaps between the conclusion and the evidence? The author assumes a link between developing a wide range of muscles/burning

calories and overall fitness, so we can check to see if any answer choice strengthens the argument by shoring up that assumption. (A) presents us with evidence of a direct connection between burning calories and overall fitness, so it is correct.

(B) is incorrect: The fact that athletic training in general is the best way to improve overall fitness doesn't strengthen an argument that one kind of athletic training (cross) is better for fitness than another (single-sport). Choice (C) is an opposite answer—it would actually weaken the argument. Tonic muscle fibers are exercised by single sport training, so increasing their value would weaken the author's argument in support of cross-training. (D) is out of scope. (E) has no effect; the fact that some slow-twitch muscles contain phasic muscle fibers is of no relevance in comparing the two types of training if we're not told which type of training targets these particular muscle fibers.

25. C

The author's claim that the editorial's argument is no good because it's poorly written depends on the assumption that an argument's validity is related to its use of language. After all, if an argument's language didn't indicate its validity, the author's argument wouldn't make any sense at all. (A) isn't assumed because the argument doesn't concern who is to blame for the bad editorial. (B) and (D) fail because the argument addresses this editorial only, so there's nothing assumed about what happens generally. And (E) goes too far: The argument isn't making a conclusion about the author's motivation for writing a bad argument.

26. A

This question asks us to infer a conclusion from the stimulus. We know the author believes that the combination of the cases will harm the defendants. We also know that the defense has argued against the combination because of supposed differences in the cases, and that the judge has rejected that argument. So it's not too great a step to Choice (A) which concludes that the judge's decision implies some similarity among the cases, and that this decision will strengthen the plaintiffs' case.

The important thing in handling inference questions is not to read anything into the passage, but rather to stick with ideas actually stated. (B) introduces a wholly new idea—that manufacturers are often able to escape individual suits on technicalities. There is nothing in the passage to support such a statement. As for (C), we have no evidence that the hundreds of plaintiffs involved have similar work histories or use similar equipment. While they all seem to have worked on computers and developed repetitive stress injuries, the similarities might well end there. Though we've been told that the defendants in this case aren't likely to do well if the suits are consolidated, we have no reason to conclude, as (D) does, that defendants in general are more likely to settle if workplace injury suits are consolidated. (E) says that publicity will prompt more suits: based on the passage we can conclude neither that consolidated cases get more publicity, nor that publicity results in further lawsuits. There is simply nothing in the passage to support such a conclusion.

27. B

The author's conclusion comes toward the end, when she says that the plant should be built inside the city limits. Despite her acknowledgment that a plant built inside the city limits will disrupt more lives, she advocates this option because it will create jobs for the city residents and offer economic benefits to the city. She's therefore deciding between two options. She concludes that one option is better than the other because it promises a certain benefit to the residents. In order for that conclusion to be valid, she must assume that the other option doesn't promise such a benefit. (B) weakens the argument by denying this assumption, stating that either alternative will create jobs for the residents of the city.

(A) doesn't do a whole lot unless you assume more than the answer choice tells you. Perhaps private-owned land is more expensive, in which case this choice would strengthen the argument, or perhaps it isn't. As it stands, there's no clear link between

(A) and the central issues of the argument. (C) says that the location of the plant doesn't matter in terms of taxation. It's wrong because taxation isn't one of the criteria determining which option the author prefers. (B) also noted a similarity between the options, but it is the correct answer because the similarity there pertains to job creation, which is central to the argument. (D) would, if anything, strengthen the argument by suggesting that the possible drawback of building inside the city, disruption, isn't so bad. (E) brings up taxes again, though this time the choice is about the workers' taxes and not the plant's. Still, the issue of taxation isn't even mentioned by the stimulus, so it's not relevant to the argument.

28. C

The evidence says that students who attend colleges with low faculty/student ratios get well-rounded educations, but the conclusion is that the author will send his kids to colleges with small student populations. Since colleges can have a small student population without necessarily having a low teacher/student ratio, (C) is correct. If you don't see this, think about a school with a small student population that has only one teacher.

(A) claims that the author confuses cause and effect. But how could getting a well-rounded education cause a low faculty/student ratio? In any event, the real problem is the scope shift from faculty/student ratios to student populations. As for (B), the author never mentions intelligence. (D) doesn't point to a problem in the reasoning, just in implementing it. And (E) claims students must do something extra to take advantage of the low faculty/student ratios. Since the author never claimed the benefits would be conferred automatically, this isn't a flaw. Remember, if you can prephrase the flaw before moving on to the answer choices, you're much less likely to be tempted by wrong answer choices.

29. B

Here's the discrepancy: Despite the fact that the rate of emphysema has declined 15 percent within the past 15 years in region A, the cost of caring for emphysema sufferers in the region is now roughly equal to what it was 15 years ago. In other words, the decline in the percentage of emphysema sufferers has not been accompanied by a corresponding decrease in the cost of treating such sufferers. (B) addresses both parts of the paradox. If improved technology has increased the cost of caring for emphysema sufferers, then a decline in sufferers wouldn't necessarily yield a decrease in costs, since the cost per patient would increase. And if the technology has been successful, then that would explain the decline in sufferers.

(A) is out because knowing that the region's overall health care costs have increased doesn't help to explain what's going on with the cost of emphysema care in particular. (C) if anything, contributes to the paradox by telling us that overall health care costs haven't increased, which makes it more unusual that emphysema costs have increased. (D) doesn't tell you that much. Just because research on emphysema has increased doesn't tell you anything about how cases could go down, while total costs increased. If, as (E) says, there were fewer expensive-to-treat cases, that would make it even harder to explain rising costs.

30. D

The author's conclusion is the companies' confidence that anemic children will be cured relatively simply with a new iron injection. The evidence is the first sentence: A new injection can apparently reverse children's anemia. Can you see any gaps between the conclusion and evidence? Notice that the evidence explains that something can be done and the conclusion states that something will be done. Just because the cure is possible doesn't mean it will automatically be administered. Any number of factors could serve to block implementation. The author assumes that children will receive the injection based on the fact that it exists.

(D) expresses this more concretely: the author assumes that children are aware of and willing to receive this injection. The argument concerns whether the cure will become available. (A) is out of scope. (B) gives us irrelevant information about

causes. The author states that iron shots reverse children's anemia, regardless of the specific cause, so (B) need not be assumed. (C) states that a managed diet would not cure anemia. But the author doesn't state that the injection is the only cure for anemia, so the argument needn't assume that no other cure exists. (E) is both extreme and out of scope. The author only claims that the injection cures anemia "relatively simply." Safety never comes up as an issue and there is no need to assume that the injections are the safest method to reverse anemia.

31. C

The conclusion here is the hypothesis: that aggressive behavior is caused by a lack of parent-led socialization in early life. And the evidence comes from animals that have been separated from their parents in the first months of their life that develop aggression disorders. The feeding example cited in the evidence is just one example of this type of behavior. To strengthen this argument you would either want to rule out other causes for the aggression or provide additional examples that fit the hypothesis. (C) fits perfectly by giving an example comparing two groups, chimps who received socialization (although simulated) and those who didn't. In this example, the chimps who did not receive socialization were more aggressive, thus strengthening the hypothesis.

(A) and (E) are opposite answers. Both directly contradict the hypothesis. In (A), the wildebeests weren't separated from their mothers, and yet still displayed aggression. Conversely, in (E), elephants that were separated did not display aggression. If you remember what the hypothesis is and that your job is to strengthen it, you won't fall for these traps. (B), to the extent that it's relevant (human studies aren't so analogous to animal studies) would probably weaken the argument. Being adopted in the first 3 months of life would not qualify as separation, yet these babies eventually display aggressive behavior. (D) isn't helpful because the polar bears aren't differentiated by whether they received any socialization.

32. A

The author makes a conclusion that the public favors solar energy based on the survey. As in all representativeness arguments, the author must be assuming that the sample is representative of the whole. And the best way to weaken this type of argument is to undermine that assumption. (A) does that by explicitly stating that this sample was unrepresentative; supporters of solar energy are far more likely than opponents of solar energy to fill out a survey. So any survey on the subject will be necessarily skewed.

(B) weakens the argument for solar power, but it doesn't weaken this author's argument, which is concerned only with public support for solar power. (C) is irrelevant, because the author isn't claiming the people who are in favor of solar energy are "right;" the author only claims that the public is in favor of solar energy. In any event, to weaken a representativeness argument, you should always try to show that the sample is not representative. Other criticisms are beside the point. If (D) were true, it may make it somewhat less likely that the Administration is being misleading in this case. But again, this gets away from the actual argument going on here: that the public is interested in solar energy as evidenced by the results of this survey. (E) has no effect on this argument.

33. D

Did you notice the scope shift here? Betty opens by saying that her opponent opposes a rule requiring the leading of the loyalty pledge. Later, however, she attacks the opponent for trying to forbid the pledge. (D) weakens the argument by pointing out the scope shift. While (A) might be something that the opponent would want to point out in her campaign, it doesn't address Betty's reasoning. (B) is out because Betty describes loyalty as the scouts' most important virtue, not its only virtue. (C) may also be a good campaign point, but it doesn't deal with the reasoning. (E) is not effective because Betty does not claim that her opponent is disloyal.

34. B

On the basis of the evidence that there was no protest to a 50-cent museum admission charge, the Board concluded that it could safely raise the price to $1.50. The unstated assumption is that since the public tolerated the 50-cent charge, it will also tolerate the higher charge. Which of the choices necessarily played a part in the Board's reasoning? Not (A). There's nothing in the passage to make us think the Board paid any attention to why the 50-cent admission charge was not protested. (B) is precisely what the Board did assume, and all it assumed. Otherwise it would not have raised the price, using the acceptance of the earlier price rise as evidence. (C) is not assumed. People may protest the price hike, but this is what the Board hopes will not happen, and so is not what the Board assumed when it raised the admission charge to $1.50. (D) is out of scope. The argument never mentions what the Board plans to do with the increased revenues. (E) is pretty silly. Future admission increases are beyond the scope, and it would be ludicrous for the Board to assume that it can triple the admission every six months without causing attendance to drop.

35. E

ERNESTO'S CONCLUSION: VCR sales will decline.

ERNESTO'S EVIDENCE: The saturation level for households has been reached.

MILTON'S CONCLUSION: VCR sales won't decline.

MILTON'S EVIDENCE: More and more films are released on videotape.

Milton simply ignores Ernesto's argument that the saturation point has been reached for VCRs. He concentrates on the new cassettes coming out, but the availability of new cassettes doesn't mean people need buy or will buy more recorders. Milton ignores the relevant issue of saturation raised by Ernesto, and simply assumes that sales of VCRs will continue as before.

(A) is wrong because Milton's evidence doesn't disprove Ernesto's evidence. The videos appearing each year have nothing to do with whether the saturation point in VCR ownership has been reached.

"Finding a gap" (B) in an argument means demonstrating that the evidence doesn't lead to the conclusion; Milton merely brings up some irrelevant information that has nothing to do with Ernesto's reasoning. Milton does cite an issue that Ernesto ignored (C), but the claim that this issue "outweighs" the issue of saturation is unsupported. Milton does fail to speak to Ernesto's point (D) but not for the bizarre reason given here. Ernesto has absolutely nothing to say about "other leisure-related products" so there's no reason for Milton to raise this issue.

36. B

THE CONCLUSION: Money spent to make the workplace more pleasant is the cause of stumbling and failing businesses.

THE EVIDENCE: New businesses almost always fail, and many established businesses show little or no profit. Workers want expensive perks like paint and radios.

The assumption here is that providing these niceties works only to the detriment or disadvantage of the businesses—that it's as simple as spending money and getting no return. We weaken the argument by denying this assumption, and showing that the perks increase productivity. In this case, the new paint, radios, and artwork might well be a wise investment.

(A) is incorrect because, even if the workers work very hard, it doesn't mean that they don't make excessive demands on their employers. With (C), it could be possible that in the past businesses went under for other reasons, and yet still be true that they're now going under because of the perks. The author hasn't claimed that different types of businesses are the same thing (D) and (E), but rather, that they're in trouble for the same reason.

37. C

THE CONCLUSION: Pharmaceutical companies have too much influence on university medical research.

THE EVIDENCE: Most of the time, only projects that promise profitable results are considered, and only scientists with lots of experience at large universities get funding.

THE DIRE PREDICTION (or ultimate conclusion): Research will continue to be conducted at the expense of human welfare.

The author believes that research would be better off without the meddling of pharmaceutical manufacturers. If, without these companies' funding, though, very little research would get done, then we're better off with their funding, even if it is selective. The companies, according to the author, are concerned with a project's potential profitability, so some actual failures (A) don't weaken the argument. The author isn't critical because the companies don't help fund students (B); the issue is which students they fund, and for what research. (D) just turns around and says "You don't like it? Then what would be better?" A poor attempt at rebuttal, and not a GMAT weakener. The idea that only large universities can support the research (E) misses the author's point: Only research of the type large universities can carry on is getting funded, and other types of research should be funded but aren't.

38. E

The key word *Therefore*, which always signals a conclusion, is a point that follows from the first sentence: *Since* heart attack victims have a higher rate of dementia, *therefore* preventing the one may help to prevent the other. Fine and dandy. But since the argument proceeds further—shifting the scope to vision loss—and ends with another conclusion, one about the greater risk of vision loss among demented elderly women, we must recognize that the last conclusion drawn is the main one. That fact of course demonstrates why (C) is wrong and (E) is correct. The point about preventing heart attacks and dementia, while of interest to elderly women perhaps, is of no interest to us analysts of the argument. (Try reading the entire paragraph with *Therefore* and the boldface statement missing. You'll see that it drops out with no damage to the logic whatsoever.)

(A) is wrong because an assumption must always be *unstated*. Since the author moves to it and follows from it, the statement is not a contradiction (B). (D) might have been tricky for you, since it often happens that an author draws a conclusion—a

"Therefore" statement—as evidence for his main conclusion to follow, as in:

Success on standardized tests depends on thoughtful practice. So you need to review thoughtfully the explanations of the questions you attempt. For that reason, Kaplan provides lots of practice questions with explanations for you to review.

The second statement acts as evidence for the final conclusion reached. However, such is not the case with the dementia argument, because of the scope shift described above.

39. C

THE POLITICIAN'S CONCLUSION: We should bring charges against the private group that's training recruits to fight against Country Z.

THE POLITICIAN'S EVIDENCE: The Neutrality Act forbids citizens from taking military action against a nation with which they are not at war.

The author assumes that this group intends to take military action, and we weaken the argument by undermining this assumption—the recruits are trained to fight only if war is declared. Civil war in Country Z (A) is way off topic, since we're concerned with a war between this country and Country Z. (B) doesn't tell us anything. We don't care how the training is being funded (D); it's the fact that it's taking place that's the issue. And the politician is calling for an investigation (E), so the fact that one is needed can't weaken his argument.

40. E

THE CONCLUSION: Implementation of a plan to convert from conventional fuels to synthetic ones will almost certainly increase the company's expenses.

THE EVIDENCE: Even if these fuels become practical, they will cost more than conventional fuels.

The author is assuming that the plan won't, in some other way, save an equal or greater amount of money than it costs. This is a classic GMAT scenario. This assumption is denied if implementing the plan makes conservation measures practical, which then compensates for the higher cost. Postponing the fuel switch (A) does nothing to alleviate the alleged increase in expenses. Showing that the expenses will be passed on to the consumer (B) doesn't change the fact that the expenses will exist. The fact that adapting the processes won't cost much (C) doesn't help, since it's the cost of the fuels themselves that the author's argument is based on. And the scarcity of raw materials (D) actually strengthens the argument by pointing out a reason for the additional costs.

CHAPTER SEVEN

Sentence Correction

Jan. 31, 2009

Serigne,

May God grant you with
Wisdom and Clear-understanding
of your Reading Comprehension.

Focus

Learn the Key skills to
guide you with Speed and
accurency.

1. By the end of the contest, the winning team had eaten nearly a dozen <u>as many pies as any of its purported</u> competitors.

    (A) as many pies as any of its purported
    (B) more pies than any of its purported
    (C) as many pies as its purported
    (D) more pies than any of its purportedly
    (E) as many pies as its purportedly

2. The self-destructive pride of Shakespeare's character Coriolanus was <u>not unlike that of the Greek hero Ajax, who killed</u> himself at Troy because Achilles' armor was awarded to Odysseus.

    (A) not unlike that of the Greek hero Ajax, who killed
    (B) not unlike the Greek hero Ajax, who killed
    (C) like the Greek hero Ajax and his killing
    (D) like that of the Greek hero Ajax for killing
    (E) as that of the Greek hero Ajax, who killed

3. The mayor was justifiably concerned about the degree <u>to which his voter support has been eroded</u>, almost to the point of obliterating his chances in the upcoming campaign, by popular opposition to his policy on the use of public parks.

    (A) to which his voter support has been eroded
    (B) to which his voter support has eroded
    (C) that his voter support has been eroded
    (D) of his voter support eroding
    (E) of the erosion of his voter support

4. Canada consumed 10,965 kilograms of energy per capita in 1995, fifty percent more than <u>the Netherlands did and nearly twice as much as France's consumption.</u>

    (A) the Netherlands did and nearly twice as much as France's consumption
    (B) the Netherlands's and nearly double what the French consumption was
    (C) the Netherlands consumed and nearly twice as much as the French did
    (D) what the Netherlands did and nearly twice as much as France's consumption
    (E) what the Netherlands consumed and nearly double the French consumption

5. The Spanish Flu pandemic that began in 1918 not only killed at least 20 million people, <u>and also sending</u> family members of the flu victims to food lines.

    (A) and also sending
    (B) it sent
    (C) it also had sent
    (D) but also sent
    (E) but also sends

6. Although the gorilla still needs to be protected from poachers, <u>its numbers are now one-and-a-half times greater than what they were when</u> Dian Fossey brought them to world attention by establishing the Karisoke Research Center in 1967.

    (A) its numbers are now one-and-a-half times greater than what they were when
    (B) its numbers now one-and-a-half times what they were when
    (C) its numbers now one-and-a-half times more than when
    (D) now with one-and-a-half times the numbers it had when
    (E) now with its numbers one-and-a-half greater since

7. Some predict that the next ice age will be caused by Egypt's Aswan Dam, <u>built to prevent the loss of fresh water into the Mediterranean Sea that would result</u> if the Nile continued its annual, uncontrolled flooding.

(A) built to prevent the loss of fresh water into the Mediterranean Sea that would result

(B) they built for preventing the loss of fresh water into the Mediterranean Sea that would result

(C) built to prevent the loss of fresh water into the Mediterranean Sea resulting

(D) they built to prevent the loss of fresh water into the Mediterranean Sea resulting

(E) built for preventing the loss of fresh water into the Mediterranean Sea that will result

8. Distributed computing, in which an otherwise overwhelming amount of data is parceled out to many computers to work on at once, is becoming a viable alternative to supercomputers, with even the humblest personal computer functioning not only as a data transmitter <u>but also as</u> a processing tool.

(A) but also as

(B) or as

(C) and as

(D) but also

(E) and also

9. As our society grows more linguistically diverse, the need <u>that translators explain cultural differences becomes</u> more apparent.

(A) that translators explain cultural differences becomes

(B) for translators to explain cultural differences became

(C) for translators to explain cultural differences becomes

(D) that cultural differences be explained by translators became

(E) that there be explanations of cultural differences by translators has become

10. A recent survey of Internet web hosting companies reported <u>effective security measures in all of them and they ranged</u> from inexpensive encryption packages to active security programs that automate compliance with a company's security procedures.

(A) effective security measures in all of them and they ranged

(B) security measures in all of them were effective and ranging

(C) the ranging of effective security measures in all of them to be

(D) that all of them had effective security measures ranging

(E) that all of them had security measures that were effective, the range was

11. Bottle-nosed dolphins have a highly developed sense of taste, enabling them to detect various chemicals in the water; however, <u>because this animal has</u> no olfactory lobe, they apparently have no sense of smell.

(A) because this animal has

(B) as these animals had

(C) those animals have

(D) because these animals have

(E) since the dolphin has

12. It has been demonstrated that individuals who participated in competitive sports <u>when they are in college tend toward remaining</u> physically active in their later years.

(A) when they are in college tend toward remaining

(B) when they were in college are likely to be

(C) when they were in college were apt to be

(D) when they are in college are apt to be

(E) when they were in college were liable to be

13. Unlike the Puritan ethic, extolling hard work as the supreme virtue, many modern psychologists focus on the goals of inner peace and self-discovery.

  (A) Unlike the Puritan ethic, extolling hard work as the supreme virtue, many modern psychologists focus on the goals of inner peace and self-discovery

  (B) Unlike believers in the Puritan ethic, which extols as the supreme virtue hard work, the goals of inner peace and self-discovery are focused on by many modern psychologists

  (C) Unlike the Puritan ethic, which extols hard work as the supreme virtue, the focus of the doctrines of many modern psychologists are the goals of inner peace and self-discovery

  (D) Unlike the Puritan ethic, which extols hard work as the supreme virtue, the doctrines of many modern psychologists focus on the goals of inner peace and self-discovery

  (E) Unlike those of the Puritans, who extol hard work as the supreme virtue, many modern psychologists focus on the goals of inner peace and self-discovery

14. The customer will not be responsible for transactions made with lost or stolen credit cards after issuing replacement cards.

  (A) The customer will not be responsible for transactions made with lost or stolen credit cards after issuing replacement cards

  (B) No customer will be responsible for transactions made with lost or stolen credit cards after they are issued replacement cards

  (C) The customer will not be responsible for transactions made with lost or stolen credit cards after replacement cards have been issued

  (D) Responsibility for transactions made with lost or stolen credit cards will not be the customer's after he is issued replacement cards

  (E) The customer will not be responsible for transactions made with lost or stolen credit cards after such time as they will have been issued replacement cards

15. Perhaps the most significant medical breakthrough of the twenties, the real story behind the isolation of insulin was not revealed for over 50 years.

  (A) Perhaps the most significant medical breakthrough of the twenties, the real story behind the isolation of insulin was not revealed for over 50 years

  (B) The real story behind the isolation of insulin was not revealed for over 50 years, even though it was perhaps the most significant medical breakthrough of the twenties

  (C) Although insulin was perhaps the most significant medical breakthrough of the breakthrough of the twenties, the real story behind it was not revealed for over 50 years

  (D) The real story behind the isolation of insulin was not revealed for over 50 years, although insulin was perhaps the most significant medical breakthrough of the twenties

  (E) Although the isolation of insulin was perhaps the most significant medical twenties, its isolation was not revealed for over 50 years

16. Ranch houses, commonly found in American suburbs, are derived from the one-floor wooden frame houses, characterized by low roofs, rectangular <u>arranging of floor plans, and the arraying of rooms in a line, that settlers built in the American West, typically when they could afford to replace</u> their original sod houses.

    (A) arranging of floor plans, and the arraying of rooms in a line, that settlers built in the American West, typically when they could afford to replace

    (B) floor plans, and rooms arrayed in a line, that settlers had built in the American West, typically when they could afford replacement of

    (C) floor plans, and consisting of rooms arrayed in a straight line, that settlers in the America West, when they were affording replacement, typically built for

    (D) floor plans, and rooms arrayed in a line, that settlers built in the American West, typically when they could afford to replace

    (E) floor plans, and rooms arrayed in a line, that settlers built in the American West, typically being done when they could afford replacing

17. The United States and France helped Hissene Habre become the President of Chad in 1982 because they <u>sought his help in opposing Chad's northern neighbor, Libya, which they viewed</u> as a conduit of unwanted Soviet influence and a sponsor of international terrorism.

    (A) sought his help in opposing Chad's northern neighbor, Libya, which they viewed

    (B) sought their help in opposing Chad's northern neighbor, Libya, which they viewed

    (C) were seeking to oppose Chad's northern neighbor, Libya, and they wanted help against it,

    (D) were seeking his help in opposing Chad's northern neighbor, Libya, which it viewed

    (E) opposed Chad's northern neighbor, Libya, and sought help from it against what they viewed

18. The Vickers-Armstrong Company's A-10 tank of 1934, with its driver's compartment in the front, turret in the center, and engine in the rear, introduced <u>what is becoming tank's dominant design form</u> for the rest of the 20th Century.

    (A) what is becoming tank's dominant design form

    (B) what became their dominant design form

    (C) what became the dominant design form of tanks

    (D) its dominant design form

    (E) the tank's dominant design form, becoming so

19. Due to geological constraints, the gold discovered in South Africa in 1886 could not easily be mined by the sort of independent fortune-seeking adventurers <u>whom had prospered</u> without the aid of large machinery in previous gold rushes in other lands.

    (A) whom had prospered

    (B) whom prospered

    (C) whom achieved prosperity

    (D) who will have prospered

    (E) who had prospered

20. The only mammals capable of true flight, <u>bats have often been reliant on a sensitive system of acoustic orientation, known as echolocation</u>.

    (A) bats have often been reliant on a sensitive system of acoustic orientation, known as echolocation

    (B) bats often rely on a sensitive system of acoustic orientation, known as echolocation

    (C) known as echolocation, sensitively and systematically orienting acoustics are often relied on by bats

    (D) a sensitive system of acoustic orientation, known as echolocation, is often relied on by bats

    (E) it is known as echolocation, a sensitive system of acoustic orientation, often relied on by bats

21. In the last five years, sales of foreign-language-instruction software have increased sharply, though <u>not as sharply as that</u> of books and tapes that fulfill the same purpose.

    (A) as sharply as that
    (B) as sharply as those
    (C) as sharp as sales
    (D) as sharply when compared to sales
    (E) so much as sales of

22. Many of Stravinsky's best known works are large-scale programmatic pieces such as the *Rite of Spring*, but the trailblazing Russian-born composer also wrote a great deal of chamber music, <u>some liturgical works, and even a piece written for jazz ensemble</u>.

    (A) some liturgical works, and even a piece written for jazz ensemble
    (B) some liturgical works, and even wrote a piece for jazz ensemble
    (C) some liturgical works, even a piece for jazz ensemble
    (D) some liturgical works, and even a piece for jazz ensemble
    (E) also some liturgical works, and even a piece for jazz ensemble

23. Rather than scratch furniture, <u>like most cats do</u>, the family's new kitten preferred to sharpen his claws on the living room carpet.

    (A) like most cats do
    (B) just like most cats do
    (C) just as most cats do
    (D) as is the case with most cats
    (E) as most cats do

24. Popular child psychologists have advocated that parents discipline male children <u>similarly to the fashion in which they discipline</u> daughters.

    (A) similarly to the fashion in which they discipline
    (B) in the same manner that they would use with
    (C) like they would handle
    (D) as they discipline
    (E) as they would

25. <u>Added to worries about budget cuts and cost of living increases</u>, the administrators of public health care facilities must contend with the possibility of a strike by employees.

    (A) Added to worries about budget cuts and cost of living increases
    (B) Added to budget cuts and increases in the cost of living
    (C) In addition to worry about cuts in the budget and as the cost of living increases
    (D) Added to their worrying about budget cuts and cost of living increases
    (E) In addition to worrying about budget cuts and increases in the cost of living

26. Medical researchers, who have identified a genetic abnormality in parents of children with Down's syndrome, <u>which they believe, instead of the age of the mother, may be</u> the cause of this congenital birth defect.

    (A) which they believe, instead of the age of the mother, may be
    (B) which, they believe, may be more important than the age of the mother as
    (C) believe this abnormality and not the age of the mother as being
    (D) believe that this abnormality, other than how old the mother is, may be
    (E) believe that this abnormality, rather than the age of the mother, may be

27. <u>More adeptly handling responsibilities than his predecessors were</u>, the new owner of the property rapidly increased the production rate of the land.

(A) More adeptly handling responsibilities than his predecessors were

(B) Being that he was more adept at handling responsibilities than were his predecessors

(C) Handling more adeptly responsibilities than are his predecessors

(D) More adept than his predecessors at handling responsibilities

(E) Since he handled responsibilities in a manner more adeptly than had his predecessors

28. <u>Rockets, like the airplane and the jet, were</u> rapidly improved during World War II.

(A) Rockets, like the airplane and the jet, were

(B) The rocket, like airplanes and jets, was

(C) Rockets, like airplanes and jets, was

(D) The rocket, like the airplane and the jet, were

(E) The rocket, like the airplane and the jet, was

29. <u>Unlike other scholars, the eminent mythologist has concluded</u> that the stories of Gilgamesh and Osiris record the transition from the age of matriarchal religious authority to that of patriarchal political power.

(A) Unlike other scholars, the eminent mythologist has concluded

(B) Unlike other scholars, the eminent mythologist's conclusion

(C) Unlike other scholars, the eminent mythologist's conclusion is

(D) Unlike those of other scholars, the eminent mythologist's conclusions are

(E) The eminent mythologists, unlike those of other scholars, has concluded

30. The combination of technical expertise, commercial enterprise, and <u>that the government backs them judiciously should ensure Italian firms continuing</u> to innovate and gain competitively in world markets.

(A) that the government backs them judiciously should ensure Italian firms continuing

(B) the government backing them judiciously should ensure Italian firms of being about to continue

(C) judicious government backing should ensure that Italian firms will continue

(D) the government's judicious backing should ensure Italian firms that they will continue

(E) the government to back them judiciously should ensure Italian firms of continuing

ANSWER KEY: SENTENCE CORRECTION

1. B	11. D	21. B
2. A	12. B	22. D
3. A	13. D	23. E
4. C	14. C	24. E
5. D	15. C	25. E
6. A	16. D	26. E
7. A	17. A	27. D
8. A	18. C	28. E
9. C	19. E	29. A
10. D	20. B	30. C

1. B

Choices (A), (C), and (E) do not state the comparison logically. The expression "as many as" means an equal number, but the sentence indicates that the winning team out-ate its competitors by a dozen pies. *More than* in (B) and (D) makes the point of comparison clear, but (D) incorrectly uses the adverb *purportedly*. (B) correctly uses the adjective *purported* to modify the noun *competitors*. (B) is the answer.

2. A

Choices (B) and (C) present faulty comparisons: in (B), Coriolanus's pride is compared to Ajax himself, not to his pride, and in (C), his pride is compared to both Ajax and his killing himself. (D) does not make it clear whether it was Coriolanus or Ajax who showed pride in killing himself. (E) incorrectly uses *as* rather than *like* to compare two noun phrases.

3. A

Choice (A) is best: It is idiomatic, and its passive-verb construction *has been eroded* clearly indicates that the *voter support* has been acted on *by popular opposition*. In (B), the active verb *has eroded* suggests that the voter support, not the opposition, is the agency of action, and leaves the phrase *by popular opposition ...* without any logical or grammatical function. In (C), the construction *the degree that his voter support* is ungrammatical; *the*

degree must be completed by *to which*. Choice (D) incorrectly employs an active verb—*eroding*—and *degree of his voter support* is meaningless and not idiomatic. (E) contains no verb to express the action performed by the *popular opposition*.

4. C

Three things are being compared here, so they should be in parallel form. The subject of the opening phrase is *Canada*, not *Canada's consumption*, so comparing it to *France's consumption* ((A) and (D)), *the Netherlands's* (B), or the *French consumption* (E) is incorrect. Also, (D) and (E) both start with the unnecessary word *what*.

5. D

The correct idiomatic construction is *not only ... but also*. Choices (A), (B) and (C) fail to complete this construction. Both items in a *not only ... but also* construction must be in parallel form. (E) switches needlessly from the past to the present tense.

6. A

Although you should be suspicious of an answer choice that is significantly longer than the others, in this case the longer sentence is correct. If you can't spot an error in the original, scan the choices and look for reasons to eliminate them. (B), (C), (D) and (E) make incomplete sentences, lacking any verb. *[I]ts numbers are* are the subject and verb of the sentence; the other verbs—*needs*, *brought*, and *establishing*—are all contained in subordinate clauses. (B) and (D) also distort the meaning of the sentence; the present numbers are one-and-a-half times greater than before (that is, they're two-and-a-half times what they were before), not just one-and-a-half times what they were before.

7. A

You should know that about 1 out of 5 sentence corrections will be correct as written. (B) and (D) have an ambiguous pronoun: *they* seems to relate back to the *some* who *predict* in the first clause, but that isn't logical. (C) fails to capture the appropriate use of the subjunctive in the correct answer: the loss of fresh water in this case is hypothetical, not actual. In (E), the correct idiomatic phrase should be *built to prevent* not *built for preventing*, and there is no logical reason to use the future tense.

8. A

This sentence requires that the phrase *not only as* be correctly completed by the parallel phrase *but also as*. It is therefore correct as written. All other choices are unidiomatic or not parallel, or both. Choice (D) omits the word *as* which is necessary for both elements of the *not only ... but also* construction to be parallel.

9. C

The first choice is not idiomatic; the correct preposition with *need* is *for* in this sentence, so (A), (D), and (E) are out. (E) is also a fine example of verbosity and inappropriate use of the passive voice. The correct verb tense needed is present; *as our society grows ... diverse*, and (B) incorrectly uses the past. (C) is the answer.

10. D

In (A), *they* is an unclear reference, apparently relating to *them* (that is, the web hosting companies), but actually referring to the security measures. In (B), the verb *ranging* should parallel the verb *were*, since they are a pair joined by *and*. (C) is unidiomatic and distorts the sense of the sentence. On the test, the verb *found* will generally be followed by *that*, so choices (D) and (E) are most likely to be correct. Choice (E), however, is verbose and awkward, while (D) is clear and brief.

11. D

Since some of the answer choices are singular, and others are plural, first decide which number is appropriate. The non-underlined pronoun *they* in the last clause is plural, so the answer must be (B), (C), or (D). With no conjunction to make the logical relation of the clauses clear, (C) gives us a run-on sentence; eliminate it.

12. B

The main differences among the answer choices have to do with verb tense. Notice that *participated*, which is not underlined, is in the simple past tense. Since the people in question participated in sports while in college, we need the past-tense *were*; that means (A) and (D) are out. Next have to determine whether *tend toward remaining* should be past or present. *It has been demonstrated* tells us we need the present; and (B) is the only answer choice which does that.

13. D

This sentence makes a comparison, so we have to make sure it's logical. You can't compare *the Puritan ethic* with *many modern psychologists* as in (A), or with *the focus of the doctrines of many modern psychologists*, in (C). You can't compare *believers in the Puritan ethic* with *the goals of inner peace and self-discovery* in (B). Only (D) makes a logical comparison, between *the Puritan ethic* and the *doctrines of many modern psychologists*.

14. C

The problem here is one of ambiguity. *Who* or *what* will issue replacement cards? Not the customer, certainly, but that's what (A) seems say. (B) and (E) have a pronoun reference problem: the plural *they* refers to the singular *customer*. *Responsibility...will not be the customer's* in (D) is more awkward than *the customer will not be responsible*.

15. C

This sentence tests modification. It is the *isolation of insulin* that's perhaps the most significant medical breakthrough of the twenties, not *insulin*, as in (D) and (E)), and not *the real story behind the isolation of insulin*, as in (A) and (B).

16. D

The underlined section continues a list of items that began in the non-underlined section. So the continuing items must be in a similar form. The list begins with *...low roofs*, so the answer will have the list items phrased as nouns. (A) doesn't do this, so it's out. (C), which begins with *consisting*, is out as well. Now, how do (B), (D), and (E) differ? Well, they each express the act of replacing *original sod houses* differently. (B) and (E) use awkward phrasing. (D) not only does this, but also maintains a parallel list structure. It is correct.

17. A

There doesn't seem to be a problem in the question stem—the many pronouns contained in it are all clearly defined. But let's run through the remaining choices to make sure. In (B), the pronoun *their* is incorrect. The United States and France seek the help of only one person (Habre). (C) is awkwardly written, with *wanted help against it*. It also changes the meaning of the original sentence by stating that the United States and France were seeking to oppose Chad rather than seeking Habre's help. (D) incorrectly uses *it* instead of they. And (E) is badly worded. (At the same time, it fails to even communicate that the two countries sought Habre's help.) Choice (A) is correct.

18. C

This sentence uses a present verb tense to refer to something that took place in the past. (A) is out right away. (D), too, is out, as it uses no verb at all. (E) is very awkward. So now between (B) and (C), (C) is preferred; it uses a past tense verb form and also clearly describes *what became* (the dominant design form of tanks). (B) incorrectly uses *their* to refer to the *company*.

19. E

The underlined portion is a clause; that is, it contains a subject and verb. The subject of the verb *had prospered* must be a subjective case pronoun. *Who* is subjective case—as opposed to *whom*, the objective case. (A), (B), and (C) are out. And the future tense in (D) is incorrect because the sentence is in the past.

20. B

An introductory phrase must modify what comes directly after it. Here, the phrase is modifying *bats* so you can eliminate (C), (D), and (E). The fact that bats rely on echolocation is an ongoing

phenomenon, so the present tense of (B) is correct. There is no need for the present perfect tense *have been reliant* so you can eliminate (A).

21. B

The sentence compares the increased sharpness of one thing (sales of software) with another (sales of books and tapes). The phrase *not as sharply as* makes this comparison clear. (A) incorrectly uses *that* to refer to sales, which, because it is plural, should be replaced by *those*, as in (B). The word *that* needs to be handled carefully on the GMAT; it can be used in several ways. Here, it's an incorrectly used pronoun. In (C), the adjective *sharp* should be *sharply*, an adverb. (D) omits the second *as*, which is needed in the paired idiom "as X as Y." (E) uses the construction *so much as*, which is almost always incorrect.

22. D

This sentence tests parallelism in several ways. The first item in the list of things that Stravinsky wrote is *a great deal of chamber music*. Second is *some liturgical works*. (E) confuses matters by using the word *also* for this second item, rather than for the final one. The word *and* needs to be used for the third item ("a piece for jazz ensemble"), so (C) is out. Be on the lookout for redundancy on the GMAT; it shows up here in (A) and (B), which unnecessarily use the words *written* and *wrote*, respectively. The non-underlined part of the sentence sets up the list with the phrase *...composer also wrote...*, so its redundant to use any form of *to write* again.

23. E

When making a comparison between verbs, you must use the conjunction *as*. That means (A) and (B) are out. Eliminate (D) because it doesn't correctly make the comparison between the actions. In (C), the word *just* is unnecessary.

24. E

Here, the main things to look for are clarity and brevity. The shortest choice, (E), is best: none of the other, longer, choices is any clearer. In (A), *discipline* isn't needed twice. (B) uses an

unnecessarily wordy construction. (C) uses *like* instead of *as*. You should use *like* when there's no verb—implied or stated—in the second half of the comparison. (D) changes the sentence's meaning.

25. E

An intro phrase set off by a comma is your signal to watch out for modification errors. Simply put, that means make sure the sentence is logical. Here, you have a 3–2 pattern in the answer choices, so you can use this to quickly narrow down the possibilities. It's not the *administrators* that are added to worries, budget cuts, or worrying, so (A), (B), and (D) are out. (C) may seem to make sense, but look at it closely: "worry" is wrong, and administrators are worrying about cuts in the budget *and* as the cost of living increases. "And" must link similar terms, but it doesn't in (C).

26. E

To tackle a sentence correction question, you have to cut through the wordiness. One way to do this is to ignore parts of the sentence that are set off by commas. Here, that's *who have identified...with Down's syndrome* and also *instead of the age of the mother*. The rest of the sentence should make sense and be complete without these. So now you have *Medical researchers ... which they believe ... may be the cause of this congenital birth defect.* In (C), (D) and (E), the subject, *medical researchers* has a verb, *believe*. In (C), *believe...as being* is unidiomatic. (*Being* is wordy and often appears in wrong choices.) In (D), you need *rather* instead of *other*, and *how old the mother is* isn't parallel to *abnormality*.

27. D

You might start by noticing that *more adeptly handling responsibilities* in (A) sounds odd, as does *handling more adeptly responsibilities* in (C). The verb *were* in (A) also suggests that his predecessors were handling responsibilities at the same time the new owner was (in which case, they wouldn't be predecessors). The present-tense *are*, in (C), is even worse. (B), like (A), uses the simple past-tense again, suggesting illogically that the activities of the new owner and his

predecessor took place at the same time. Also, *being that he was* is the kind of wordy phrase you should suspect immediately. (E) logically uses *had* to refer to the actions of predecessors, but it wrongly uses *adeptly*, an adverb. to describe the new owner's manner. (D) correctly gives us an introductory phrase that correctly modifies the subject *owner*.

28. E

Here, a modifying phrase comes between the subject and the verb, so you should know to start by checking for subject-verb agreement. *Rockets was* and *the rocket were* are clearly wrong, so you can cross out (C) and (D). Now, with respect to the modifying phrase that begins with *like,* things being compared should be parallel. That is, we can't compare the plural *rockets* with the singular *the airplane and the jet*, in (A); nor can we compare *the rocket* with *airplanes and jets*, in (B).

29. A

The underlined portion of the stem sentence contains a modifier (*Unlike other scholars*), so be on the lookout for modification errors. Start with the stem sentence. Is the modifier correctly placed? Yes—the *eminent mythologist* Is being compared to *other scholars*, so this sentence appears to be OK. Before accepting (A), though, let's check out the other choices. (B) and (C) incorrectly compare *scholars* to *conclusions*. (E) compares *mythologists* to *those of scholars*. For this choice to be correct, *mythologists* would need to belong to *scholars*. That's illogical. (D) offers a correct modifier, but it also contains an awkward verb construction— *conclusions are that*. Choice (A) is preferable and is the correct answer.

30. C

When you see a list or series, ask yourself, Are all the listed items similar grammatically and logically? The phrase that matches *technical expertise* and *commercial enterprise* is *judicious government backing*, in (C). (D) is close but it's not as compact, and GMAT often rewards compact language. Also, (D)'s *ensure Italian firms that they will* is unclear.

CHAPTER EIGHT
Reading Comprehension

Questions 1–7 are based on the following passage:

The field of medicine is going through unprecedented changes. Physicians, in response to increased government regulations and declining reimbursements from insurance
(5) companies, are seeking to form or join complex healthcare entities rather than work independently. As physicians turn away from the autonomy that historically characterized the medical profession, they are encountering
(10) situations commonly found in the business world, such as disagreements with their employers and colleagues. To respond to these changes in the medical profession, healthcare professionals should consider the benefits of
(15) employing Alternative Dispute Resolutions (ADR).

ADRs are mechanisms for settling disputes between parties that do not involve litigation. Examples include arbitration,
(20) mediation, early neutral evaluation, and other methods of conciliation. ADRs are often productive alternatives to lawsuits, given the costs and prolonged timeframes of the legal process. To apply them in a healthcare setting,
(25) one must consider the specific physician arrangement at hand. When an entity consists of physician partners, ADR programs may not be mandatory. When an entity consists of physician employees, each physician must
(30) individually agree to participate in such a program.

Arbitration and mediation are the most commonly used forms of ADR, and therefore are recommended starting points. While there
(35) are some distinctions between the two, they are conceptually similar. Arbitration generally refers to a process that ends in a decision, not a recommendation. Hence, arbitration is usually legally binding on the parties involved. It is a
(40) process similar in format to a trial, but involves only limited discovery and very simplified rules of evidence. Arbitration hearings last only a few hours and the opinions are not public record.

Arbitration has long been used in labor,
(45) construction, and securities regulation cases.

Mediation is a process whereby an independent third party facilitates resolution of a dispute between two parties. The mediator is neither a judge nor a referee. Rather, he is a
(50) conciliator who improves the negotiating atmosphere by emphasizing the common ground between the parties and helping to remove obstacles to communication. Mediators can accomplish this by working with the parties
(55) to reduce irrationality, explore alternative solutions, provide opportunities for graceful retreat, and regulate public intervention. The mediator is not primarily responsible for the resolution of the impasse, but rather helps the
(60) parties resolve it themselves. Of course, the ultimate measure of the effectiveness of mediation is whether the process produces a settlement.

The different forms of ADR successfully
(65) provide acceptable solutions to many disputes within healthcare organizations. But if a physician is not happy with the outcome of an ADR process, he or she may still leave the organization or pursue alternatives such as
(70) litigation.

1. The author's primary purpose in the passage is to

    (A) Demonstrate that arbitration and mediation are good forms of alternative dispute resolution regardless of the conflict at hand

    (B) Suggest that certain methods of conflict resolution used in business are also applicable to medicine

    (C) Prove that mediation can be as effective as arbitration but that the latter should be tried first

    (D) Discuss ways that healthcare entities can keep their employees from leaving

    (E) Prove that courtroom costs are increasing

2. According to the passage, which of the following is true of most arbitration hearings?

   (A) They are similar to court hearings but are shorter and not public record.

   (B) They have been extremely successful in settling disputes in the fields of labor, construction, and securities regulation.

   (C) The outcomes are always enforceable by law.

   (D) They are the first method of ADR that is usually tried.

   (E) An arbitration hearing prevents an employee or employer from taking further action.

3. It can be inferred from the passage that

   (A) Most physicians have moved into large healthcare organizations

   (B) Decisions about when to use ADR methods to settle conflicts must be made by the management of a healthcare entity

   (C) Employed physicians can refuse to settle disputes using an ADR method

   (D) Employees in the business world always choose to settle disputes using ADR methods

   (E) All partners in a group practice have to reach agreement on using an ADR method to settle a dispute that arises between two physicians

4. Which of the following provides the most appropriate title for the passage?

   (A) Are Arbitration and Mediation Good for Healthcare?

   (B) The Recent Growth of Alternative Dispute Resolutions in Healthcare Settings

   (C) Mediation and Arbitration: Good Alternatives for Medical Professionals

   (D) The Relation of Complex Healthcare Entities to Alternative Dispute Resolutions

   (E) The Business of Healthcare Disputes

5. Which of the following does the author suggest was an important reason that physicians have begun joining complex healthcare entities?

   (A) Because large organizations have established means to settle disputes

   (B) To increase reimbursement from insurance companies

   (C) To improve their understanding of the business side of medicine

   (D) Because patients are seeking out larger over smaller practices

   (E) Because various pressures have made it difficult to work as a solo practitioner

6. The author states that which of the following is always true about mediation?

   (A) It can be followed or preceded by arbitration.

   (B) Its results are enforceable by law.

   (C) It occurs in a courtroom.

   (D) It is not a binding decision.

   (E) Mediators work with both parties until a settlement is reached.

7. Which of the following most accurately describes the organization of the passage?

   (A) A presentation of data leading to an overall conclusion

   (B) A general recommendation, followed by specific examples of its application

   (C) A historical presentation of two proposals for solving a problem

   (D) A comparison of two methods, followed by a rejection of both

   (E) An argument based on a sequence of logical implications from an initial premise

Questions 8–14 are based on the following passage:

In 1943, Baade obtained photographs of stars in the galaxy Andromeda. Using these photographs, Baade divided stars into two groups. The brightest members of Population I
(5) were hot, blue stars with surface temperatures up to 30,000 degrees Kelvin. The brightest Population II stars (called "red giants") were large, cool and red, and fainter than Population I stars. Later observations showed that most
(10) Population I stars occur in the arms of spiral galaxies, while Population II stars are most common between the arms and in the centers of spiral galaxies, and in elliptical galaxies. According to Baade, the two populations
(15) compose distinct stellar age groups. Since the rate at which stars consume their fuel is directly proportional to their brightness, and brightness increases with mass, large, bright stars burn their fuel more quickly than dimmer stars.
(20) Baade concluded that the brightest Population I stars were probably less than one million years old while Population II stars were older.

Baade found support for his views in the distribution of red giants. It is believed that
(25) most of a star's hydrogen fuel is gradually converted to helium. When the helium core comprises about one-tenth of a star's mass, the star expands and its surface cools. This phase lasts until the red giant consumes all of its fuel
(30) and disintegrates in either a single explosion or a series of outbursts. Most red giants occur in Population II.

The composition of red giants supports Baade's conception. It is thought that all
(35) elements evolved from hydrogen as a result of nuclear reactions in stars. When a star explodes, it throws out heavy elements. Thus, the dust and gas from which new stars are produced gradually become richer in heavier elements.
(40) Studies of red giants in both populations reveal that heavier elements are more abundant in Population I giants. Thus, Population II stars evolved from material poor in heavier elements and are older.

(45) While Baade's basic insights have been sustained, analyses of stars in our galaxy have shown variations in concentrations of heavy elements, indicating that the stars must be of assorted ages. As a consequence, stars are now
(50) classified into five distinct populations.

8. The primary purpose of this passage is to

(A) explain how to determine the age of a star
(B) describe a system of star classification and some of the evidence supporting it
(C) discuss Population II stars
(D) compare and evaluate competing theories of stellar evolution
(E) examine the importance of Baade's contributions to astronomy

9. According to the passage, Baade considered all of the following to be characteristics of Population I stars EXCEPT:

(A) They are relatively young stars.
(B) The brightest members are hot, blue stars.
(C) They are found mainly between the arms of spiral galaxies.
(D) They are brighter than Population II stars.
(E) They have surface temperatures of up to 30,000 degrees Kelvin.

10. According to the passage, when the core in which hydrogen has been totally consumed amounts to approximately one tenth of a star's mass, then

    (A) the star will expand and its outer layer will cool
    (B) its life as a normal star will end
    (C) the star may disintegrate in a single explosion
    (D) the star will throw out the heavy elements it has produced
    (E) its classification will change from Population I to Population II

11. Which of the following statements can be inferred from the passage as characteristic of red giants?

    I.   They are all Population II stars.
    II. Each red giant is cooler than it once was.
    III. They all have a low percentage of heavy elements.

    (A) I only
    (B) II only
    (C) I and II only
    (D) I and III only
    (E) I, II, and III

12. The passage provides support for all of the following statements EXCEPT:

    (A) The death of a star involves either one major or several minor explosions.
    (B) The chemical compositions of red giants support the classification of stars into different age groups.
    (C) Population II stars are older than Population I stars.
    (D) Elliptical galaxies have existed for a longer period of time than spiral galaxies.
    (E) The chemical composition of a star is indicative of its age.

13. The author would most probably agree that

    (A) astronomers can ascertain with ease to which of the five populations a star belongs
    (B) more recent information has discredited Baade's early ideas about stars
    (C) eventually the spiral arms of the galaxies will be devoid of interstellar dust
    (D) the classification of stars has helped to lend order to their study
    (E) the present classification of stars into five populations is outdated

14. From the information presented in the passage, it can be inferred that stars that have not yet formed will

    (A) comprise a distinct population of stars
    (B) be brighter and hotter than those already in existence
    (C) have a greater mass than those already in existence
    (D) do so between the arms of the spiral galaxies
    (E) evolve from material richer in heavier elements than did earlier ones

Questions 15–21 are based on the following passage:

Congress has had numerous opportunities in recent years to reconsider the arrangements under which federal forest lands are owned and managed. New institutional
(5) structures merit development because federal forest lands cannot be efficiently managed under the hierarchical structure which now exists. The system is too complex to be understood by any single authority. The
(10) establishment of each forest as an independent public corporation would simplify the management structure and promote greater efficiency, control, and accountability.

To illustrate how a system for
(15) independent public corporations might work, consider the National Forest System. Each National Forest would become an independent public corporation, operating under federal charter, which gives it legal authority to manage
(20) federal land in the same manner that other federal corporations manage communications, transportation, or electrical generation facilities. The charter would give the corporation the right to establish its own
(25) production goals, land uses, management practices, and financial arrangements, within the policy constraints set by the Public Corporations Board. To assure economic efficiency in making decisions, the Public
(30) Corporations Board would establish a minimum average rate of return to be earned on assets held by each corporation. Each corporation would be required to organize a system for reporting revenues, costs, capital
(35) investments and recovery, profits, and the usual measures of financial health normally required of any private corporation. While the financial objective would not necessarily be to maximize profit, there would be a requirement to earn at
(40) resources under the corporations's control.

The primary advantage of this approach to federal land management lies in the potential for achieving greater efficiency in the utilization of land, capital, and labor. A second advantage
(45) stems from the potential stabilization of the personnel involved in managing federal lands. A positive program of advancement, more flexible job classifications, professional training, and above all, countering outside bids with
(50) higher salary, would enable a corporation to develop a more stable professional workforce. A third advantage is that federal land management would become less vulnerable to the politics of special interest groups.

15. The primary purpose of this passage is to

   (A) suggest that the National Forest System is plagued by many problems
   (B) argue that it is necessary to restructure the management of federal forest lands
   (C) insist that private corporations be allowed to manage the country's natural resources
   (D) discuss the role of private corporations in the management of the National Forest System
   (E) highlight the competing needs of public agencies managing communications, transportation, and national forests

16. According to the passage, all of the following are potential benefits of forming public corporations to manage federal forest lands EXCEPT

   (A) a more stable labor force
   (B) more effective management of natural resources
   (C) the ability to offer competitive salaries
   (D) less vulnerability to special interest groups
   (E) expansion of federal forest land boundaries

17. According to the passage, the responsibilities of a corporation authorized to manage a National Forest should include which of the following?

    I. Establishing formal procedures for making official reports of the corporation's financial well-being

    II. Earning at least a minimum return on the corporation's resources and assets

    III. Achieving a maximum level of profits on the corporation's capital investments

    (A) I only

    (B) II only

    (C) III only

    (D) I and II only

    (E) I, II, and III

18. The author suggests that administrators of federal forest lands have been handicapped by which of the following?

    (A) The public expectation that federal forest lands will remain undeveloped.

    (B) The failure of environmental experts to investigate the problems of federal forest lands.

    (C) The inability of the federal government to compete with private corporations for the services of skilled professionals.

    (D) The unwillingness of Congress to pass laws to protect federal forest lands from private developers.

    (E) The difficulty of persuading citizens to invest their capital in a government-run endeavor.

19. According to the passage, the present problems of federal forest lands derive mainly from

    (A) overuse by the population

    (B) inefficient organization

    (C) hostility from special interest groups

    (D) the corporate mentality of Congress

    (E) opposition to reform by government employees

20. The author's attitude toward the "hierarchical structure" mentioned in line 7 can best be characterized as

    (A) resigned

    (B) admiring

    (C) skeptical

    (D) bitter

    (E) ambivalent

21. Which of the following best describes the organization of the passage?

    (A) A proposal is made and then supporting arguments are set forth.

    (B) One claim is evaluated and then rejected in favor of another claim.

    (C) A point of view is stated and then evidence for and against it is evaluated.

    (D) A problem is outlined and then various solutions are discussed.

    (E) Opposing opinions are introduced and then debated.

Questions 22–24 are based on the following passage:

Any species participates in what biologists call a "specific ecology," a relationship to its environment described by measurement both of environmental factors affecting the
(5) species, and of the species' response to these factors. Environmental factors include such variables as amount of light and abundance of food; species' responses typically include changes in the rates of birth, death,
(10) immigration and emigration.

Since environmental stresses limit population growth, variations in environment correlate directly with variation in local species population density. The relationship between
(15) particular environmental stresses and specific modes of response are difficult to define and predict; however, the relationship between the various response modes and changes in population density is relatively simple. The rate
(20) of change in population density is equal to the immigration rate plus the birth rate, minus the death rate, minus the emigration rate.

Introduction of iodine into an area populated by sea urchins, for example, might affect the
(25) birth rate and immigration rate negatively, and the death rate and emigration rate positively, shifting the rate of change of population density toward the negative.

22. The purpose of this passage is to

(A) question the existence of specific ecologies

(B) reveal the effects of the introduction of iodine into a population of sea urchins

(C) discuss the specific factors which limit sea urchin population growth

(D) predict the relationship between various environmental factors and specific modes of response

(E) define "specific ecology" and illustrate how local population density changes when certain factors are altered

23. The author discusses the introduction of iodine into a population of sea urchins in order to

(A) question the usefulness of statistical approaches to ecology

(B) illustrate how population density is affected by species response modes

(C) explain the concept of "specific ecology"

(D) demonstrate how chemical pollutants affect a marine environment

(E) show that population density remains constant over time despite environmental changes

24. It can be inferred that ecologists probably have the LEAST precise understanding of which of the following?

(A) The relationship between variation in environment and variations in local population density

(B) How species response modes affect population density

(C) The effect of introducing a toxin into an area on the immigration rate into the area

(D) What types of behavior comprise species responses to environmental stresses

(E) The relationship between a given environmental stress and a given mode of response

Questions 25–27 are based on the following passage:

The relevance of formal economic models to real-world policy has been a topic of some dispute. The economists R.D. Norton and S.Y. Rhee achieved some success in applying
(5) such a model retrospectively to theKorean economy over a fourteen-year period; the model's figures for output, prices, and other variables closely matched real statistics. The model's value in policy terms, however, proved
(10) less clearcut. Norton and Rhee performed simulations in which, keeping long-term factors constant, they tried to pinpoint the effect of short-term policy changes. Their model indicated that rising prices for imported oil
(15) would increase inflation; reducing exports by five percent would lower Gross Domestic Product and increase inflation; and slowing the growth of the money supply would result in slightly higher inflation.
(20) These findings are somewhat startling. Many economists have argued that reducing exports will lessen, not increase, inflation. And while most view escalating oil costs as inflationary, few would think the same of
(25) slower monetary growth. The Norton–Rhee model can perhaps be viewed as indicating the pitfalls of a formalist approach that stresses statistical "goodness of fit" at the expense of genuine policy relevance.

25. The author is primarily concerned with

(A) proposing a new type of economic analysis
(B) criticizing an overly formal economic model
(C) advocating the use of statistical models in determining economic policy
(D) suggesting an explanation for Korean inflation
(E) determining the accuracy of Norton and Rhee's analysis

26. The author mentions "a fourteen-year period" (line 6) in order to

(A) indicate how far into the future Norton and Rhee's model can make accurate predictions
(B) acknowledge the accuracy of Norton and Rhee's model in accounting for past events
(C) explain the effect of reducing exports on inflation
(D) demonstrate the startling nature of Norton and Rhee's findings
(E) expose the flaws in Norton and Rhee's model

27. The most significant criticism leveled against Norton and Rhee's model is that it

(A) excludes key statistical variables
(B) is too abstract to be useful in policy making
(C) fails to adjust for Korea's high rate of inflation
(D) underestimates the importance of economic growth
(E) fails to consider the effect of short-term variations in the economy

Questions 28–30 are based on the following passage:

Today there are an estimated 4-6 million undocumented immigrant workers and their families in the United States. These workers are caught in a web of ambiguity of U.S. attitudes
(5) and policies: they are attracted to a society in which many will reside in an underclass, defined by the illegal status of its members. Concern about an ever-increasing flow of immigrants has been a central factor behind
(10) recent legislative initiatives. Various economic and humanitarian arguments have figured in the debate over immigration reform. Some support regularizing the status of immigrants so that they can be reached by institutions like
(15) schools, courts, and public health services. Those supporting more stringent immigration controls assert that organized labor would benefit from elimination of the negative pressure that undocumented workers exert on
(20) wages and working conditions, and that unemployed U.S. workers are unfairly burdened by competition with immigrant workers. Manufacturers, on the other hand, argue that they can compete internationally only with
(25) access to the cheap labor provided by immigrants. Civil libertarians and community groups, fearing increased discrimination against immigrants, oppose legal sanctions designed to prevent hiring of undocumented
(30) workers.

Clearly, policies and attitudes regarding immigrant workers are based on broad, often conflicting social values and priorities. Because the situation of immigrants raises ethical
(35) questions about social justice and the right to decent living conditions, we must examine issues related to the social meaning and use of illegal status. Those issues involve the present use of the illegal status of immigrants to deny
(40) them treatment equal to that of other workers, and the possible use of access to social services as a reward for behaving in a prescribed

manner. Immigration policy raises questions about our national responsibility to people who
(45) are pushed from their own countries and pulled to ours by the effects of our own economy and of our foreign and domestic policies. If we are concerned with fairness, then we must attempt to meet the needs of those whose lives are
(50) distorted and disrupted by the present ambivalence of our immigration policies.

28. According to the passage, the dilemma faced by immigrants in the U.S. is the result of

(A) A dramatic increase in their numbers in recent years

(B) ambiguity of present U.S. attitudes and policies

(C) willingness of employers to hire undocumented immigrants

(D) ineffective enforcement of laws protecting immigrant workers

(E) support they have received from advocates of immigrant rights

29. Which of the following, if true, would most WEAKEN the argument of those who say greater regulation of immigration would aid U.S. workers?

    (A) Most undocumented immigrants take low-paying jobs that other workers will not consider

    (B) Wages offered by certain employers would rise in order to attract U.S. workers

    (C) Many U.S. workers of foreign origin oppose regulation, saying it could lead to discrimination

    (D) The imposition of regulation would require all workers to supply proof of documentation

    (E) Many undocumented workers are hired by employers that offer no employee benefits

30. The author implies any consideration of the conditions of immigrants should include an examination of

    (A) comparative wage scales of U.S. and foreign industries

    (B) population statistics of legal and illegal immigrants

    (C) methods by which illegal immigrants are denied equal treatment in the workplace

    (D) impact on U.S. citizens of entitling immigrants to receive public benefits

    (E) responsibility of U.S. employers toward legal immigrants

ANSWER KEY: READING COMPREHENSION

1. B	11. B	21. A
2. A	12. D	22. E
3. C	13. D	23. B
4. C	14. E	24. E
5. E	15. B	25. B
6. D	16. E	26. B
7. B	17. D	27. B
8. B	18. C	28. B
9. C	19. B	29. A
10. A	20. C	30. C

1. B

If you created a good roadmap for the passage, you already have a sense of the author's purpose. She attempted to show that arbitration and mediation—two forms of alternative dispute resolution—should be considered for resolving conflicts in the medical profession. The answer choice that best captures this idea is (B).

(A) is too broad—some conflicts may not be amenable to arbitration or mediation, as the last paragraph indicates. (C) suggests a comparison between the two methods that is never made. (D) and (E) are outside the scope of the passage.

2. A

Paragraph 3 states that arbitration hearings are similar to a trial, last only a few hours, and that the opinions are not public record. Choice (A) is correct because it states the facts conveyed in paragraph 3.

(B) is incorrect because although we learn in paragraph 3 that arbitration has been used for labor, construction, and securities regulation disputes, the author doesn't tell us whether such hearings have been successful. In (C), the word *always* makes it too extreme. The author states that arbitration is "*usually* legally binding on the parties involved." The GMAT loves to offer overly extreme

wrong answers—be careful! (D) is not supported by anything in the passage; arbitration is mentioned first, but we aren't told that it's usually tried first. (E) is contradicted by the last paragraph.

3. C

The last three sentences of paragraph 2 introduce the idea that implementation of ADR programs may be different depending on whether the physicians in an organization are partners or employees. The author states that in employed situations, each physician must decide whether or not she or he wants to participate in an ADR program. This makes choice (C) the best answer.

(A) is incorrect because the author does not us any idea how many physicians are employed by organizations. (B) is outside the scope of the passage. (D), too, expands beyond the scope of the passage and uses the extreme adverb, *always*. Although the passage suggests that these methods were first used by businesses, we aren't told if they are the only ones chosen. In (E), we aren't given any clues in the passage about how partner physicians decide to use ADR programs. We're only told that ADR programs may not be mandatory.

4. C

A question that asks for a title for the passage is a global question, because a good title will sum up the main idea. In this case, the main idea could be stated thus: "Arbitration and mediation should be considered for resolving disputes within the medical profession."

(A) is out because the scope is too broad—the passage doesn't concern the effects of arbitration and mediation on healthcare overall, but on their use in disputes between physicians who are members of large medical organizations. In (B), the passage doesn't address the growth of these methods in healthcare settings; it only suggests that they be tried. (D) does not correctly capture the broad discussion of the passage. (E) is too broadly worded—it goes outside of the scope of the passage. (C) is correct because it mentions the two ADR methodologies detailed in the passage, and it suggests that they are good alternatives (this follows from the recommendation at the end of paragraph 1 that healthcare professionals should consider ADR).

5. E

(A) is out because we aren't told that large organizations have established means for dispute resolution. The author's suggestion of mediation and arbitration implies that many large healthcare entities have not yet embraced them. (B) distorts a detail mentioned in paragraph 1. (C) is too vague, and outside the scope of the passage, as is (D). (E) is correct: the first paragraph lists two reasons why physicians are joining larger practices and shunning solo practice.

6. D

(A) and (C) are incorrect because the passage does not state either of these facts about mediation. (B) is a distortion: the passage says that arbitration is *usually* legally binding, but the legal aspects of the results of mediation are not discussed. (E) is incorrect because, again, a settlement is not always the outcome of a mediation process. (D) is correct; in paragraph 4, we learn that mediators do not enforce decisions, and in fact a settlement may not be reached in all cases.

7. B

The passage opens by describing the movement of physicians into larger medical practices, and the problems that follow. It then recommends ADR, and outlines two examples of ADR in action. (A) and (E) both describe passage structures that are very different from the one here. (C) is incorrect because there is no historical presentation. With (D), while certain aspects of arbitration and mediation are compared, neither is rejected. The last paragraph does suggest that some physicians might not be happy with ADR outcomes, but this doesn't represent a rejection by the author.

8. B

The purpose of the passage is something like "describe Baade's star categories and show how evidence supports them." (B) contains these ideas, though in more general terms. (A) ignores the first and last paragraphs, which aren't concerned with star ages. (C) focuses only on Population II stars, while the passage clearly differentiates between Population I and II stars. No theories of stellar evolution are presented, so (D) is wrong. (E) is tempting because it focuses on Baade, but it does so without mentioning his star categories, which are the main focus of the passage: (E) would be appropriate for a more general and biographical passage than this.

9. C

"According to the passage" indicates a detail question, so the answer will be found in the text itself. Population I stars are discussed in the first two paragraphs: They are bright (brighter than Population II stars), hot (up to 30,000 degrees Kelvin), the brightest among them are blue, they are young, and they occur in the arms of spiral galaxies. Since this is an "all/EXCEPT" question, the correct answer cannot be one of these facts. This eliminates (A), (B), (D) and (E). That leaves (C), which is indeed correct, because it is Population II stars that are found between the arms of spiral galaxies.

10. A

This development is discussed in the third paragraph. "When the helium core comprises about onetenth of a star's mass, the star expands and its surface cools." (A) paraphrases this development. Notice that (B), (C), and (D) come from either too far along in the third paragraph or from the fourth paragraph. (E), logical as it may appear, is never mentioned at all.

11. B

According to the passage, red giants occur primarily among Population II stars, and they are older, cooler, dimmer and redder than Population I stars.

Their hydrogen has mostly changed to helium, and they are poorer in heavier elements than other stars. Option I is not a valid inference because of the word "all." The author says at the end of the third paragraph that "most," but not "all," red giants are in Population II. (B), then, must be the answer. Option II is supported by information in the third paragraph. Option III, on the other hand, is another absolute assertion that the passage doesn't support; the passage says that Population I red giants have "more abundant" heavy elements than Population II red giants. They are not all alike, nor do we know anything about a "low percentage."

12. D

You meed the choice that is NOT supported by information in the passage. (A) appears nearly verbatim at the end of the third paragraph. (B) and (E), which get at the same point, constitute the principal focus of the fourth paragraph. (C)'s point is made several times in the passage. (D), however, looks different immediately. Elliptical galaxies are mentioned only once—at the end of the first paragraph—where it's stated that older Population II stars are found in them. But these stars are found in spiral galaxies as well, so it can't be concluded that elliptical galaxies are older than spiral galaxies. (D), therefore, is correct.

13. D

The answer here must relate to the author's purpose—in this case, something about Baade's classification of stars. (A) goes too far with the words "with ease." While the author says that there are five classifications of stars, actually classifying them requires analysis that may or may not be easy. (B) is contradicted by the passage, which says that Baade's basic insights have been "sustained," not "discredited." (C) wrongly mixes details from two separate paragraphs. (D), however, looks good because the thrust of the passage is that increasing precision in classifying stars has made it easier to study them. Finally, (E) is completely unsupported— the author says that Baade's two, original classifications have been increased to five. But the

author doesn't say that these five categories are now "outdated."

14. E

The only part of the passage that mentions stars that have not yet formed is the sentence in the fourth paragraph that refers to "the dust and gas from which new stars are produced." This sentence says that this dust and gas becomes richer in heavier elements over time. Thus, the correct answer is (E).

(A) is wrong because, while it is clear that five age classifications now exist, it cannot be inferred that new stars will be put into a new star class. (B) and (C) refer to characteristics of Population I stars, but the author makes no claim that these characteristics will also apply to future stars. (D) refers to Population II stars.

15. B.

The author's purpose, clear from paragraph 1, is that managing forests as public corporations would have several advantages over the present system. The closest choice is (B), which mentions restructuring forest management. The author mentions the problems referred to in (A), but the focus is the solution, not the problems. (C) and (D) refer to *private* corporations—never discussed in the passage. (E) distorts a detail—all the passage suggests is that forest lands and other public agencies should be similarly managed.

16. E

For the benefits of forming public corporations to manage forests, check paragraph 3, which names three: efficiency, stable personnel, and less vulnerability to politics. You're looking for something that's not one of these benefits. (A), (B), (C) and (D) all paraphrase the author. (E), forest land expansion, was never mentioned.

17. D

The first half of paragraph 2 deals with the legal authority of a public corporation, and the second half deals with its obligations, primarily financial.

 149

The responsibilities are to earn a minimum, "public utility" rate of return, and to report financial activities as do private corporations, both expressed in options I and II. With option III, paragraph 2 explicitly states that the primary goal is not "to maximize profit." Choice (D)—options I and II only—is correct.

18. C

This question is harder to locate because much of the passage talks directly or indirectly about forest management problems. Paragraph 1 mentions complexity, while paragraph 3 indicates inefficiency, personnel problems, and political issues, any of which could be the answer. (A), (B), (D) and (E) are never mentioned, while (C) corresponds to the personnel issue. The best approach to a question like this is to aggressively skim the choices—look for one that relates to information in the passage. If you don't find the answer quickly, skip the question and score easier points elsewhere.

19. B

Your work with the previous question helps here. You know the passage is about forest land management. The main problem, says paragraph 3, is structural inefficiency. (B) "jumps out" with its paraphrase of the author's main criticism. (A), public overuse, and (E), opposition to reform by government workers, are never mentioned. (C) and (D) can be stretched to fit the idea of "political vulnerability" but they're poor choices: First, they stray from the passage by getting too specific, and second, the passage presents "political vulnerability" as only one effect of inadequate management.

20. C

Paragraph 1 cites "hierarchical structure" as the basic problem. So the answer must be negative—strongly negative—but consistent with the passage's unemotional tone. (B) and (D) sound too emotional. (A) is out because the author is not resigned—he's advocating a change. (E) is wrong because ambivalence implies mixed feelings—

some positive, some negative. The author never expresses any positive feelings toward the current hierarchy. The answer is (C), which is both negative and purposeful.

21. A

This question is global in character and easier to answer if you jot down a brief 2–4 word summary of paragraphs as you skim: That gives you a rough map of how the key ideas build an argument. For example—Paragraph 1: "need better forest mgmt"; paragraph 2: "how pub corps work"; and paragraph 3: "advantages." The structure is summarized as: a proposed solution, detailed explanation of solution, and finally some advantages. The closest paraphrase is (A), which mentions "proposal" and "support" for the proposals. Checking the other choices, the author evaluates a "claim" or proposal, in (B), but never rejects it for another. (C) is off because the author never gives evidence against the proposal. Nor does he mention other solutions (D), or opposing opinions (E).

22. E

The first sentence of the passage defines "specific ecology," while the first paragraph ends by giving examples of the environmental factors that would impact on a species. The second paragraph begins by stating how population density is affected by variations in environment. The passage then ends with a specific example—that of sea urchins reacting to the introduction of iodine into their environment. (A) is out, as specific ecologies are actually presented as fact in the passage. (B) is a detail included in the passage, but isn't the main point. (C) is also too narrow. And predictions were not part of the passage, so (D) doesn't work. (E) is the best answer.

23. B

"Purpose of detail" questions, like this one, often focus on specific illustrations of a more general point. Relating the detail to its context is the best approach. In the second sentence of paragraph 2, the author says, "The relationship between the various response modes and changes in population density is relatively simple." The third sentence spells out the relationship and the final sentence, about the sea urchins, functions to illustrate the specific relationship in sentence 3 and the more general statement in sentence 2. (B) focuses on the latter. (A) is wrong because the author does not question the usefulness of statistical approaches; he seems to prefer them, when possible, as in the sea urchin example. (C) is mentioned and explained in the first paragraph; it is not the topic here. (D) seizes on one possible lesson of the sea urchin case, but completely misses the author's purpose in introducing it into the passage—the author is interested in methods of study, not in pollution. (E) is contradicted: sea urchin population density does change.

24. E

This question refers to the relationship that is "difficult to define and predict" (second sentence of paragraph 2). If it is difficult to define and predict then ecologists do not have a precise understanding of the relationship. All the others are, inferably, understood more precisely. (A) is described in the first sentence of paragraph 2 as involving a direct correlation. (B) is described in detail in the third sentence of paragraph 2. (C), apparently, is well understood, since the hypothetical example of the sea urchins involves the effect of introducing iodine, presumably a toxin for sea urchins. And (D) is described in the last sentence of paragraph 1.

25. B

The passage begins by posing the question of how useful formal models are, and concludes by calling Norton and Rhee's model an example of the "pitfalls" of formalism. (B) captures this critical approach, though it misses the broader implications hinted at in the opening sentence. There's nothing that indicates that Norton and Rhee's method of analysis was "new" (A), nor is the author "proposing" it; on the other hand, he/she doesn't propose any other approach. (C) is what the author

is very skeptical about; certainly he/she doesn't "advocate" using such models. (D) is a mess. N & R were not trying to explain Korean inflation as a whole, but to see how various economic factors would affect inflation; and the author is not even trying to do that, but to discuss N & R's work. (E) is something the author does do, but it is incidental to the broader purpose of criticizing "formalism."

26. B

The passage says that Norton and Rhee "achieved some success in applying such a model retrospectively to the Korean economy over a fourteen-year period." In other words, the model is fairly effective in analyzing past events, as (B) suggests. Since the "fourteen-year period" refers to the past, not the future, (A) is clearly wrong; in fact, one of the main points of the passage is that Norton and Rhee's model is not particularly useful for predicting the future. (C), (D), and (E) refer to matters discussed later in the passage.

27. B

The whole passage is critical of Norton and Rhee, but the last sentence offers the only explicit criticism: their approach is "formalist" (or abstract) and lacks "policy relevance." (B) paraphrases this criticism. The only economic factors specifically excluded from the model (A) are the long-term factors mentioned in the middle of paragraph 1; there is no suggestion that N & R should be criticized for this procedure. (C) is something that the model does do, since it is aimed at finding the effect of various factors on inflation. The "importance" of economic growth (D) is not discussed at all and certainly not underestimated. (E) is contradicted by paragraph 1: these are exactly the factors N & R did consider.

28. B

The question basically restates the final sentence of the passage, and it's (B) which accurately represents the author's stance. (A), (C) and (E) are minor points mentioned as evidence, not conclusions.

29. A

A tough question on the surface, it appears to be slumming from the critical reasoning section. This is a great question to *pre-phrase*; that way you won't get caught up and confused in the long, tiresome answers. According to the passage, those who say greater regulation of immigration would aid U.S. workers argue that undocumented workers depress wages and that U.S. workers therefore can't compete (Paragraph 2). So, in order to weaken the argument, we'd have to show that either undocumented workers don't depress wages OR that U.S. workers aren't in competition with undocumented workers.

(A) very kindly agrees with our pre-phrase. Keep it. (B) strengthens the argument. If wages would rise to attract U.S. workers, they must currently be lower because of the presence of undocumented workers. (C) and (D) are out because, even though they are related to parts of the passage, they have nothing to do with the argument *in question*. Choice (E) also seems related to our pre-phrase.

So, of our three remaining choices, which is the best? (E) has a logical error: Many undocumented workers are hired by employers who offer no employee benefits, but it doesn't say whether or not U.S. workers are hired by the same firms. If so, it agrees with the argument in question, rather than weakening it. (A) agrees much more readily to the prephrase; it weakens the argument is the best answer.

30. C

This is another good spot for a prephrase. In Paragraph 3, the author writes, "...we must examine issues relating to the social meaning and use of illegal status. Those issues involve the present use of the illegal status of immigrants to deny them treatment equal to that of other workers...." It's fair to say, given this context, that the author is most concerned with unequal treatment of undocumented workers based on their illegal status, and would likely insist on such a discussion to be included in consideration of the conditions of immigrants. So a good prephrase might be: "The author implies any consideration of the conditions of immigrants should include an examination of the denial of equal status to immigrants based on their illegal status."

Given this prephrase, (A), (B), and (D) are out. (E) mentions the responsibility of U.S. employers toward immigrants, but it doesn't mention what this includes. (C) fits our prephrase almost exactly, and it's the best answer choice.

This question demonstrates the importance of prephrasing; if you hadn't previously decided what you were looking for, it might be easy to be swept up in the answer choices, since all the choices are mentioned somewhere in the passage. Careful examination of the author's tone should lead to the crucial section mentioned, and a prephrase helps you locate the answer quickly.

CHAPTER NINE

Problem Solving

1. In 1995, a basketball team won 30 percent of the 20 games it played. In 1996, it won 28 percent of its 25 basketball games. What was the percent increase from 1995 to 1996 in the number of basketball games team won?

    (A) 5%

    (B) $14\frac{2}{7}$%

    (C) $16\frac{2}{3}$%

    (D) $23\frac{1}{3}$%

    (E) 60%

2. A stamp collector receives a shipment of 1,000 stamps, of which x are damaged. If 33 of the undamaged stamps are English, then, in terms of x, the undamaged English stamps are what fraction of the total number of undamaged stamps?

    (A) $\dfrac{x - 33}{1,000}$

    (B) $\dfrac{x - 33}{1,000 - x}$

    (C) $\dfrac{33}{1,000 - 33\,x}$

    (D) $\dfrac{33}{1,000 - x}$

    (E) $\dfrac{33 - x}{1,000}$

3. Water is dripping into a bathtub so that the bathtub is being filled at the constant rate of approximately 0.5 cubic feet per hour. If the rectangular tub is 5 feet long, 2.5 feet wide, and 2 feet deep, how long will it take to fill the tub?

    (A) 5 hours

    (B) 19 hours

    (C) 25 hours

    (D) 50 hours

    (E) 125 hours

4. A plumber has only synthetic pipe sections and copper pipe sections. Each synthetic pipe section weighs 5 pounds, and each copper pipe section weighs 9 pounds. If the average (arithmetic mean) weight of all of the pipe sections the plumber has is 6 pounds, and the plumber has 27 synthetic pipe sections, how many copper pipe sections does the plumber have?

    (A) 5

    (B) 7

    (C) 9

    (D) 12

    (E) 81

5. Two cars, *J* and *K*, started simultaneously from opposite ends of the same road, 210 miles apart, and drove towards each other. Car *J* traveled at a constant speed of 30 miles per hour, and car *K* traveled at a constant speed of 35 miles per hour. How far had car *J* traveled when car *K* reached the opposite end of the road?

(A) 105 miles
(B) 140 miles
(C) 150 miles
(D) 180 miles
(E) 195 miles

6. Last year, MegaCorp International had revenue in France of 48 million dollars. This amount represented 16 percent of the company's total revenue for the year. What was the company's total revenue last year, in millions of dollars?

(A)   3
(B)   30
(C)   150
(D)   300
(E) 1,500

7. The average (arithmetic mean) of 31, 33, and 35 equals the average of 32, 34, and

(A) 30
(B) 32
(C) 33
(D) 34
(E) 36

8. A restaurant serves a 16-ounce drink that contains only orange juice and pineapple juice. The ratio of orange juice to pineapple juice is 3:5. If the size of the drink is increased to 24 ounces, how many ounces of pineapple juice must be added in order to maintain the same ratio?

(A) 5
(B) 6
(C) 9
(D) 12
(E) 15

9. Copier *A* produces copies at a uniform rate of 110 every 11 seconds, and Copier *B* produces copies at a uniform rate of 100 every 25 seconds. If the two copiers run simultaneously, how many seconds will it take for them to produce 280 copies?

(A) 18
(B) 20
(C) 25
(D) 28
(E) 36

10. The length of a rectangular garden is twice its width and its area is 800 square feet. If a fence is to be placed around three sides of the garden, including the two longer sides and one of the shorter sides, how many linear feet of fencing will be required?

(A) 40
(B) 60
(C) 75
(D) 80
(E) 100

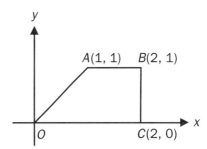

11. In the figure above, which of the following is NOT the equation of a line which contains all the points of a side of quadrilateral *ABCO* ?

(A) $y = 0$
(B) $x = 2$
(C) $x = 1$
(D) $y = 1$
(E) $y = x$

12. If the number *x* of cars sold each week varies with the price per car *y* in dollars according to the equation $x = 800{,}000 - 50y$, what would be the total weekly revenue, in dollars, from the sale of cars priced at $15,000?

(A)   50,000
(B)   750,000
(C)   850,000
(D)   7,500,000
(E)   750,000,000

13. If integers x, y and z are consecutive positive multiples of 3, and $x < y < z$, which of the following must be true?

    I. $z - x = 6$

    II. xy is an even integer

    III. $\dfrac{x + y + z}{3}$ is an integer

  (A) I only

  (B) II only

  (C) I and II only

  (D) I and III only

  (E) I, II and III

14. How many multiples of 5 are there between 50 and 200 exclusive?

  (A) 28

  (B) 29

  (C) 30

  (D) 31

  (E) 32

15. If $x^2 < x^3$, which of the following must be true?

  (A) $x = 0$

  (B) $x < 0$

  (C) $x > 1$

  (D) $x = 1$

  (E) $x < 1$

16. If x, y, and z are nonzero numbers and $\dfrac{y + z}{x} = 1$, which of the following must be true?

  (A) $x = y - z$

  (B) $x = z - y$

  (C) $y = x - z$

  (D) $y = x + z$

  (E) $z = x + y$

17. In which of the following pairs are the numbers reciprocals?

    I. $\dfrac{1}{2}$ and $\dfrac{-1}{2}$

    II. $\sqrt{2}$ and $\dfrac{\sqrt{2}}{2}$

    III. 2 and $\dfrac{1}{2}$

  (A) I only

  (B) II only

  (C) I and II

  (D) I and III

  (E) II and III

18. Which of the following is the best approximation of $\sqrt{0.000063}$?

  (A) 0.004

  (B) 0.008

  (C) 0.025

  (D) 0.04

  (E) 0.08

19. The average (arithmetic mean) of two integers is 18. If the larger integer is 5 times the smaller, what is the value of the larger integer?

    (A) 6
    (B) 12
    (C) 18
    (D) 24
    (E) 30

20. If $1 < st$, which of the following cannot be true?

    (A) $s < t < 0$
    (B) $0 < t < 1 < s$
    (C) $s < -1 < 0 < t$
    (D) $t < s < -1$
    (E) $-1 < t < 1 < s$

21. A family of seven goes to a certain restaurant on a night when children 2-years old or younger eat free, and children over 2 but under 5 eat for $2. All other dinners cost $8. The family also uses coupon to receive 25% off of their entire bill. If the family is made up of two parents and five children of ages 1, 3, 4, 7, and 9, how much does the family pay for dinner?

    (A) 9
    (B) 24
    (C) 27
    (D) 32
    (E) 36

22. Which of the following is a solution to $10x^2 + 10x = 20$?

    (A) -2
    (B) -1
    (C) $\frac{3}{2}$
    (D) 2
    (E) 10

23. If the average (arithmetic mean) of 6 consecutive even integers is 37, what is the difference between the greatest and the least of the 6 integers?

    (A) 5
    (B) 10
    (C) 12
    (D) 32
    (E) 34

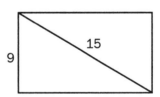

24. What is the perimeter of the rectangle shown above?

    (A) 12
    (B) 21
    (C) $18 + 2\sqrt{206}$
    (D) 42
    (E) 108

25. If $7y + 3z = 30 + 12y - 2z$ and $z = 9$, then $y =$
    (A) $\frac{5}{19}$
    (B) 3
    (C) $4\frac{2}{5}$
    (D) 6
    (E) $7\frac{4}{5}$

26. $\frac{6}{8} + \frac{4}{6} =$
    (A) $\frac{1}{2}$
    (B) $\frac{5}{9}$
    (C) $\frac{5}{7}$
    (D) $\frac{5}{4}$
    (E) $\frac{17}{12}$

27. A plumber charges a flat fee of z dollars for a house visit, even if she performs no work. Once at the house, she charges $\frac{z}{2}$ dollars for each half-hour of work plus the cost of supplies. Lewis hires the plumber to come to his house. The plumber is there for 1.5 hours to replace three fittings. The cost of supplies for each fitting is $\frac{2z}{3}$. If Lewis pays the plumber $270, how much does the plumber charge for each half-hour of work?

    (A) $20
    (B) $30
    (C) $40
    (D) $60
    (E) $120

28. The cost in dollars to manufacture y tables is $25,000 + 125y$. Each of these tables can be sold for $250. What is the smallest number of tables that must be manufactured and sold so that the amount received is at least equal to the manufacturing cost?

    (A) 100
    (B) 150
    (C) 200
    (D) 250
    (E) 300

29. If $r \neq s$ and $r + \dfrac{r(s + r)}{s - r} = 2s + \dfrac{2s(s + r)}{s - r}$, then $\dfrac{r}{s} =$
    (A) -1
    (B) $\frac{1}{2}$
    (C) 1
    (D) 2
    (E) 3

30. The product of two positive numbers is $12yz + 4y^2$. The larger number is $4y$. What is the difference between the larger number and the smaller number?

    (A) $5y - 3z$
    (B) $3(y - z)$
    (C) $4y - 3z - 1$
    (D) $3z + y$
    (E) $3(z - y)$

31. Childcare workers at a certain daycare center are paid a basic rate of w dollars per hour plus a bonus of B dollars per hour for each child that a worker watches. On a certain day, there are 60 children in the center from 8:00 AM until 6:00 PM. From 8:00 AM until noon, there are 10 childcare workers in the center, and from noon until 6:00 PM there are 12 childcare workers. If the children in the center are divided evenly among the childcare workers in the center at any time, how much does a childcare worker earn for the day if she works the entire 10 hours?

   (A) $10w + 54B$
   (B) $10w + 60B$
   (C) $60w + 10B$
   (D) $10w + 22B$
   (E) $8w + 56B$

32. If s and t are positive odd numbers, which of the following must be odd?

   I. s^t

   II. $(s + 1)^{(t + 1)}$

   III. $(s + t)^t$

   (A) I only
   (B) II only
   (C) I and III only
   (D) II and III only
   (E) I, II, and III

33. If x and y are not equal to 0, which of the following represents the reciprocal of $\dfrac{1}{x} - \dfrac{x}{y}$?

   (A) $x - \dfrac{y}{x}$

   (B) $\dfrac{1}{xy - x}$

   (C) $\dfrac{y - x^2}{xy}$

   (D) $\dfrac{yx}{x - y}$

   (E) $\dfrac{xy}{y - x^2}$

34. If the sum of two distinct integers is zero, which of the following could be the product of the two integers?

   (A) 9
   (B) 4
   (C) 1
   (D) 0
   (E) –1

35. If y and x are positive numbers, and $y - x$ is between $-x$ and -1, then which of the following must be true?

   (A) y is less than x
   (B) x is less than y
   (C) x is less than 0
   (D) x is greater than 1
   (E) x is equal to y

ANSWER KEY: PROBLEM SOLVING

1. C	13. E	25. B
2. D	14. B	26. E
3. D	15. C	27. B
4. C	16. C	28. C
5. D	17. E	29. D
6. D	18. B	30. B
7. C	19. E	31. A
8. A	20. C	32. A
9. B	21. C	33. E
10. E	22. A	34. E
11. C	23. B	35. A
12. E	24. D	

1. C

We need to use the formula Percent Increase = $\frac{\text{Increase in value}}{\text{Original value}} \times 100\%$. The increase in value is the increase in number of games won from 1995 to 1996, and the original value is the number of games won in 1995.

In 1995, the team won 30% of 20 games, which is $(0.30)(20) = 6$ games. In 1996, the team won $(0.28)(25) = 7$ games. Thus, the percent increase was $\frac{7-6}{6} \times 100\% = \frac{1}{6} \times 100\% = \frac{100}{6}\% = \frac{50}{3}\% = 16\frac{2}{3}\%$.

2. D

A fraction is $\frac{\text{Part}}{\text{Whole}}$. In this case, the numerator is the number of undamaged English stamps and the denominator is the total number of undamaged stamps. We are told that 33 of the undamaged

stamps are English, so we know that numerator must be 33. We can eliminate all choices except (C) and (D).

There are 1,000 stamps in total, of which x stamps are damaged, so the total number of undamaged stamps is $1,000 - x$. That's our denominator, so the correct choice is (D), $\frac{33}{1,000 - x}$.

3. D

At any point in time, the amount of water in the tub is equal to the rate at which it is being filled multiplied by the amount of time elapsed. We know that the rate is 0.5 cubic meters feet per hour, so at any point: Volume = (0.5 cubic feet per hour) × Time. We want to solve for the Time.

To begin, we can determine the volume.

The tub will be full when the volume of water equals the total volume of the tub. The volume of a rectangular solid is the product of its length, width, and depth. So, the volume of this tub is $5 \times 2.5 \times 2 = 25$ cubic feet. Thus, we can replace Volume with 25 cubic feet in the equation Volume = (0.5 cubic feet per hour) × Time. We then have 25 cubic feet = (0.5 cubic feet per hour) × Time.

$$\text{Time} = \frac{25 \text{ cubic feet}}{\left(0.50 \frac{\text{cubic feet}}{\text{hour}}\right)} = \frac{25}{0.5} \text{ hours}$$

$$= \frac{25 \times 2}{0.5 \times 2} \text{ hours} = 50 \text{ hours.}$$

4. C

The average weight of all pipe sections is equal to the total weight of all the sections divided by the total number of sections. There are 27 synthetic sections, so if we use c to represent the number of copper sections, the total number of sections will be $27 + c$.

The total weight will be the weight of the synthetic sections plus the weight of the copper sections. The synthetic sections weigh 5 pounds each, so the total weight of these sections is $27 \times 5 = 135$. The copper sections weigh 9 pounds each, so their total weight is $9c$ pounds. Thus the combined total weight is $135 + 9c$.

Now we can set up an equation for the average weight and solve for c.

Average Weight $= \dfrac{\text{Total Weight}}{\text{Total Pipes}}$, so $6 = \dfrac{135 + 9c}{27 + c}$. To solve for c, start by cross-multiplying to get $6(27 + c)$ $= 135 + 9c$. At this point, we can multiply out the left side, but we can also divide everything by 3 to simplify the arithmetic. Doing so will give us $2(27 + c)$ $= 45 + 3c$, or $54 + 2c = 45 + 3c$. Subtracting 45 and $2c$ from both sides gives us $9 = c$, so (C) is correct.

5. D

We need to take the problem in two steps. First, we'll figure out how long it took car K to reach the opposite end, a distance of 210 miles. Then we will calculate how far car J traveled in that amount of time.

Since Distance = Speed × Time, Time $= \dfrac{\text{Distance}}{\text{Speed}}$.

Car K traveled 210 miles at an average speed of 35 miles per hour, so Time $= \dfrac{210 \text{ miles}}{35 \text{ mph}} = 6$ hours.

The average speed for car J was 6 miles per hour, so in 6 hours, the distance traveled is $30 \times 6 = 180$ miles, choice (D).

6. D

The 48 million in revenue from France represented 16% of total revenue, so if we let r be the total revenue, we have this equation: 48 million = 16%

of r. Since 16% is equivalent to 0.16, this becomes 48 million = 0.16r, or $\dfrac{48}{0.16}$ million = r.

Since 0.16 is equivalent to $\dfrac{16}{100}$, we can write $\dfrac{48}{0.16}$ as $\dfrac{48}{\left(\frac{16}{100}\right)}$. Dividing by a fraction is the same as multiplying by the reciprocal of the fraction, so the expression $\dfrac{48}{\left(\frac{16}{100}\right)}$ becomes $48 \times \dfrac{100}{16}$, or $3 \times 100 = 300$. Thus, $r = 300$ million. (D) is correct.

7. C

If the averages of two sets of three numbers are equal, then the sums of the two sets must also be equal. If x is the missing value from the second set of three numbers, we can say that $31 + 33 + 35 = 32 + 34 + x$, or $99 = 66 + x$. So, $x = 33$.

Here's another approach. In the first set, the average must be 33 because 31 and 35 are 2 less and 2 more than 33, respectively. The average of the second set can only be 33 if missing number is itself 33.

8. A

Let's start by calculating how many total ounces of liquid are added. The new size is 24 ounces and the old size was 16 ounces, so $24 - 16 = 8$ ounces are added. Thus, we can eliminate (C), (D), and (E), since they are all greater than 8.

Now we need to know how many ounces of the 8 additional ounces are pineapple juice. Since the ratio of orange juice to pineapple juice is 3:5, we know that 5 out of every 8 ounces are pineapple juice. We are adding a total of 8 ounces, so 5 ounces must be pineapple juice. Choice (A) is correct.

9. B

If we convert the two rates to number of copies per second, we can add the two rates together to get an overall rate at which the two copiers produce copies. We can then use this combined rate to determine the time required to produce 280 copies.

If Copier *A* produces 110 copies every 11 seconds, it can produce $\frac{110}{11}$ = 10 copies per second. Similarly, Copier *B* produces $\frac{100}{25}$ = 4 copies per second. Thus, running simultaneously, the two copiers produce 10 + 4 = 14 copies per second.

The total output of the two copiers together will be the product of their combined rate and the time. If we want to find the time needed to produce 280 copies, we have 280 copies = (14 copies per second) × Time. So, Time = $\frac{280 \text{ copies}}{14 \text{ copies per second}}$ = 20 seconds.

10. E

We need enough fencing to equal the two longer sides plus one of the shorter sides. We know that the longer sides are exactly twice the length of the shorter sides, so if we can find the length of the shorter sides, we'll have all the information we need.

If we use *x* to represent the length of the shorter sides, then 2*x* will be the length of the longer sides. Since the area of a rectangle is the product of the shorter and longer sides and we know that this rectangle has an area of 800 square feet, we can say that 800 = (*x*)(2*x*), or 800 = 2*x*². We can solve this equation for *x* as follows.

First, divide both sides by 2 to get 400 = *x*². Taking the square root of both sides gives us $\sqrt{400}$ = *x*. Since 20 × 20 = 400, $\sqrt{400}$ = 20. Therefore, *x* = 20 (we can ignore the possibility of *x* = –20, since we are dealing with lengths which must be positive).

So, if the shorter sides are 20 feet, the longer sides are 40. For two longer sides and one shorter side, we will need (2)(40) + 20 = 100 feet of fencing. Choice (E) is correct.

11. C

Since this is a "which of the following question," let's begin with choice (E).

(E): The line with the equation *y* = *x* goes through the points (0, 0) and (1, 1). Side *OA* also passes through these same points. So the line with the equation *y* = *x* contains all the points of side *OA*. Eliminate choice (E).

(D): The line with the equation *y* = 1 goes through the points (1, 1) and (2, 1). Side *AB* also passes through these same points. So the line with the equation *y* = 1 contains all the points of side *AB*. Eliminate choice (D).

(C): The line with the equation *x* = 1 is parallel to the *y*-axis. This line actually crosses side *OC* perpendicular to side *OC*. This line will contain point *A* whose coordinates are (1, 1). However, since this line is parallel to the *y*-axis and all the points on this line have an *x*-coordinate of 1, the line with the equation *x* = 1 will not contain all the points of any side of quadrilateral *OABC*. Choice (C) is correct.

12. E

We are given an equation with two variables, *x* (number of cars sold) and *y* (price of each car). The question provides us with the price of each car, $15,000, which we can substitute for the variable *y*.

So the equation becomes *x* = 800,000 – 50(15,000), or *x* = 800,000 – 750,000 = 50,000. So *x* equals 50,000 cars sold. This number appears as choice (A), which is a trap answer. We need the weekly revenue, not the number of cars sold.

To find the weekly revenue, we multiply the number of cars by the price per car: (50,000 cars)($15,000/car) = $750,000,000. Therefore (E) is correct.

13. E

For Roman Numeral questions, start by testing the statement that shows up in the most answer choices. Here, statement II appears three times. If we find that statement II must be true, we'll know that the answer must be (B), (C) or (E). If statement II does not have to be true, the answer must be (A) or (D).

Let's pick numbers for x, y and z to help us test statement II. The values $x = 3$, $y = 6$ and $z = 9$ will work; they are all positive integers, they are consecutive multiples of 3 and $x < y < z$. So, using these values, is xy an even integer? Yes, $(3)(6) = 18$, which is even. In fact, xy will always be even. If x is even, the product xy must be even, since anything multiplied by an even number will be even. If x is odd, $x + 3 = y$ must be even, since odd + odd = even, and thus xy will again be even. So we know that II must be true and we can eliminate (A) and (D).

Now let's test statement I, since it's in 2 of the remaining 3 choices. Using the same chosen values, $z - x = 9 - 3 = 6$, so statement I appears to be true. In fact, since all the numbers are consecutive multiples of 3, z must always be 6 greater than x. Thus, $z - x$ will always be 6, which is even, so statement I must be true. Now we can eliminate (B) since it does not include statement I.

Finally, test III. If it must be true, (E) will be correct.

If not, (C) will be correct. Again using our chosen values, $\frac{x + y + z}{3} = \frac{3 + 6 + 9}{3} = 1 + 2 + 3 = 6$, which

is an integer. Since all three numbers are multiples

of 3, they all give integers when divided by 3 and the

sum of 3 integers must be an integer. So statement

III must also be true; (E) is correct.

14. B

We are looking for the number of multiples of 5 between 50 and 200, exclusive of 50 and 200 themselves. The first such multiple is 55 and the largest is 195. Thus, we can also think of this as finding the number of multiples of 5 between 55 and 195 inclusive.

The easiest way to figure out the number of multiples in a sequence such as this is to factor the endpoints. In this case, $55 = 5 \times 11$ and $195 = 5 \times 39$. Now we just need to know how many integers there are between 11 and 39 inclusive, since each

such integer, when multiplied by 5, represents one multiple of 5 between 55 and 195 inclusive. The number of integers between 11 and 39 inclusive is $39 - 11 + 1 = 29$. We need to add in the 1 to make sure we are counting the number 11 itself. If we didn't add back the 1, we would be counting only numbers larger than 11. Consider a simpler example: How many integers are there between 2 and 5 inclusive? There are 4 (2, 3, 4, and 5), which is $5 - 2 + 1 = 4$.

So, there are 29 integers between 11 and 39 inclusive. Each integer represents a multiple of 5, so there are 29 multiples of 5 between 55 and 195 inclusive.

15. C

Since we know that any number, when squared, results in a positive value, x^2 must be positive. Thus, we can divide both sides of $x^2 < x^3$ by x^2 without reversing the sign of the inequality. Doing so will give us $1 < x$, which is equivalent to the expression $x > 1$ in choice (C). Therefore (C) is correct.

We could also have tested the choices to find the one that must be true. We'll pick numbers if necessary.

(E): $x < 1$: Let's try $x = -1$, giving us $x^2 = (-1)^2 = 1$ and $x^3 = (-1)^3 = -1$. In this case, $x^2 < x^3$ is not true, so $x < 1$ does not have to be true. Eliminate (E).

(D): $x = 1$: If this is true, $x^2 = (1)^2 = 1$ and $x^3 = (1)^3 = 1$. Again, $x^2 < x^3$ is not true, so $x = 1$ cannot be true. Eliminate (D).

(C): $x > 1$. Let's try $x = 2$, which gives us $x^2 = (2)^2 = 4$ and $x^3 = (2)^3 = 8$. So, $x^2 < x^3$ is true if $x = 2$, and it will still be true for any larger values of x. Thus, (C) must be true; it is the correct choice.

Looking at the other answers:

(B): $x < 0$: If $x = -1$, $x^2 = (-1)^2 = 1$ and $x^3 = (-1)^3 = -1$. Thus, $x^2 < x^3$ would not be true, so $x < 0$ cannot be true. Eliminate (B).

(A): $x = 0$: If true, then $x^2 = (0)^2 = 0$ and $x^3 = (0)^3 = 0$ and $x^2 < x^3$ is not true, so we can also eliminate (A).

16. C

This problem gives us an equation with a fraction, but none of the choices have fractions, so let's rearrange the equation to get rid of the fraction. We can do this by multiplying both sides by x to get $y + z = x$. Now we can test the choices, starting with (E). If we solve our original equation for z, by subtracting y from both sides, we get $z = x - y$. That is not equivalent to (E), so (E) is not necessarily true.

To test (D), let's solve our original equation for y by subtracting z from both sides to get $y = x - z$. That does not match (D), so let's move on to (C).

When we tested (D), we solved the original equation for y, and we saw that $y = x - z$. That matches the equation given in (C), making it the correct choice.

Picking numbers is also a good option here. Since $y + z = x$, if $y = 2$ and $z = 3$, $x = 5$. Using these values in choice (E), we get $3 = 5 + 2$, which is not true, so we eliminate (E). In choice (D), we get $2 = 5 + 3$, which is also not true. In choice (C), we have $2 = 5 - 3$, which is true, so (C) is correct.

17. E

For Roman Numeral questions, start with the statement that shows up in the most choices. Here, that's statement II.

By definition, two numbers are reciprocals of each other only if their product is 1. So, we'll test the statements by multiplying the numbers together. For statement II, that gives us $(\sqrt{2})\left(\dfrac{\sqrt{2}}{2}\right) = \dfrac{(\sqrt{2})(\sqrt{2})}{2}$ $= \dfrac{2}{2} = 1$, so the numbers in statement II are reciprocals. We can eliminate choices (A) and (D) because they don't include statement II.

In the remaining choices, statement I and statement III both appear once, so start with statement I. Multiplying the numbers gives us $\left(\dfrac{1}{2}\right)\left(\dfrac{-1}{2}\right) = -\dfrac{1}{4}$, which is not 1. Thus, the numbers in

statement I are not reciprocals, so the correct choice cannot include statement I. Eliminate (C).

Testing statement III, we have $(2)\left(\dfrac{1}{2}\right) = \dfrac{2}{2} = 1$, so the numbers are reciprocals. Thus (E) must be correct. The pairs in statements II and III are reciprocals of each other, but the pair in statement I is not.

18. B

A good way to deal with an expression such as $\sqrt{0.000063}$ is to rewrite it as an equivalent expression than doesn't include the decimal. In this case, $0.000063 = \dfrac{63}{1,000,000}$, so we can write the radical as $\sqrt{\dfrac{63}{1,000,000}}$, or $\dfrac{\sqrt{63}}{\sqrt{1,000,000}}$. The numerator is approximately equal to $\sqrt{64}$. The square root of 64 is 8, so $\sqrt{63} \approx 8$. In the denominator, the square root of 1,000,000 is 1,000 (because $1,000,000 = 10^6$ and $\sqrt{10^6} = \sqrt{(10^3)(10^3)} = 10^3 = 1,000$).

So, $\sqrt{0.000063} = \dfrac{\sqrt{63}}{\sqrt{1,000,000}} \approx \dfrac{8}{1,000} = 0.008$.

Choice (B) is correct.

19. E

First, translate the question piece by piece into an equation. Let's call the smaller integer x. Then the larger integer is 5 times the smaller integer, so the larger integer is $5x$.

We are also told that the average of the two integers is 18. Since $\frac{\text{Sum of the Terms}}{\text{Number of Terms}}$ = Average, we can say that $\frac{x + 5x}{2} = 18$. Cross-multiplying, we find that $x + 5x = 36$, or $6x = 36$. Dividing both sides by 6, we see that $x = 6$.

However, this is the value of the smaller integer, and the question asked for the larger integer, which is $5x = (5)(6) = 30$. So (E) is correct. Notice that 6 appears as trap answer (A).

20. C

We're told that st must be greater than 1, so the choice that *cannot* be true will be the choice that limits the possible values of s and t in such a way that st cannot be greater than 1. So, we can test any choice by picking numbers for s and t. If we can find values such that st is greater than 1, we can eliminate that choice. Since this is a "which of the following" question, start with choice (E).

For choice (E), if $t = \frac{1}{2}$ and $s = 4$, $st = (4)\frac{1}{2} = 2 > 1$. (E) is not the answer.

In (D), both s and t are negative, so their product will be positive, and both are greater than one in absolute value, their product will be greater than 1. For example, if $t = -3$, and $s = -2$, $st = (-2)(-3) = 6$. Eliminate (D).

In (C), s must be negative and t must be positive. Thus, their product must be negative, so st cannot be greater than 1. Therefore (C) cannot be true; this is the correct choice.

21. C

Be careful and systematic when working through a question like this. First, determine how much the family would pay prior to the 25% discount and then apply the discount. The family has one child aged 2 years or less, who will eat free, and two children over 2 but under 5, who will eat for $2. The parents and the other 2 children are over 5 and will eat for $8.

So before the 25% discount, the cost for dinner will be $(1 \times \$0) + (2 \times \$2) + (4 \times \$8) = \$4 + \$32 = \$36$. Notice that this is a trap answer, choice (E).

Now let's apply the 25% discount. 25% of $36 is $(0.25)(\$36)$, or $9. So, the cost after the discount is $\$36 - \$9 = \$27$. (C) is correct.

22. A

This is a typical quadratic equation. To find the solution(s) to a quadratic, put it into standard form (i.e. set it equal to zero) and factor the other side. Keep in mind that in many cases, there will be two solutions to a quadratic equation.

In this case, we subtract 20 from both sides to get $10x^2 + 10x - 20 = 0$. Then:

Factor out a 10:	$10(x^2 + x - 2) = 0$
Use reverse FOIL:	$10(x + 2)(x - 1) = 0$
Set the factors equal to 0:	$x + 2 = 0$ or $x - 1 = 0$
Determine the solutions:	$x = -2$ or $x = 1$

The two solutions are 1 and –2. Only –2 appears in the choices, so (A) is correct.

23. B

We can solve this by setting up an algebraic equation, but there's a quicker way. Think about what a series of 6 consecutive even integers would look like. Each number would be greater than the previous number by 2, so the last number must be larger than the first number by 10. Regardless of the actual numbers or their average, the difference between the greatest and least will be 10.

Here is the algebraic solution. If n is the smallest term, the second is $n + 2$, the next is $n + 4$ and so on. Using the average formula, we know that the sum of the terms = average times the number of terms:

$n + (n + 2) + (n + 4) + (n + 6) + (n + 8) + (n + 10)$
$= (37)(6)$

$6n + 30 = (37)(6)$

$\frac{6n + 30}{6} = 37$

$n + 5 = 37$

$n = 32$, which is trap answer (D)

$n + 10 = 32 + 10 = 42$, or trap answer (E).

We want to find the difference between these terms, so $42 - 32 = 10$, choice (B).

24. D

First note that the sides of the rectangle are also the sides of a right triangle where one side is 9 and the hypotenuse is 15. Since 9 is 3×3 and 15 is 3×5, this 9:15 ratio indicates that the sides of the triangle have the ratio 3:4:5. Thus, the missing side must be $3 \times 4 = 12$.

Now we know that our rectangle has a length of 12 and a width of 9, so the perimeter is $9 + 9 + 12 + 12 = 42$. Choice (D) is correct.

25. B

We're given two equations and two variables, and we want to solve for y. We're told that $z = 9$, so we can replace z with 9 in the first equation, then simplify and solve.

$7y + 3(9) = 30 + 12y - 2(9)$

$7y + 27 = 30 + 12y - 18$

$7y + 27 = 12y + 12$

Subtract 12 from each side and subtract $7y$ from each side. We're left with $15 = 5y$, or $y = 3$. (B) is correct.

26. E

Adding or subtracting fractions requires a common denominator. In this case, 24 is the least common multiple of 6 and 8, so it is the common denominator:

$$\frac{6}{8} + \frac{4}{6} = \frac{6(3)}{9(3)} + \frac{4(4)}{6(4)} = \frac{18}{24} + \frac{16}{24} = \frac{34}{24} = \frac{17}{12}$$

If we had simply added the numerators and denominators without finding a common denominator, we would have arrived at trap answer (C).

If we had tried to cancel out terms in the two fractions—which is permissible when multiplying fractions but not when adding them—we might have arrived at trap answer (A) or (B). Choice (E) is correct.

27. B

We need to find a value for $\frac{z}{2}$, so the most direct approach is to set up an equation for the amount the plumber charges and solve it for z. The amount she charged, \$270, must be equal to the flat fee of z plus $\frac{z}{2}$ for each half-hour she worked plus $\frac{2z}{3}$ for the supplies for each fitting.

She worked 1.5 hours, which is equivalent to 3 half-hours, so she charged $3 \times \frac{z}{2} = \frac{3z}{2}$ dollars for the time she spent at the house. She replaced 3 fittings, so the cost for the supplies was $3 \times \frac{2z}{3} = 2z$.

Combining everything into one equation, we have $z + \frac{3z}{2} + 2z = 270$.

Let's start by multiplying everything by 2, to eliminate the fraction. This gives us $2z + 3z + 4z = 540$, or $9z = 540$, Dividing both sides by 9, we have $z = 60$.

We need the rate *per half hour* which is $\frac{z}{2} = \frac{60}{2} = 30$. (B) is correct.

Since there are numbers in the answer choices, we can also backsolve here. The choices give us possible values for $\frac{z}{2}$; we need to find the one that makes the total cost \$270. Starting with choice (C), if $\frac{z}{2}$ is \$40, then z is \$80. The total cost will be $80 + (3)(40) + 3\left(\frac{(2)(80)}{3}\right)$, or $80 + 120 + 160$, which is 360. That's too large, so let's try (B).

If $\frac{z}{2}$ is \$30, then z is \$60. The total cost will be $60 + (3)(30) + 3\left(\frac{(2)(60)}{3}\right)$, or $60 + 90 + 120$, which is 270. Thus (B) is correct.

28. C

We want the amount received from the sale of the tables, $250y$, to be at least equal to the cost of manufacturing them, $25{,}000 + 125y$. In other words, we want $250y \geq 25{,}000 + 125y$. Subtracting $125y$ from both sides gives $125y \geq 25{,}000$, or $y \geq \dfrac{25{,}000}{125}$. Since $125 \times 100 = 12{,}500$ and $12{,}500 \times 2 = 25{,}000$, $125 \times 200 = 25{,}000$.

Thus $y \geq 200$. So the smallest possible value for y is 200, and (C) is correct.

29. D

Because we have two variables and one equation, we can't solve for the actual values of r and s. But we need only their ratio, so let's try to solve the equation for $\dfrac{r}{s}$.

Let's first try to get rid of the fractions. Multiply both sides of the equation by $(s - r)$. We're left with $r(s - r) + r(s + r) = 2s(s - r) + 2s(s + r)$.

When we multiply out all the terms, we get $rs - r^2 + rs + r^2 = 2s^2 - 2rs + 2s^2 + 2rs$.

Combining like-terms, we have $2rs = 4s^2$. We want the ratio of r to s, so we divide by $2s^2$ to get $\dfrac{2rs}{2s^2} = \dfrac{4s^2}{2s^2}$, or $\dfrac{r}{s} = 2$. Choice (D) is correct.

30. B

We're told that $4y$ times an unknown number is $12yz + 4y^2$. We can write this as $4y(\quad) = 12yz + 4y^2$, where the blank space represents the unknown number. How do we know what goes in the blank space? If we factor $4y$ out of $12yz + 4y^2$, we'll have $4y$ times *something* on both sides of the equation.

$4y(3z + y) = 12yz + 4y^2$. So, $12yz + 4y^2$ is the product of $4y$ and $(3z + y)$.

We need the difference between two numbers, and we know that $4y$ is the larger number. So the difference we need is $4y - (3z + y) = 4y - 3z - y = 3y - 3z = 3(y - z)$. This is choice (B).

Another approach is to let some other variable such as x represent the unknown number. This gives us $4y(x) = 12yz + 4y^2$. Now just divide both sides by $4y$ to find that $x = 3z + y$. The difference we need is $4y - x$, or $4y - (3z + y)$, which is $3y - 3z$, or $3(y - z)$.

31. A

First, the worker earns the basic rate of w dollars per hour for 10 hours, so that's a total of $10w$ before bonus. So the answer must include $10w$, and we can eliminate (C) and (E).

Now let's consider the bonus. From 8 AM to noon, a span of 4 hours, there are 60 children and 10 workers, or 6 children per worker. The bonus is B dollars per child watched per hour, so from 8 AM to noon the bonus is (6 children)(4 hours)(B per child per hour) = $24B$.

From noon to 6 PM, a span of 6 hours, there are 60 children and 12 workers, or 5 per child. Thus the bonus is (5 children)(6 hours)(B) = $30B$.

Adding everything together, her total for the day is $10w + 24B + 30B = 10w + 54B$. Choice (A) is correct.

32. A

We can approach this by applying the odd/even rules, or by picking numbers, which will always work on number properties problems. Let's try picking numbers. Both variables must be positive and odd, so we let's use the smallest possible numbers: $s = 3$ and $t = 1$. We'll use the smaller number for t since it is the exponent in the statements. The smaller t is, the easier the calculations will be.

All of the statements appear in three choices, so we can start with whichever one looks simplest. That is statement I.

Statement I must be odd. With $s = 3$ and $t = 1$, $s^t = 3^1 = 3$, which is odd. In fact, if s is odd, then for any positive integer value of t, s^t will be odd, since it will simply be the product of 1 or more odd numbers, and (odd × odd) is always odd. Since I must be odd, it must appear in the correct choice. Eliminate (B) and (D).

Statement II: $(s + 1)^{(t + 1)} = (3 + 1)^{(1 + 1)} = 4^2 = 16$, which is even, so statement II cannot be odd, and we can eliminate any remaining choice containing II. Eliminate (E).

Statement III: $(s + t)^t = (1+3)^3 = 4^3 = 64$, which is even. So, III is also not in the correct choice. We eliminate (D), leaving (A) as the answer.

33. E

The reciprocal of a fraction is found by switching the numerator and denominator. To find the reciprocal of the expression given in this question, we first need to combine the 2 fractions into 1 by finding a common denominator and then adding the fractions. The common denominator of x and y is xy, so we will multiply $\frac{1}{x}$ by $\frac{y}{y}$ and multiply $\frac{x}{y}$ by $\frac{x}{x}$. The result will be the following:

$$\frac{1}{x} - \frac{x}{y} = \left(\frac{1}{x}\right)\left(\frac{y}{y}\right) - \left(\frac{x}{y}\right)\left(\frac{x}{x}\right) = \frac{y}{xy} - \frac{x^2}{xy} = \frac{y - x^2}{xy}.$$

Now just switch the numerator and denominator to find the reciprocal: $\frac{xy}{y - x^2}$. Choice (E) is correct.

.34. E

If the sum of two distinct integers is zero, one must be positive and the other must be negative. So the product of the two numbers must be negative. Only choice (E) is negative, so it must be correct.

Alternatively, we can pick numbers. 1 and –1 gives a sum of zero and a product of –1; 2 and –2 yields a product of –4; 3 and –3 gives a product of –9. The pattern of the negative products becomes evident, pointing to choice (E) as correct.

Note that (D) cannot be correct because the 2 integers must be distinct. If one of the integers is zero, their product would be zero, but their sum could not be zero.

35. A

Since x is positive, $-x$ must be negative. So, the condition "$y - x$ is between $-x$ and -1" tells us that $y - x$ is between two negative numbers ($-x$ and -1) and thus $y - x$ must itself be negative. If both numbers are positive and $y - x$ is negative, y must be less than x. For example, if $x = 2$ and $y = 1$, $y - x = 1 - 2 = -1$. But if $x = 2$ and $y = 3$, $y - x = 3 - 2 = 1$, which is positive. So choice (A) is correct.

CHAPTER TEN
Data Sufficiency

Choose answer choice:

A. if statement (1) BY ITSELF is sufficient to answer the question, but statement (2) by itself is not;

B. if statement (2) BY ITSELF is sufficient to answer the question, but statement (1) by itself is not;

C. if statements (1) and (2) TAKEN TOGETHER are sufficient to answer the question, even though NEITHER statement BY ITSELF is sufficient;

D. if EITHER statement BY ITSELF is sufficient to answer the question;

E. if statements (1) and (2) TAKEN TOGETHER are NOT sufficient to answer the question, requiring more data pertaining to the problem.

---

1. In triangle *ABC*, side *AB* has length 7. Is the perimeter of triangle *ABC* less than 14?

    (1) Side *BC* has length 6.
    (2) The shortest side of the triangle has length 5.

    (A)
    (B)
    (C)
    (D)
    (E)

2. What is the value of *w* ?

    (1) $\dfrac{w^3}{27} = 1$

    (2) $\dfrac{1}{w^2} = \dfrac{1}{9}$

    (A)
    (B)
    (C)
    (D)
    (E)

3. If *y* is a positive integer, is 3*y* odd?

    (1) *y* + 319 is even.
    (2) *y* cannot be evenly divided by any odd number other than 1.

    (A)
    (B)
    (C)
    (D)
    (E)

4. Is $1 \leq d$?

    (1) $d^3 \geq 1$
    (2) $de > 1$ when $e > 0$

    (A)
    (B)
    (C)
    (D)
    (E)

Choose answer choice:

A. if statement (1) BY ITSELF is sufficient to answer the question, but statement (2) by itself is not;

B. if statement (2) BY ITSELF is sufficient to answer the question, but statement (1) by itself is not;

C. if statements (1) and (2) TAKEN TOGETHER are sufficient to answer the question, even though NEITHER statement BY ITSELF is sufficient;

D. if EITHER statement BY ITSELF is sufficient to answer the question;

E. if statements (1) and (2) TAKEN TOGETHER are NOT sufficient to answer the question, requiring more data pertaining to the problem.

5. What is the value of the prime number p ?

(1) $20 \leq p \leq 30$

(2) $p - 21$ is an even integer.

(A)

(B)

(C)

(D)

(E)

6. Is the positive integer x prime?

(1) x is an odd integer less than 24.

(2) $\sqrt{x} \neq 3$

(A)

(B)

(C)

(D)

(E)

7. If the integer x is positive, is $x > 17$?

(1) When x is divided by 4 or 5, the remainder is 3.

(2) x is evenly divisible by 21.

(A)

(B)

(C)

(D)

(E)

8. If y is an integer, is y odd?

(1) $4y$ is an even integer.

(2) $3y$ is an odd integer.

(A)

(B)

(C)

(D)

(E)

Choose answer choice:

A. if statement (1) BY ITSELF is sufficient to answer the question, but statement (2) by itself is not;

B. if statement (2) BY ITSELF is sufficient to answer the question, but statement (1) by itself is not;

C. if statements (1) and (2) TAKEN TOGETHER are sufficient to answer the question, even though NEITHER statement BY ITSELF is sufficient;

D. if EITHER statement BY ITSELF is sufficient to answer the question;

E. if statements (1) and (2) TAKEN TOGETHER are NOT sufficient to answer the question, requiring more data pertaining to the problem.

---

9. What is the value of b ?

(1) $b^4 = 16$

(2) $7^{3b-4} = 49$

(A)

(B)

(C)

(D)

(E)

10. What is the value of j ?

(1) $j = -|j|$

(2) $2j^2 = 18$

(A)

(B)

(C)

(D)

(E)

11. At Sammy's cookout, every guest ate at least one hamburger, some ate two hamburgers, and none ate more than two. How many guests ate only one hamburger?

(1) A total of 90 hamburgers were eaten.

(2) 25 percent of the guests ate 2 hamburgers.

(A)

(B)

(C)

(D)

(E)

12. Mary sells industrial equipment. For her commission, she received 5 percent of the selling price of a certain piece of equipment. How much was her commission?

(1) If the selling price had been 10 percent higher, her commission would have been $16,500.

(2) The selling price was 20 times Mary's commission.

(A)

(B)

(C)

(D)

(E)

Choose answer choice:

A. if statement (1) BY ITSELF is sufficient to answer the question, but statement (2) by itself is not;

B. if statement (2) BY ITSELF is sufficient to answer the question, but statement (1) by itself is not;

C. if statements (1) and (2) TAKEN TOGETHER are sufficient to answer the question, even though NEITHER statement BY ITSELF is sufficient;

D. if EITHER statement BY ITSELF is sufficient to answer the question;

E. if statements (1) and (2) TAKEN TOGETHER are NOT sufficient to answer the question, requiring more data pertaining to the problem.

---

13. In a certain triangle, the degree measures of the three angles are a, b, and c. What is the value of c?

(1) $a + c = 100$

(2) $b + c = 120$

(A)

(B)

(C)

(D)

(E)

14. Does company X own 64 trucks?

(1) If the company does not buy any new trucks and 10 of the existing trucks are sold, the company will own fewer than 55 trucks.

(2) If the company buys 20 new trucks and does not sell any of the existing trucks, it will own no less than 83 trucks.

(A)

(B)

(C)

(D)

(E)

15. Is $3(x - y) + z$ less than $-z + 3x + y$?

(1) $x = 5$

(2) $z = 2y$

(A)

(B)

(C)

(D)

(E)

16. A certain company decreased the price of its two most popular products, Product A and Product B. In dollars, which product received the smaller decrease in price?

(1) The price of Product A was reduced by 20 percent.

(2) The price of Product B was reduced by 40 percent.

(A)

(B)

(C)

(D)

(E)

Choose answer choice:

A. if statement (1) BY ITSELF is sufficient to answer the question, but statement (2) by itself is not;
B. if statement (2) BY ITSELF is sufficient to answer the question, but statement (1) by itself is not;
C. if statements (1) and (2) TAKEN TOGETHER are sufficient to answer the question, even though NEITHER statement BY ITSELF is sufficient;
D. if EITHER statement BY ITSELF is sufficient to answer the question;
E. if statements (1) and (2) TAKEN TOGETHER are NOT sufficient to answer the question, requiring more data pertaining to the problem.

---

17. In a certain rectangle, the lengths of the sides are the integers x and y. What is the area of the rectangle?

    (1) If the longer side were 1 unit shorter, the rectangle would be a square.
    (2) $x + y = 49$

    (A)
    (B)
    (C)
    (D)
    (E)

18. If set N consists of the elements $\{t, r, u, s, v\}$, is the range of the numbers in set N less than 8?

    (1) s is the greatest number in the set.
    (2) $t - r > 8$

    (A)
    (B)
    (C)
    (D)
    (E)

19. If set $X = \{a, 30, -2, 40\}$, what is the median of set X?

    (1) $a > 30$
    (2) $a > 40$

    (A)
    (B)
    (C)
    (D)
    (E)

20. Anne must randomly select one ball from a bag. What is the probability that the ball she selects will be green?

    (1) If the number of green balls were increased by 400 percent without changing the number of other balls, the probability of choosing a green ball would be $\frac{5}{11}$.

    (2) The ratio of the number of green balls to the total number of balls in the bag is 1:7.

    (A)
    (B)
    (C)
    (D)
    (E)

Choose answer choice:

A. if statement (1) BY ITSELF is sufficient to answer the question, but statement (2) by itself is not;

B. if statement (2) BY ITSELF is sufficient to answer the question, but statement (1) by itself is not;

C. if statements (1) and (2) TAKEN TOGETHER are sufficient to answer the question, even though NEITHER statement BY ITSELF is sufficient;

D. if EITHER statement BY ITSELF is sufficient to answer the question;

E. if statements (1) and (2) TAKEN TOGETHER are NOT sufficient to answer the question, requiring more data pertaining to the problem.

---

21. During a certain sale at a tire store, each of the customers bought either a two-tire set or a four-tire set. How many customers bought tires during the sale?

    (1) 25 percent of the customers bought 4 tires.
    (2) 200 total tires were sold.

    (A)
    (B)
    (C)
    (D)
    (E)

22. Carla ran in her town's 5-kilometer road race last year and this year. By what percentage did the time in which she completed the run decrease from last year to this year?

    (1) Last year, Carla ran the 5-kilometer race in 15 minutes.
    (2) This year, Carla ran the race in 2 minutes less than she did last year.

    (A)
    (B)
    (C)
    (D)
    (E)

23. A window shade is pulled part of the way down a window. How many square feet of the window does the shade cover?

    (1) The window shade covers half of the window's area.
    (2) The window is 3 feet wide.

    (A)
    (B)
    (C)
    (D)
    (E)

24. Is it true that $m > n$?

    (1) $m - n > m - 1$
    (2) $m - n > 0$

    (A)
    (B)
    (C)
    (D)
    (E)

Choose answer choice:

A. if statement (1) BY ITSELF is sufficient to answer the question, but statement (2) by itself is not;

B. if statement (2) BY ITSELF is sufficient to answer the question, but statement (1) by itself is not;

C. if statements (1) and (2) TAKEN TOGETHER are sufficient to answer the question, even though NEITHER statement BY ITSELF is sufficient;

D. if EITHER statement BY ITSELF is sufficient to answer the question;

E. if statements (1) and (2) TAKEN TOGETHER are NOT sufficient to answer the question, requiring more data pertaining to the problem.

---

25. Andrea makes hot chocolate mix by combining only dry milk powder and cocoa powder. What is the ratio of cocoa powder to dry milk powder in the mix?

    (1) Andrea uses 3 times as much milk as cocoa.

    (2) 48 ounces of the hot chocolate mix contains 12 ounces of cocoa powder.

    (A)
    (B)
    (C)
    (D)
    (E)

26. In what year was Jordan born?

    (1) Jordan's 16th birthday was in 1996.

    (2) Jordan's brother Bill, who was born in 1979, is $1\frac{1}{2}$ years older than Jordan.

    (A)
    (B)
    (C)
    (D)
    (E)

27. Of the 30 books purchased by the Smith family last year, how many were read by Jane Smith?

    (1) Jane Smith has read 70% of the books owned by the Smith family.

    (2) The Smith family owns 400 books.

    (A)
    (B)
    (C)
    (D)
    (E)

28. If x is an integer, and $100 < x < 150$, what is the value of x?

    (1) The sum of the hundreds digit of x and the tens digit of x is less than the units digit of x.

    (2) The units digit of x is 4, and x is not evenly divisible by 4.

    (A)
    (B)
    (C)
    (D)
    (E)

Choose answer choice:

A. if statement (1) BY ITSELF is sufficient to answer the question, but statement (2) by itself is not;

B. if statement (2) BY ITSELF is sufficient to answer the question, but statement (1) by itself is not;

C. if statements (1) and (2) TAKEN TOGETHER are sufficient to answer the question, even though NEITHER statement BY ITSELF is sufficient;

D. if EITHER statement BY ITSELF is sufficient to answer the question;

E. if statements (1) and (2) TAKEN TOGETHER are NOT sufficient to answer the question, requiring more data pertaining to the problem.

29. On Monday, one share of stock in Company X sold for a certain amount of money. On Tuesday, that price increased. How much profit could have been made by selling 500 shares of Company X stock on Tuesday instead of Monday?

   (1) On Monday the stock sold for $56.50 per share.

   (2) On Tuesday the stock sold for $58.00 per share.

   (A)
   (B)
   (C)
   (D)
   (E)

30. What is the value of $x + y$?

   (1) $x = y - 4$
   (2) $(x + y)^2 = 64$

   (A)
   (B)
   (C)
   (D)
   (E)

31. In triangle XYZ, the lengths of the three sides are x, y and z. In this triangle, does $x^2 + y^2 = z^2$?

   (1) The angle across from side X is equal to the angle across from side Y.

   (2) The angle across from side X is one-fourth of the triangle's total angle measure.

   (A)
   (B)
   (C)
   (D)
   (E)

32. Is the perimeter of triangle T equal to the perimeter of rectangle R?

   (1) The ratio of the perimeter of T to the sum of the lengths of any two adjacent sides of R is 2:1.

   (2) The perimeter of R is 24.

   (A)
   (B)
   (C)
   (D)
   (E)

Choose answer choice:

A. if statement (1) BY ITSELF is sufficient to answer the question, but statement (2) by itself is not;

B. if statement (2) BY ITSELF is sufficient to answer the question, but statement (1) by itself is not;

C. if statements (1) and (2) TAKEN TOGETHER are sufficient to answer the question, even though NEITHER statement BY ITSELF is sufficient;

D. if EITHER statement BY ITSELF is sufficient to answer the question;

E. if statements (1) and (2) TAKEN TOGETHER are NOT sufficient to answer the question, requiring more data pertaining to the problem.

33. Set S contains the elements $\{x,y,z\}$, $x < y < z$, and the arithmetic mean of S is 12. What is the median of set S?

    (1) x is ten less than z, which is eight greater than y.
    (2) $2x + 2 = z$

    (A)
    (B)
    (C)
    (D)
    (E)

34. Is $-9 < t < 4$?

    (1) $0 < t < 5$
    (2) $-6 < t < 1$

    (A)
    (B)
    (C)
    (D)
    (E)

35. If $50 \leq r \leq 60$, what is the value of r?

    (1) There is a remainder of 2 when r is divided by 7.
    (2) There is a remainder of 28 when r is divided by 30.

    (A)
    (B)
    (C)
    (D)
    (E)

ANSWER KEY: DATA SUFFICIENCY

1. D	13. C	25. D
2. A	14. E	26. A
3. D	15. B	27. E
4. A	16. E	28. C
5. E	17. C	29. C
6. E	18. B	30. E
7. D	19. B	31. C
8. B	20. D	32. A
9. B	21. C.	33. A
10. C	22. C.	34. B
11. C	23. E	35. B
12. A	24. B	

1. D

Since this is a yes–no question, we don't need the exact perimeter of the triangle; we just need to know whether it is or is not less than 14. The perimeter is the sum of the side lengths, so we need information about the other sides of the triangle.

Statement (1): If side *AB* is 7 and side *BC* is 6, then by the triangle inequality theorem, the third side must be greater than 7 – 6 = 1. The sum of *AB* and *BC* is 13, and the third side is greater than 1, so the sum of the three sides must be greater than 13 + 1 = 14. Therefore, the answer to the questions is "no." The perimeter cannot be **less** than 14. Statement (1) is sufficient; eliminate (B), (C) and (E).

Statement (2): We know that two sides of the triangle add up to 7 + 5 = 12. The remaining side must be greater than 5, since the shortest side is 5. Thus, the perimeter must be more than 12 + 5 = 17, which is greater than 14. So Statement (2) is also sufficient. Choice (D) is correct.

2. A

Other than telling us that this is a value question, the stem doesn't give us much to work with, so let's go directly to the statements.

Statement (1) is sufficient. We can isolate w^3 by multiplying both sides by 27. This gives us $w^3 = 27$. Since $3 \times 3 \times 3 = 27$, $w = 3$. Because the *w* is raised to an odd exponent, we know that *w* cannot be –3. Eliminate (B), (C), and (E).

Statement (2) seems similar, but be careful—this exponent is even, so that might make a difference. To solve for w^2, cross-multiply to get $w^2 = 9$. In this case, *w* could be either 3 or –3, so we there is more than one possible value for *w*. Thus (2) is not sufficient. Eliminate (D). The correct choice is (A).

3. D

This is a yes–no question. So we'll need to show that either 3*y* is always odd OR never odd in order to have sufficiency. Before going on to the statements, let's see what else we can get from the stem.

Notice that we are multiplying *y* by 3, which is an odd number. Therefore, if *y* is an even integer, 3*y* must be even, since the product of any integer and an even must be even (for example, $3 \times 4 = 12$). If *y* is odd, 3*y* will be odd, since odd × odd = odd (for example, $3 \times 7 = 21$).

Statement (1): Since 319 is odd, *y* must also be odd, because their sum is even and odd + odd = even but odd + even = odd. We can pick numbers if necessary to confirm this. If *y* = 3, 319 + *y* = 319 + 3 = 322, which is even, but if *y* = 4, 319 + *y* = 323, which is odd. So, *y* must be even and therefore 3*y* cannot be odd. Statement (1) is sufficient.

Statement (2): If *y* can't be divided by any odd number other than 1, *y* must be the product of only even numbers, and therefore *y* must be even. Thus, 3*y* cannot be odd, and Statement (2) is also sufficient. Since both statements are sufficient, the answer is (D).

4. A

In order for $1 \le d$ to be false, *d* would have to be negative, zero, or a fraction between zero and 1. We may need to test all these cases when evaluating the statements.

Statement (1): sufficient. If $d^3 \geq 1$, then d cannot be negative, since a negative number raised to an odd exponent would be negative. We also know that d cannot be 0, since 0 raised to any nonzero exponent is 0. Additionally, d cannot be a positive fraction less than one, since any such fraction cubed would also result in a positive fraction less than one. Thus, d must be greater than or equal to 1. Eliminate choices (B), (C), and (E).

Statement (2): insufficient. If e is positive and de is also positive, then d itself must be positive. But just knowing that d is positive is not enough to answer the question; d could be greater than or equal to 1, but it could also be a positive fraction between 0 and 1. For example, if $d = 0.5$ and $e = 5$, then $de = 2.5$, and 2.5 is greater than 1. So (2) is not sufficient; choice (A) is correct.

5. E

The question stem tells us that p is a prime but not much else, so let's go directly to the statements.

Statement (1): insufficient. Between 20 and 30, there are two prime numbers: 23 and 29. We therefore cannot determine the single value of p based on statement (1). Eliminate (A) and (D).

Statement (2): insufficient. This simply tells us that p is an odd integer (since odd – odd = even). Thus, p could be any prime number other than 2. Eliminate (B).

Statements (1) and (2): insufficient. From statement (1), you know that $p = 23$ or 29. From statement (2), you know that p is odd. Since 23 and 29 are both odd, there is still no way to determine one single value for p. Choice (E) is correct.

6. E

This is a yes–no question involving number properties, so picking numbers may help. There's not much in the stem, so go let's go directly to the statements.

Statement (1): Let's pick numbers. One possible value for x is 9, which is not prime. But x could also

be 3, 5, or 7, which are all prime. So we can't answer the question definitively; statement (1) is insufficient. We can cross off (A) and (D).

Statement (2) can be translated into $x \neq 9$, so all we know about x is that it is a positive integer other than 9. Thus statement (2) is also insufficient; eliminate (B) and combine the statements.

When we combine the statements, we know that x must be odd and less than 24, but it can't be 9. So, some possible values of x are 3, 5, and 7, which are all prime. But x could also be 1, 15, or 21, none of which are prime. We still don't have enough information to answer the question, so the answer is (E).

7. D

If x is ALWAYS greater than 17 or NEVER greater than 17, we'll have sufficiency. Otherwise, the statements will not be sufficient. There's not a lot to work with in the question stem, so let's go to the statements. In this case, statement (2) seems a little simpler, so let's start there.

Statement (2): If x is positive and evenly divisible by 21, then x must be at least equal to 21. Thus, x must be greater than 17, so statement (2) is sufficient. Eliminate choices (A), (C), and (E).

Statement (1): Since x has the same remainder when divided by 4 or 5, x must be three greater than some multiple of 4 and also three greater than some multiple of 5. Therefore, x must be three greater than some common multiple of 4 and 5. The least common multiple of 4 and 5 is 4×5, or 20, so x must be equal to at least $20 + 3 = 23$. That's greater than 17, so statement (1) is also sufficient. Choice (D) is correct.

8. B

This is a number properties question. We can approach it by remembering the rules for multiplying odds and evens, or we can pick numbers if we need to.

In Statement (1), the integer y times the even integer 4 is even. Since *any integer* times an even integer is even, y could be either odd or even. Pick a couple of numbers to confirm this. If $y = 2$, $4y = 4(2) = 8$, which is even. But if $y = 3$, $4y = 4(3) = 12$, which is also even. We can't say for sure whether y is odd or not, so statement (1) is not sufficient. Eliminate choices (A) and (D).

In Statement (2), the integer y times the odd integer 3 is odd. Thus y can't be even; if it were, $3y$ would be even, but statement (2) says it must be odd. Pick a couple of numbers to confirm this. If $y = 2$, $3y = 3(2) = 6$, which is even. But if $y = 5$, $3y = 3(5) = 15$, which is odd. We can only get an odd value for $3y$ if y is odd, so statement (2) is sufficient to say that y must be odd. Choice (B) is correct.

9. B

This is a value question, so we'll only have sufficiency if we find that there can be exactly one possible value for b. The question stem doesn't give us much to work with, so let's go on to the statements.

Statement (1): Because of the even exponent, we won't be able to find one exact value for b. It could be 2, because $2^4 = 16$, but it could also be -2, because $(-2)^4$ is also 16. Statement (1) is insufficient. Eliminate (A) and (D).

Statement (2): The right side of the equation is 49, which is the same as 7^2. If we replace the 49 with 7^2, the equation becomes $7^{3b-4} = 7^2$. Since both sides of the equation have the same base, both sides must also have the same exponent. This means that $3b - 4$ must be equal to 2, or $3b - 4 = 2$. We could solve this equation for b and find one exact value for b, so statement (2) is sufficient. We would not want to spend the extra time actually solving for b; all we need to know is that we *could* find the single possible value for b.

Finally, notice that although 49 is also equivalent to $(-7)^2$, this will not affect our result. Because $(-7)^2 = 7^2 = 49$, it is still correct to rewrite Statement (2) as $7^{3b-4} = 7^2$.

10. C

This is a value question, so we'll only have sufficiency if we can find exactly one possible value

for j. The stem doesn't give us much to work with, so let's go on to the statements.

Statement (1): The absolute value of any number must be nonnegative. The word nonnegative means not negative. So the absolute value of any number is 0 or positive. The equation $j = -|j|$ is equivalent to $|j| = -j$. So $-j$ must be 0 or positive. Therefore j must be 0 or negative. But that's not enough to find a specific value for j, so (1) is insufficient.

Statement (2): We can solve this for j. Divide both sides by 2 to get $j^2 = 9$. So, j could be 3, but it could also be -3. We don't have a specific value for j, so (2) is also insufficient.

Statements (1) and (2) together are sufficient. From (1), we know that j is 0 or negative. From (2), we know j is 3 or -3. There is only one possibility, $j = -3$, that makes both statements true. Thus j must be -3. So, (1) and (2) together are sufficient.

11. C

This is a value question—to have sufficiency, we need to be able to find one exact value for the number of guests who ate only one hamburger. Because we have two unknowns here (the number of guests eating one hamburger and the number eating two hamburgers), we will need to find two different equations in order to have sufficiency.

Let's evaluate statement (1) first. Suppose x is the number of guests eating one hamburger and y is the number of guests eating two hamburgers. Knowing that 90 hamburgers in total were eaten, we can say that $x + 2y = 90$, but that's only one equation. So statement (1) is not sufficient. We eliminate (A) and (D) and move on to consider statement (2).

From statement (2), we know that 25% of the guests ate 2 hamburgers. Again, let's let x be the number of guests eating one hamburger and let's let y be the number of guests eating two hamburgers. Then $x + y$ is the total number of guests. Since y is 25% of all the guests, we can write the equation $y = 0.25(x + y)$. But again, we have only one equation, so statement (2) by itself is not sufficient. We eliminate (B). Now let's consider statements (1) and (2) together.

Using both statements (1) and (2) gives us two different first-degree (or linear), equations, so the statements taken together are sufficient to answer the question. So (C) is correct.

Remember: don't actually solve the equations for *x* and *y*. It's enough to know that we COULD solve them.

12. A

We have a value question here; we need an exact value for the commission in order to have sufficiency. To find an exact value, we will need information that either gives us the commission amount directly or gives us the selling price. If we know the selling price, we can calculate the commission. In this case, statement (2) looks slightly simpler, so let's start there.

Does statement (2) really give us any new information? We can conclude from this statement that Mary's commission is $\frac{1}{20}$ of the selling price. Now $\frac{1}{20}$ is equivalent to 5 percent, and we already know that the commission is 5 percent of the selling price. Statement (2) is just another way of saying that Mary received a commission of 5 percent of the selling price, which is information given in the question stem. So statement (2) tells us nothing new and therefore cannot be sufficient. We can eliminate (B) and (D).

Now we can evaluate statement (1). We have more information here, so maybe we can set up an equation for the commission or the selling price. If we let *s* represent the selling price, in dollars, then the selling price, in dollars, plus 10% of that number will be 1.10*s*. If the selling price had been 10% higher, or 1.10*s* dollars, the commission would have been $16,500. Since the commission is 5% of the selling price, it must be the case that 5% of (1.10*s*) = 16,500, or (0.05)(1.10*s*) = 16,500. So we have an equation that we could use to find the selling price. And if we know the selling price, we

can find the commission, so statement (1) is sufficient and (A) is correct.

Don't spend time solving for *s*.

13. C

We will need to find a specific value for *c* in order to have sufficiency. Let's start by evaluating statement (1).

We know that the sum of the measures of the three angles in any triangle is 180 degrees. From statement (1), we also know that *a* + *c* = 100, so the degree measure *b* of the remaining angle must be 180 − 100 = 80. But that's as far as we can go; there is no way to determine the exact value of *c*, so statement (1) is insufficient. We can discard choices (A) and (D).

Similarly, statement (2) tells us that *b* + *c* = 120, so the degree measure *a* of the remaining angle must be 180 − 120 = 60. But again, we can't go any farther; there is no way to determine the exact value of *c*, so statement (2) by itself is insufficient. Eliminate (B).

Combining statements (1) and (2), we know that *b* = 80 and *a* = 60. Since *c* must equal 40, we could find the value of *c*. So statements (1) and (2) together are sufficient and the correct choice is (C).

14. E

This is a yes–no question. Only if the number of trucks must be equal to 64 or can never be equal to 64 will we have sufficiency.

Let's use *n* to represent the number of trucks owned by the company. From statement (1), we know that if they sell 10 trucks and buy no new ones, they will have less than 55. We can write this as an inequality: *n* − 10 < 55, or, adding 10 to both sides, *n* < 65. Does that imply that *x* is always 64 or never 64? No; *n* **could** be 64, but it could also be any other integer greater than or equal to 10 and less than 65. (The reason that *n* ≥ 10 is that in order to sell 10 trucks, the company had to own at least 10 trucks.) So statement (1) is insufficient. Eliminate (A) and (D).

From statement (2), we can write another inequality: $n + 20 \geq 83$, or $n \geq 63$. Again, this is not enough to say that n is always 64 or never 64; it could be 63, or 64, or 65, or any greater integer. So statement (2) is also insufficient; eliminate (B).

Now combine statements (1) and (2). From statement (1), we know that $10 \leq n < 65$. From statement (2), we know that $n \geq 63$. So n must be either 63 or 64; those are the only 2 values that satisfy both statements (1) and (2), which must always be consistent with each other. But that's still not enough; we can't say that n is **always** or **never** 64. So even together, statements (1) and (2) are not sufficient. The correct choice is (E).

15. B

Before evaluating the statements, let's work with the stem to find out what the question is really asking. We are asked if $3(x - y) + z < -z + 3x + y$. Simplify this by first multiplying out the 3 on the left side. That gives us $3x - 3y + z < -z + 3x + y$. Now subtract $3x$ from both sides to get $-3y + z < -z + y$. Since there are no longer any x terms, we know that any information about x will be irrelevant. Continue simplifying by adding $3y$ to both sides, and then adding z to both sides. The result will be $2z < 4y$, or $z < 2y$. This last inequality is much easier to work with than what we started with. All we really need to know is whether z is less than $2y$. Noting that this is a yes–no question, let's evaluate statement (1).

Statement (1) only provides information about x, which can't help us determine whether z is less than $2y$. So statement (1) is insufficient; (A) and (D) can be eliminated.

Statement (2) tells us that z is in fact equal to $2y$. This means that z can't be **less** than $2y$, so statement (2) is sufficient to answer the question in the negative: no, z is never less than $2y$. Thus (B) is the correct choice.

16. E

This is a value question. We would need to know either the actual dollar prices of both products or the ratio of the dollar prices of both products in order to determine which dollar decrease was smaller.

Let's look at statement (1). The statement tells us nothing about the price of Product B, so there's no way we can determine which price decrease was smaller. Statement (1) is not sufficient, so we can eliminate choices (A) and (D) and evaluate statement (2).

Statement (2) tells us nothing about the price of Product A. Thus, statement (2) by itself is also insufficient. We can eliminate choice (B) and evaluate the 2 statements together.

Even taken together, the statements only tell us about the percent changes in price. Neither gives us any information about the original prices, so the statements together are still insufficient. The correct choice is (E).

17. C

We need to find the area of the rectangle, so this is a value question. The formula for the area of a rectangle is the product of the length and width, or xy in this case. So any information that allows us to solve for both x and y OR their product will be sufficient.

Statement (1) does not provide enough information. In a square, all sides are equal. If we assume that x is the longer side, then $x - 1 = y$. But that leaves us with 2 variables and only one equation. There is no way to solve for x and y, so statement (1) is insufficient. We can eliminate choices (A) and (D). Note that there is another possibility: y could be the longer side. However, our conclusion would have been the same. We would have found that $y - 1 = x$, which is still only 1 equation.

From statement (2), we know only that the sum of the lengths of a pair of adjacent sides of the rectangle is 49. Because there are many pairs of integers that add up to 49, there is no way to solve for x and y or for xy, so statement (2) must be insufficient as well. Cross off (B) and evaluate the 2 statements together.

From statement (1), we know that either $x - 1 = y$ OR $y - 1 = x$. From statement (2), we know that $x + y = 49$. Since we don't which equation from statement (1) is true, there is no way to solve for x and y. But remember that it would be enough just to find xy—we don't actually need to know the sides, just the area. Because x and y must be integers, one of them must be 1 greater than the other and their sum must be 49, the only possibilities are $x = 25$ and $y = 24$ or $x = 24$ and $y = 25$. Either way, the area will be the same: (24)(25) or (25)(24). So we can find one specific value for the area. This means statements (1) and (2) together are sufficient, and the answer is choice (C).

18. B

We will have to be able to say that either the range of the set is ALWAYS greater that 8 or NEVER greater than 8 in order to have sufficiency. The range of a set is the difference between the largest and smallest values in the set, so we'll be looking for information about the highest and lowest values in set N.

Statement (1) tells us which of the variables represents that largest value in the set, but that's not enough. We don't actually know what the largest value is or how it compares to the smallest value, so we have no way to answer any questions about the range. Statement (1) is insufficient; eliminate (A) and (D).

Statement (2) tells us that the difference between two of the elements is greater than 8. We don't know that $t - r$ is in fact the range of the set, but since there is at least one pair of numbers in the set whose difference is greater than 8, there is no way for the range to be less than 8. Because the range of a set is the difference between the largest and smallest values in the set, the range must also be the largest difference between any two numbers in the set. If $t - r$ itself is not the range, then the range must be even larger than $t - r$. Either way, the range will be greater than 8, meaning that the answer to the question will always be NO. So, (2) is sufficient, and (B) is correct.

19. B

For a set with an even number of elements, the median is the average of the two middle values. So the median of {1, 3, 5, 7} is 4, which is the average of the two middle values, 3 and 5.

For this value question, we'll need to be able to find one specific value for the median in order to have sufficiency. We don't yet know where the variable a fits into the set, but let's start by putting the other values in ascending order: {–2, 30, 40}. Now we can evaluate the statements.

For Statement (1), let's pick numbers. If $a = 36$, then the set would be {–2, 30, 36, 40} and the median would be 33. But suppose $a = 50$. Then the set would be {–2, 30, 40, 50} and the median would be 35. So we can't find one exact value for the median; (1) is insufficient. We can eliminate (A) and (D).

Statement (2): If $a > 40$, then the set must be {–2, 30, 40, a}. Regardless of the actual value of a, the median will always be 35. So (2) is sufficient and (B) is correct.

20. D

$$\text{Probability} = \frac{\text{\# of desired outcomes}}{\text{\# of total outcomes}}$$

$$= \frac{\text{\# of green balls}}{\text{total \# of balls}}.$$

To find the probability of choosing a green ball, we need the number of green balls and total balls, or at least the proportion of green balls in the bag. Statement (2) looks a little easier to work with, so let's start there.

Ratios are another way of expression proportions, so if the ratio of green balls to total balls is 1:7, then the proportion of green balls is $\frac{1}{7}$. We have an exact value for the probability of choosing a green ball; Statement (2) is sufficient.

Statement (1): The probability we want is $\frac{\text{\# of green balls}}{\text{total \# of balls}}$. If g = green balls and t = total balls (before any balls are added), the probability is $\frac{g}{t}$. Now, the number of green balls is increased by 400%. That's (400%)(g), or $4g$. To find the new probability, $\frac{5}{11}$, we have to add $4g$ balls to both the numerator and the denominator. (No other balls are added, so the total number of balls increases by the number of green balls added.) So we have this equation: $\frac{5}{11} = \frac{g + 4g}{t + 4g} = \frac{5g}{t + 4g}$. We have 2 variables, so we can't solve for g and t, but we don't have to; all we need is the fraction $\frac{g}{t}$. We **can** solve this equation for $\frac{g}{t}$, so Statement (1) is also sufficient, and (D) is the correct choice.

It's not necessary to go through the steps of solving for $\frac{g}{t}$, but it would be done as follows: first, cross-multiply to get $5(t + 4g) = 55g$, or $5t + 20g = 55g$. Subtract $20g$ from both sides to get $5t = 35g$. Now divide both sides by t to get $5 = \frac{35g}{t}$. Finally, dividing both sides by 35, we have $\frac{5}{35} = \frac{g}{t}$, or $\frac{1}{7} = \frac{g}{t}$. Note that this fraction is consistent with Statement (2).

21. C

Let x represent the number of customers who bought two-tire sets, and let y be the number of customers who bought four-tire sets. In order to answer the question, we must be able to solve for both x and y or their sum.

Statement (1): Since $x + y$ = the total number of customers and we are told that 25% of the customers bought 4-tire sets, we can say the y = 25% of $(x + y)$, or $y = 0.25(x + y)$. That only gives us one equation, so it's insufficient. We can eliminate (A) and (D).

Statement (2): Since x represents customers buying 2 tires and y represents customers buying 4 tires, the total number of tires sold must be $2x + 4y$. So, Statement (2) tells us that $2x + 4y = 200$. Again, that's only one equation, so Statement (2) by itself is also insufficient.

If we combine the two statements, we have 2 distinct linear equations and 2 variables, so we could solve for x and y. Thus Choice (C) is correct. There is no need to solve the equations to find the actual values of x and y.

22. C

To find a percent decrease, we need both the original value (her time last year) and either the new value (her time this year) or the decrease in her time. Only if we have all of this information will we have sufficiency.

Statement (1) only tells us her original time, so it is not sufficient.

Statement (2) only tells us the decrease in her time, so it is not sufficient.

If we take the statements together, we will know both the original value and the decrease, which is sufficient to answer the question. Choice (C) is correct.

23. E

We could find the square feet covered by the shade if we know the length and width of the covered region OR if we know the total area of the window and the percentage of the window that is covered.

Statement (1) gives us the percentage covered but not the total area of the window, so it is insufficient.

Statement (2) gives us one of the dimensions of the window, but that is not enough to determine the total area of the window or the covered area, so it is also insufficient.

When we combine the statements, we only know that the shade covers half of a window that is three feet wide. We can't find the total area of the window or the covered region, so both statements together are still insufficient. Therefore (E) is correct.

24. B

Because this is a yes–no question, we will have sufficiency only if m is always or never greater than n.

Statement (1): If we add m to both sides of the inequality, we get $-n > -1$. This means that Statement (1) actually provides no information about m, so we can't say whether m is greater than n or not. So Statement (1) is insufficient.

Statement (2): If we add n to both sides of the inequality, we get $m > n$, which is exactly what we are looking for. Since m must be greater than n, Statement (2) is sufficient.

25. D

To find the ratio of cocoa powder to milk, we need to find the proportions of the 2 ingredients or the specific amounts of the ingredients.

From Statement (1), we know that any given amount of the hot chocolate mix contains 3 parts dry milk powder and 1 part cocoa powder. Thus the ratio of cocoa to milk is 1:3. Statement (1) is sufficient; we can eliminate (B), (C) and (E).

Statement (2): if 48 ounces of the mix contains 12 ounces of cocoa powder, it must contain 48 – 12 = 36 ounces of milk powder. So, the ratio of cocoa to milk is 12:36, or 1:3. Statement (2) is also sufficient, so Choice (D) is correct.

26. A

This is a value question, so we need to find exactly what year Jordan was born in order to have sufficiency.

Statement (1): If he turned 16 in 1996, he must have been born 16 years earlier, or 1996 – 16 = 1980. So, (1) is sufficient. Eliminate (B), (C) and (E).

Statement (2): Suppose Bill was born in February 1979. One and a half years (or 18 months) later would be August 1980, so Jordan could have been born in 1980. But suppose Bill was born in December 1979. One and a half years later would be May 1981, so, based on Statement (2), Jordan could also have been born in 1981. Thus (2) is insufficient; (A) is correct.

27. E

To have sufficiency, we need to be able to calculate the exact number of books read by Jane Smith. We'll be looking for any information that helps us find that value.

Statement (1) tells us that Jane has read 70% of the books **owned** by the family. That does not imply that Jane read 70% of the books they **purchased** last year. She may have read some, all, or none of the books they purchased, so (1) is insufficient.

Statement (2) has no information about how many books Jane read, so it is also insufficient.

Combining (1) and (2), we know that Jane has read 70% of the 400 books the family owns. But this doesn't tell us many of the 30 bought last year were read by Jane, so (1) and (2) together are also insufficient. (E) is correct.

28. C

For this question, we will have sufficiency only if we can find a specific value for x. From the stem, we know only that x is an integer between 100 and 150, so let's move on to the statements.

Statement (1): Since x is between 100 and 150, the hundreds digit of x must be 1 and the tens digit could be 0, 1, 2, 3 or 4. Their sum could be 1, 2, 3, 4 or 5. The fact that the units digit must be greater than the sum of the other digits doesn't help us find a value for x. For example, x could be 102 or 113 or 129 or 136 or many other values. So (1) is insufficient.

If the units digit is 4, x could be 104, 114, 124, 134 or 144. Two of these, 114 and 134, are not divisible by 4. Thus, x could be 114 or 134, so (2) by itself is also insufficient.

Combining (1) and (2), we know $x = 114$ or $x = 134$. Only 114 meets the conditions given in (1), so x must be 114. Thus (1) and (2) together are sufficient, and (C) is correct.

29. C

The profit per share that could be made by selling on Tuesday rather than Monday is the Tuesday price minus the Monday price, and the total profit is the number of shares sold multiplied by this price difference. Since we are given the number of shares in the stem, we'll need to find the two prices (or their difference) in the statements in order to have sufficiency.

Statement (1) only tells us the Monday price, so it's insufficient.

Statement (2) only tells us the Tuesday price, so it's also insufficient.

Taking (1) and (2) together, we have all the information we need. Therefore (C) is the correct choice. There is no need calculate the actual amount of profit that could be made; it's enough to know that we could calculate it.

30. E

This is a value question, but notice from the stem that we don't actually need the individual values of x and y. That would certainly be sufficient, but all we really need is their sum. That would also be sufficient.

Statement (1): We have 2 variables and only 1 equation, so clearly we can't solve for x and y. Can we rearrange the equation to find $x + y$? We can add 4 to both sides to get $x + 4 = y$. Now subtract x from both sides to get $4 = y - x$. That looks closer to what we want, but it's not close enough. We can't actually rearrange this equation to isolate $x + y$, so Statement (1) is insufficient.

In Statement (2), $x + y$ is already set apart in the equation, but it is also squared. If we take the square root of both sides of the equation, we find that $x + y$ equals either 8 or –8. We can't find one specific value for $x + y$, so (2) is also insufficient.

When we combine the statements, it may be tempting to think that we have 2 equations and 2 unknowns, so we should be able to solve for x and y, leading to Choice (C). But remember that the n-unknowns/n-equations rule requires that all the equations be linear. One of the equations here is quadratic, so we cannot actually solve for x and y. Thus Choice (E) is correct.

Another way to see that we can't find a value for $x + y$ even using both statements is to notice that (2) gives us 2 possible values for $x + y$ (8 or –8). Since Statement (1) tells us nothing about $x + y$ (if it did, it would have been sufficient), it can't help us determine whether $x + y$ equals 8 or –8.

31. C

The equation $x^2 + y^2 = z^2$ is the Pythagorean Theorem, which is only valid for right triangles. So, the question becomes: is XYZ a right triangle? If we can answer YES or NO definitively, we will have sufficiency.

Statement (1) tells us that the triangle has at least 2 equal angles. This could be a right triangle, but it could also be an equilateral triangle with three 60-degree angles. So (1) doesn't give us enough information. We can eliminate (A) and (D).

For Statement (2), remember that the sum of the angles in a triangle is 180 degrees. We know that one of the three angles is one-fourth of 180 degrees, or 45 degrees. This could be a right triangle, but it doesn't have to be; for example, the three angles could be 45, 65 and 70 degrees. Thus, (2) is also insufficient.

Combining (1) and (2), we know that the angle opposite side X is 45 degrees. It's also equal to the angle opposite side Y, so that angle must also be 45 degrees. Thus, the sum of 2 of the angles is 45 + 45 = 90, so the third angle must be 180 – 90 = 90. Therefore this is in fact a right triangle.

Statements (1) and (2) together are sufficient, so (C) is correct.

32. A

We will have sufficiency only if the two perimeters are always or never equal. The perimeter is the sum of the lengths of the sides, so we'll be looking for information about side lengths as we evaluate the statements. For this question, Statement (2) looks simpler than (1), so let's start there.

Statement (2) tells us the perimeter of the rectangle but says nothing about the triangle. The perimeter of the triangle could be less than, equal to or greater than 24, so (2) is insufficient. We can eliminate (B) and (D).

Statement (1): Since the perimeter of rectangle R is the sum of the 4 side lengths, the sum of any 2 adjacent sides must be half the perimeter. Thus, the ratio of the perimeter of T to the sum of the lengths of any two adjacent sides of R is the same as the ratio of the perimeter of T to half the perimeter of R. This ratio is 2:1, so the ratio of the two perimeters must be 1:1. If their ratio is 1:1, the perimeters must be equal, so the answer to the question is YES, and Statement (1) is sufficient. Choice (A) is correct.

33. A

Since $x < y < z$, y must be the middle value of the three elements of the set. Since the median is by definition the middle value (when there are an odd number of terms), all we need is the value of y. Also, since the mean (or average) equals the sum of the terms divided by the number of terms, we know from the stem that $(x + y + z) \div 3 = 12$. Multiplying both sides by 3 gives us $x + y + z = 36$. Now let's evaluate the statements to see if we can find a value for y. Since we have one equation involving three unknowns, we'll probably need 2 more equations in order to solve for any of the unknowns.

Statement (1) gives us just what we need. We can write these equations: $x = z - 10$, and $y + 8 = z$. Now we have three unknowns and three equations, so we could solve for y. So (1) is sufficient; we can eliminate (B), (C) and (E).

Statement (2) only gives us only one more equation, $2x + 2 = z$. We can't solve for y, so (2) is not sufficient. (A) is the correct choice.

34. B

We will have sufficiency if we can say for certain that t is either always or never between –9 and 4. Also, keep in mind that picking numbers can be very helpful when evaluating inequalities.

Statement (1): insufficient. One possible value for t is 2, in which case the answer would be yes, but t could also be 4 or 5, in which case the answer would be no. Eliminate (A) and (D).

Statement (2): sufficient. If $–6 < t < 1$ is true, then $–9 < t < 4$ must also be true because any number that is between –6 and 1 will also be between –9 and 4. So the answer is "yes" and Choice (B) is correct.

35. B

The question stem only tells us that we have a value question and that r is between 50 and 60, inclusive, so we can move on to the statements.

Statement (1): How can we find values for r that will give us a remainder of 2 when r is divided by 7? We need to pick numbers that are equal to (some multiple of 7) + 2. For example, $(7 \times 7) + 2 = 51$, so $51 \div 7 = 7$, Remainder 2. So one possible value of r is 51. Are there any other values between 50 and 60 inclusive which will work? Adding another 7 to 51 gives us 58, and $58 \div 7 = 8$, Remainder 2. Thus 58 is also a possible value for r. So, we can't pick one single value. (1) is insufficient; eliminate (A) and (D).

We can approach (2) the same way. The possible values for r must be equal to (some multiple of 30) + 28. Start with $(1 \times 30) + 28 = 58$. That gives us one possible value. The next possible value is $58 + 30 = 88$, which is outside the permissible range. So there's only one possible value for r that is between 50 and 60 inclusive. (2) alone is sufficient, and (B) is correct.

CHAPTER ELEVEN

Analytical Writing

The AWA is designed to assess your ability to think critically and communicate your ideas. It consists of two 30-minute writing tasks: *Analysis of an Issue* and *Analysis of an Argument*. For these essays, no specific knowledge will be required—only your ability to write analytically is evaluated. Whether you agree or disagree with the claims presented is irrelevant; what matters is that you convincingly support your view with appropriate examples and statements.

For the *Issue* essay (30 minutes), you'll be given a sentence or paragraph that expresses an opinion on a general topic. Your job will be to analyze the issue and explain your point of view. There is no correct answer. Use relevant reasons and/or examples drawn from your experience or observations to develop your position. Make sure in your essay to consider other perspectives (pro and con).

For the *Argument* essay (30 minutes), you'll be presented with a paragraph that argues a certain point. You'll need to analyze the reasoning behind the argument, and write a critique of that argument. You aren't being asked for your own opinion on the subject. Your essay should discuss how well-reasoned you believe the argument is.

Each essay will be graded on a scale from 1–6. (A score of 0 means that your essay is off-topic.) This score is computed and reported separately from the multiple-choice section, and has no effect on your Verbal, Quantitative, or total score. The schools to which you are sending your GMAT results may ask for a copy of your essay answers; however, your own copy of your score report will not include the completed text.

For the AWA, you will be evaluated on how well you:

- Organize, develop, and express your ideas about the argument presented
- Provide relevant supporting reasons and examples
- Control the elements of standard written English

Here are some proven strategies for a high score on the AWA section of the GMAT:

KAPLAN METHOD FOR ANALYTICAL WRITING

		Spend:	
Step 1	Digest the issue/argument	2 minutes	
Step 2	Select the points you will make	5 minutes	
Step 3	Organize	1 minute	
Step 4	Write/type your essay	20 minutes	
Step 5	Proofread your work	2 minutes	

KAPLAN'S 22 PRINCIPLES OF EFFECTIVE WRITING

1. Avoid wordiness
2. Don't be redundant
3. Avoid needless qualification
4. Do not write sentences just to fill up space
5. Avoid needless self-reference
6. Use the active voice
7. Avoid weak openings
8. Avoid needlessly vague language
9. Avoid clichés
10. Avoid jargon
11. Pay attention to subject-verb agreement
12. Pay attention to modification
13. Use pronouns carefully
14. Use parallelism carefully
15. Do not shift narrative voice
16. Avoid slang and colloquialisms
17. Watch out for sentence fragments and run-on sentences
18. Use commas correctly
19. Use semicolons correctly
20. Use colons correctly
21. Use hyphens and dashes correctly
22. Use the apostrophe correctly

SIX TIPS FOR WRITING A "6"

Your essay isn't expected to be perfect. You can still get a 6 and have a few minor errors.

1. Keep sight of your goal: to demonstrate that you can think logically and communicate clearly.
2. Use language effectively; watch for words that add nothing to the sentence.
3. Keep your word choice, sentence structure, and argument simple (but not simplistic).
4. Resist the temptation to use inflated language in your essays; big words that don't fit the tone or context of your essays won't impress anyone.
5. Be strong and convincing in your choice of arguments, words, and sentence style.
6. Don't worry too much about making minor mistakes.

The remainder of this chapter includes sample prompts for each type of prompt. Try your hand at each. We have also included sample student essays—both of score 6—for your review. By evaluating how these essays address the assigned topic, you will get a better understanding of what the graders are looking for.

Notice the use of strong transitions, logical organization, and effective word choice in the sample essays. All of these factors contribute to their receipt of a top score.

ANALYSIS OF ISSUE ESSAY

(30 minutes)

"The quality of a business can best be judged by looking at the quality of its highest-level managers."

From your perspective, is this an accurate observation? Why or why not? Explain, using reasons and/or examples from your experience, observations, and reading.

_____

_____

_____

_____

_____

_____

_____

_____

_____

_____

_____

_____

_____

_____

ANALYSIS OF ARGUMENT ESSAY

(30 minutes)

The following appeared in a report from a management-consulting firm to the CEO of Telamon Industries.

"Ten years ago, Telamon Industries had factories in 11 states. Over the last decade, as Telamon has centralized all of its operations in one plant located in its home state, it has also become less profitable. Thus we recommend that Telamon reduce the size of the central facility in its home state and open smaller facilities in other states. Doing so will enable the company to increase profitability by taking advantage of the lower labor costs in other states."

Discuss how well-reasoned you find this argument. In your discussion be sure to analyze the line of reasoning and the use of evidence in the argument. For example, you may need to consider what questionable assumptions underlie the thinking and what alternative explanations or counter-examples might weaken the conclusion. You can also discuss what sort of evidence would strengthen or refute the argument, what changes would make it more logically sound, and what, if anything, would help you better evaluate its conclusion.

_____

_____

_____

_____

_____

_____

_____

_____

_____

Sample Issue Essay (Score 6)

"The quality of a business can best be judged by looking at the quality of its highest-level managers."

From your perspective, is this an accurate observation? Why or why not? Explain, using reasons and/or examples from your experience, observations, and reading.

Many people, especially those following the news, judge the quality of a business by its highest-level managers. It is true that top management can set standards for the quality of a business's products and services; it is also true that highest-level management can help create a climate conducive to quality with incentives. However, that alone cannot create a culture of quality. I will argue that the best way of judging the overall quality of a business is not to look at the quality of the highest-level management but to look at the quality of its rank-and-file employees.

Bad conduct in corporate officers may create negative public opinion for their business as a whole and lead to a loss in sales and investor confidence. Indeed, the Enron scandals involving CEO Kenneth Lay and other corporate officers led to a formerly strong company's bankruptcy in 2001. Equally true is the fact that "superstars," such as CEOs Bill Gates and Steve Jobs, lent an air of innovation and excitement to their products that helped propel their businesses to success in the 1980s. However, most good managers are usually not that visible. They are aware that they will be judged primarily by how well the people they manage do their jobs, and are usually too busy working to give press conferences.

Most customers never meet the CEO of a company; few know his or her name. They do, however, meet or talk to sales clerks, tellers, call center personnel, and receptionists. These people are hardly at the highest-level, yet their attitude, helpfulness (or not!), and work ethic are what a customer responds to. Many customers make the decision to choose one company over a competitor based on the quality of that one contact. If a teller is rude, an operator unhelpful or uninformed, or a sales person unavailable, many people simply decide to choose another product or service.

Corporate America knows the appeal of quality at the person-to-person level. Time Warner Cable in New York bases its advertising campaign on reliability and service. Competing with satellite services, the company's recent commercial shows an operator—concerned and informed—ready to help a customer with any problem. This is juxtaposed with a customer trying to deal with a frustrating bureaucracy at the competitor satellite dish company. Ads like these rarely feature the CEO or the CFO; instead, they feature an Avis clerk helpfully adjusting a customer's radio, or a waitress providing quick, cheerful service, or a technician offering clear instructions on how to use software.

In the book *Making Quality Work* by Labovitz, Chang, and Rosansky, a Japanese executive recounts that when IBM executives went to Japan to learn about creating a quality culture, they proudly announced that they viewed quality as seventy percent attitude and thirty percent quality control. Their Japanese peers were shocked: they viewed quality as ninety percent attitude. Top managers can institute procedures for quality control, but they can't institute a quality attitude. All employees must be invested in creating quality products for quality to occur.

Senior management can help grow a corporate culture of quality by providing goals, standards, incentives, and resources. They can offer competitive salaries and benefits, opportunities for advancement, challenges, and a sense of personal value to employees. These are the seeds of quality, and the managers who plant them will be worth looking at and emulating. However, the actual gauge of a quality company will be to see how employees respond.

So while looking at top management can give insight into a company, the surefire litmus test of quality is to take a hard look at the employees. What is their work ethic like? How do they treat customers? How do they solve problems? How invested are they in their jobs? Are they involved in the company as a whole, or do they take the "not-my-job" attitude? These are the factors that will determine the quality of the company.

Sample Argument Essay (Score 6)

The following appeared in a report from a management-consulting firm to the CEO of Telamon Industries.

> "Ten years ago, Telamon Industries had factories in 11 states. Over the last decade, as Telamon has centralized all of its operations in one plant located in its home state, it has also become less profitable. Thus we recommend that Telamon reduce the size of the central facility in its home state and open smaller facilities in other states. Doing so will enable the company to increase profitability by taking advantage of the lower labor costs in other states."

Discuss how well-reasoned you find this argument. In your discussion be sure to analyze the line of reasoning and the use of evidence in the argument. For example, you may need to consider what questionable assumptions underlie the thinking and what alternative explanations or counter-examples might weaken the conclusion. You can also discuss what sort of evidence would strengthen or refute the argument, what changes would make it more logically sound, and what, if anything, would help you better evaluate its conclusion.

Perhaps the greatest weakness of the argument presented by the management-consulting firm is the fact that the business conducted by Telamon Industries is never specified. Yet even with if this information were provided, the author of the report fails to include important details and often relies on unsubstantiated assumptions about the best course of action for Telamon Industries.

Without knowing what type of product or service Telamon provides, it is difficult to pinpoint why it has become less profitable. The consultant only correlates the localization of its operations to its home state to this decline in business. Clearly, other crucial information could be provided regarding the loss in profits. First, Telamon could be a manufacturer of a product that has seen decline in the last decade, for example, VHS video cassettes which are being replaced by DVDs. That alone, and not the centralization of operations could account for the loss in profits. Secondly, the loss in profits, while recognized, could be minimal. Perhaps the discrepancy between profits a decade ago and profits today is a mere $100. Without knowing exactly how much profits have declined in the last decade, there could be no reason for alarm.

Another critical issue with the statement made by the consultant pertains to the recommendation that the home state operations should be reduced and that smaller facilities in other states should be established. To further strengthen this argument, the consultant should provide specific information to show that it would indeed be cost effective to do so. For example, perhaps the home state location of Telamon is one with an ample labor supply that falls below the national average in terms of cost. In this case, the move to other states might cost more to do than it would increase profits. However, if the consultant were to provide research of other states where a significant savings would be available and that the cost of starting up new factories would be dwarfed in comparison to increased profits, the argument would be much stronger.

Again, without knowing what Telamon produces, a move to different states may prove futile in increasing profit. For example, if Telamon were a company that specialized in elevators for use in high-rise office buildings, relocation to certain parts of the country would be an unwise choice. To improve the argument for opening smaller facilities in other states, the consultant would have to take into account both the demand for the product, which may be lower in rural states, as well as the cost of shipping the product to areas where demand may be greater.

It is important to note that other than correlating the centralization of Telemon Industries and the decline in profits, the consultant gives no information about why the centralization occurred in the first place. Perhaps having several factories in 11 different states was not cost-effective. Although it is implied that profits were higher when several factories were running concurrently, it does not mean that was the best use of the company's resources. Each factory would have required its own upper management to ensure the facility ran properly, and depending on the nature of the business, shipping and operating costs could have varied widely, making some factories quite successful, while others may not have been.

The conclusion made by the consultant regarding Telamon Industries might be the best one for the success of the company. That said, there is simply not enough information or facts regarding the supply, demand, and related costs pertaining to Telamon. Only by specifying the reasons why centralizing Telamon was harmful and by outlining the costs of decentralizing the company can the consultant make a strong argument that this is the way to increase profits.

ANALYSIS OF ISSUE ESSAY

(30 minutes)

"Employees respond best to monetary compensation. No incentive will engender better performance than a raise in salary or a big bonus for a job well done."

From your perspective, is this an accurate observation? Why or why not? Explain, using reasons and/or examples from your experience, observations, and reading.

_____

_____

_____

_____

_____

_____

_____

_____

_____

_____

_____

_____

_____

_____

ANALYSIS OF ARGUMENT ESSAY

(30 minutes)

The following appeared in a letter from the circulation manager of the *Muse*, a monthly arts magazine, to the magazine's publisher.

"Our circulation has declined steadily since the launch of a competing magazine, the *Apollo*, two years ago. The *Apollo* includes more color photographs than the *Muse* does. If we want to increase our circulation to its former level, we need to add more color photographs. This will enable us to increase our circulation and therefore sell more advertising."

Discuss how well-reasoned you find this argument. In your discussion be sure to analyze the line of reasoning and the use of evidence in the argument. For example, you may need to consider what questionable assumptions underlie the thinking and what alternative explanations or counter-examples might weaken the conclusion. You can also discuss what sort of evidence would strengthen or refute the argument, what changes would make it more logically sound, and what, if anything, would help you better evaluate its conclusion.

_____

_____

_____

_____

_____

_____

_____

_____

_____

_____

Sample Issue Essay (Score 6)

"Employees respond best to monetary compensation. No incentive will engender better performance than a raise in salary or a big bonus for a job well done."

From your perspective, is this an accurate observation? Why or why not? Explain, using reasons and/or examples from your experience, observations, and reading.

Until the 1920s, employees were considered cogs in an industrial wheel, working only for wages. According to supply and demand, such workers could be relied upon to work for the highest possible wage, and respond only to monetary compensation. However, since the 1920s, researchers have found that a majority of employees value human relations factors at work more than money. I will refute the argument that the best motivator of employees is monetary compensation, and argue that human relations management can motivate employees more.

The famous Hawthorne studies conducted by Elton Mayo in the 1920s found that employees were more motivated by their attitudes than by money. With changes in shifts to fight monotony and a free meal on the company, output among the experimental workers in the study shot up, as did teamwork. Although the changes were arbitrary, the sense of freedom among the members of this group created amazing productivity.

A few decades later, the psychologist Maslow developed his hierarchy of needs to explain human motivation. Once basic needs like hunger and safety are taken care of, Maslow argued, people need self-esteem, something money alone might not provide. Work is an area in which people gain and grow in self-esteem, noted Maslow, with work seen as an opportunity to contribute to society.

Recent studies confirm the human relations theory of motivation. Most motivational studies rank monetary compensation as important to employees, but not the most important factor. For most employees, these studies find, a work environment in which they are valued, respected, and appreciated is the strongest motivator of all.

For many people, interesting work and the opportunity for increased responsibility are the keys to productivity. For others, job security or help during times of personal problems can inspire loyalty. Good working conditions can appeal to many more than money. Status, promotions, and/or growth in the organization are essential to the performance of many individuals.

Many employees respond strongly to the mission of an organization, feeling proud to help fulfill it. Even very well paid managers can sulk and slack if they feel they are not "in the loop," so the feeling of being part of something can be much more important than a big pay check. Of course, appreciation for work well done may be one of the most important motivators of all.

The psychology of optimal experience is called "flow," the sense of being completely in the moment and absorbed with full interest in an activity. Although often occurring during difficult tasks, like climbing mountains, flow is nevertheless synonymous with the feeling of being really alive. When asked to evaluate flow in their lives, most people say they feel it more at work than at home. It is not likely that flow happens when employees get their pay checks, but rather when they are engaged and involved.

Sample Argument Essay (Score 6)

The following appeared in a letter from the circulation manager of the *Muse*, a monthly arts magazine, to the magazine's publisher.

> "Our circulation has declined steadily since the launch of a competing magazine, the *Apollo*, two years ago. The *Apollo* includes more color photographs than the *Muse* does. If we want to increase our circulation to its former level, we need to add more color photographs. This will enable us to increase our circulation and therefore sell more advertising."

Discuss how well-reasoned you find this argument. In your discussion be sure to analyze the line of reasoning and the use of evidence in the argument. For example, you may need to consider what questionable assumptions underlie the thinking and what alternative explanations or counter-examples might weaken the conclusion. You can also discuss what sort of evidence would strengthen or refute the argument, what changes would make it more logically sound, and what, if anything, would help you better evaluate its conclusion.

The author of the letter intends to inform the publisher regarding the declining circulation of Muse magazine. However, the information and assumptions he or she presents are vague and unsupported. By failing to quantify the situation, and by presenting facts that are not directly relevant to the issue of declining circulation, the manager has failed to make a reasonable argument.

First, the manager mentions that circulation has declined steadily in the last two years. This statement seems bleak, but with actual quantities assigned to the steady decline, that may not be the case. For example, a decline of .00001% monthly is by definition a steady decline, but not one that would cause any concern to a circulation manager or a publisher. Because the manager never assigns a figure to the rate of decline, the argument is weak. This alone would cast the manager's statement in doubt. Unfortunately, this is only the beginning of errors in judgment.

The greatest flaw of the circulation manager's argument is the belief that the decline in circulation is a direct result of the launch of a competitor, Apollo. By linking the two, the manager has made a straw man of Apollo. Without reviewing internal factors that may be the cause of declining circulation, for example, the loss of several writers, budget cuts in the sales department, or even a trend in the world of art magazines, the manager immediately blames the emergence of a competitor. Unfortunately, by laying the foundation of the argument on the Apollo, the manager is further weakening his or her argument.

Moreover, the manager has created an incomplete argument by mentioning the fact that Apollo magazine includes more color photographs than Muse magazine. The quantity of color photographs is only one distinguishing element of the Apollo versus the Muse. The case could be that Apollo has twice as many pages, different types of art, several famous art historians and critics on staff, or even higher quality photographs, regardless of whether they are in color or black and white. All of these factors are possibilities for why Apollo is a strong competitor. However, these facts are irrelevant to the Muse. The case has not been made that the existence of the Apollo is the cause of the decline in the Muse's circulation.

Because the manager is falsely arguing that the Apollo is the cause of the Muse's decline, his or her premise that including more color photographs to Muse magazine will increase circulation is just as useless. There is no support, factual or circumstantial, that would show that adding more color photographs to Muse magazine would return circulation to its previous level. Clearly, the manager offers no evidence that readers and potential subscribers of the Muse would be more likely to purchase the magazine if it included more color photographs. If the manager were able to provide this information the argument would be significantly improved.

Up to this point, the circulation manager has failed to make convincing or even valid arguments to support his or her position that following one design element of a competitor will restore circulation levels of the Muse. From here, the manager further argues that increased circulation will then lead to increased advertising sales. Again, the manager has drawn a conclusion, that higher circulation will cause higher advertising sales, based on a false premise, that including more color photos will cause higher circulation. Everything about the manager's argument is based on inconclusive information or unsubstantiated possibilities.

Rather than blaming the competition for the Muse's decline and then directly copying the competitor to increase sales is a design for continued failure. In this case, only by recognizing internal causes for the decline in circulation, offering a clear method for remedying those causes, and thus increasing circulation can the manager make a well-reasoned argument.